HEALTH CARE & SPIRITUALITY:
Listening,
Assessing,
Caring

edited by
Reverend Richard B. Gilbert
D.Min., BCC, FAAGC, CPBC

Death, Value and Meaning Series
Series Editor: John D. Morgan

Baywood Publishing Company, Inc.
AMITYVILLE, NEW YORK

Library of Congress Catalog Number: 00-063056
ISBN: 0-89503-250-3 (paper)

Library of Congress Cataloging-in-Publication Data

Gilbert, Richard B.
    Health care & spirituality : listening, assessing, caring / edited by Richard B. Gilbert.
      p. cm. - - (Death, value, and meaning series)
    Includes bibliographical references and index.
    ISBN 0-89503-250-3 (paper)
     1. Patients- -Religious life. 2. Spirituality. 3. Medical care- -Religious aspects. I. Title: Health care and spirituality. II. Title. III. Series.

BL625.9.S53
[G55 2000]
291.'78321- -dc21

                                            00-063056

Foreword

Linking health care to spirituality is not a modern discovery. So wedded is health to spiritual life that the first professional health care advisers were doctor/priests who interceded with the deities or interpreted divine will as expressed in dreams and visions. Known as shamans, these ancient healers of both spirit and body were active in a wide variety of cultures and historical eras. The shaman attempts to reestablish, in the patient, a sense of connectedness with the universe by entering into and closely identifying with the wounded soul of the person who is ill. The term "wounded healer," which Henri Nouwen has made popular in Christian circles, was originally ascribed to the shaman in the vast literature on this most universal and widely practiced form of healing in the history of the world.

Though not new, the link between health care and spirituality is certainly modern. Page through recent issues of almost any popular magazine, and you are likely to find an article on spirituality and health. It's a hot topic of conversation in our current culture, fueled by the media and self-help books.

More surprising is the interest of medical scientists, who throughout this century have insisted on health care based solely on biomedical science. Its attitude toward spirituality has been dismissive. Nowhere is that clearer than the systematic scientific effort to eliminate it as a factor in healing. Double-blind clinical trials are designed to identify the placebo effect as a non-therapeutic factor (inert, nothing). The spiritual term for the placebo effect is faith or expectant trust. What is being measured is not a pharmacological agent vs. nothing, but a pharmacological agent plus faith vs. faith alone. This attitude of indifference, if not disdain, toward spirituality is changing in the world of medicine, as is evident in medical literature, course offerings in medical schools, and above all in clinical settings. The changes are not dramatic, but what was once a closed system of biomedical science is now more open to the role of spirituality in health care.

How can we account for the modern interest in spirituality as a factor in health care? For one thing, people are voting with their feet and their pocketbook, flocking to complementary methods of health care in record number. Many if not most of these methods have either a spiritual basis or a spiritual component in their therapy. The interest of medical science has been prompted by a plethora of mind/body studies, which have produced among other things a new sub-discipline in medicine, psychoneuroimmunology. There is new respect for spirituality in medical circles, a recognition that an exclusive focus on material remedies is too narrow a perspective on healing. What that means for treatment is being sorted out, often on a case-by-case basis. This book is a major contribution toward charting the changes that have taken place and mapping the course we must follow for spirituality to have its rightful place in health care.

Reverend Tom Droege, Ph.D.
Interfaith Health Program, The Carter Center

Preface

The December 1995 conference on "Spirituality and Healing in Medicine," sponsored by the Harvard Medical School, serves as a striking example of the interest in relating health care to spirituality. Just under 1,000 people attended this conference, attracted by the topic and intrigued that it was being sponsored by the prestigious Harvard Medical School. The traditions of medicine and spirituality were given equal standing at this conference, which kept it from being what one might have expected from a medical school: a detached, objective rehearsal of scientific findings about spirituality and medical outcomes. Instead, a full day was given to representatives from various faith traditions who gave moving testimonies to spiritual healings, their own and those they had witnessed. It was obvious to everyone present—health professionals, religious practitioners, and research scientists—that more was happening in spiritual healing practices than science could capture with its methodology. And, for the most part, the spiritual practitioners were open to scientific investigation of their practices, eager to have the validation of science for what they already knew to be true through personal experience and the narratives of those who had been healed. That's a far cry from the attitude of both science and religion that neither had anything to contribute to the other.

This is not the place to review the extensive literature linking spirituality and health. I will, however, give one representative example. It is a study that involved 232 patients over fifty-five years of age, all of whom had elective open-heart surgery for coronary artery or aortic valve disease. Those who said they found at least some strength and comfort from their religious feelings were three times more likely to survive than those who had no comfort from religious faith. Those who participated in social and community groups had three times the survival rate of those who didn't take part in any organized activity. Those seniors who were protected by both spiritual factors—religious and social support—enjoyed a ten-fold increase in survival [1]. Not all studies are that dramatic, but they are consistent in identifying spirituality, and more particularly religion, as a positive indicator for health and healing.

A definition of spirituality and its relation to religion is of utmost importance for understanding the issues being discussed in this volume. The authors of individual chapters will offer their definitions and distinctions as they address particular topics, but it may be useful to the reader if I indicate in general terms the meaning of spirituality and religion and how they are distinguished from each other.

Spirituality is the uniquely human capacity for self-conscious reflection, for relationships of trust and loyalty, and for meaning and purpose. It's in a distinction between the structure and content of spirituality that we can see the relationship between religion and spirituality. The structure of spirituality is the human capacity to love, to remember and anticipate, and above all to experience "the holy." Jung and Frankl speak of an instinctual drive for meaning and purpose. I would prefer to say that human beings are born with a hunger or a need for meaning, for purpose, for belonging. The great Abrahamic faith traditions (Judaism, Christianity, and Islam) understand this native spirituality as reflecting the image of God.

The content of spirituality, on the other hand, is the particular form it takes as the story of a person's life unfolds. The content of spirituality is what a person trusts and is loyal to, especially at the center of his/her life. The content of spirituality is the belief system and values that shape the meaning and purpose of a person's life. The content of spirituality is the formation of a person's identity, his/her self-understanding and self-worth.

The content of spirituality is not necessarily religious. Everybody is spiritual; not everybody is religious. Everybody has spiritual needs, the need for meaning and purpose, for forming relationships, for reassurance, for forgiveness, for hope, for self-esteem, and so forth. Those needs can be met on both a horizontal and a vertical level. The horizontal level refers to all the ways that spiritual needs are met in our common life together through relationships we form, through life goals we set for ourselves, through all the ways we find meaning in our shared lives. The vertical level refers to all the ways our spiritual needs are met in relation to God, and one of the functions of spiritual care is to help people access the resources of their faith tradition to meet those needs.

I trust it's obvious from these remarks that spirituality is not the sole province of pastors, rabbis, and imams, though they need to claim it as their specialty. Health care professionals are beginning to recognize their responsibility for providing spiritual care to patients. That is cause for rejoicing, even though managed care makes it more difficult than ever to practice.

Nurses are far ahead of physicians in their sensitivity to spiritual needs for all the reasons one might suspect. They have more patient contact than physicians, especially in institutional settings. Their profession has historically been oriented more to care than cure. Though changing somewhat, traditional gender differences between physicians and nurses are linked to the differences between objective scientist (physician) and caretaker (nurse). Articles on spiritual care appear regularly in nursing journals but are rarely found in medical journals.

This volume of chapters is a major step forward in putting spirituality in the forefront of discussions about the future of health care. The timing could not be better, given the economic and political factors that are driving the industry toward managed care and capitation. If managed care means the cheapest and most efficient way to deliver traditional medical treatment, there is no future for spirituality in health care, and that includes the role of chaplains. However, if a convincing case can be made that attending to patients' spiritual needs lowers treatment costs and keeps people out of the hospital, then spirituality will play a vital role in the future of health care. Rather than whining about using such a crass economic indicator to judge the worth of spirituality, those of us who are convinced of its worth need to promote studies that demonstrate its cost effectiveness.

Parents do not need to be convinced of the value of spirituality in health care, as polls consistently show. In fact, the biggest threat to managed care is the growing protest of patients to a system of "managed costs" that takes the "care" out of health care. Too often discussions about health care are discussions among medical professionals, politicians, and insurance agents. The patient becomes a factor in these discussions only in relation to treatment of disease and payment of services. Patients as persons with unique spiritual, cultural, ethnic, and gender perspectives are lumped together as a generic patient that is the object of treatment and a source of revenue. The strength of this volume is that the patient's perspective is not only respected but given its rightful place at the center of discussions about the future of health care.

For all the value in giving spirituality the attention it deserves in health care, a caveat is in order. In many current popular books and articles, spirituality is little more than one of many tools that individuals can pull out of their self-help kit. At its best, spirituality is perceived as a complementary technique to be used alongside medical treatment. In other words, spirituality has relevance within a whole-person approach to health care. Not only chaplains, but all health care professionals should not only recognize but nurture this spirituality by being attentive to spiritual needs and providing spiritual care. As indicated, this is a major advance.

However, it is too limited a perspective and if not placed within a broader context can lead to a distorted understanding of health care outcomes. In all faith traditions spirituality is much more than a means of healing. It is the power of God that impels one to service. If spirituality is nothing more than a means to achieving personal health outcomes (both absence of disease and whole-person wellness), then it may well be contributing to a modern form of idolatry. The danger of the wellness movement, especially in a culture that values individual over community health, is that personal health is treated as an end in itself rather than as the means to serving both God and neighbor. Within this broader perspective, spirituality is empowerment for such service.

The editors of this volume, well-known leaders in the field of pastoral care and chaplaincy, deserve high marks for the diversity of perspectives in this volume and their choice of authors. We owe them and the individual authors our gratitude for giving patients a voice and making us all more sensitive to their needs, and particularly their spiritual needs. It is my hope that this volume will not only aid practitioners in care giving but also contribute to policy discussions about the future of health care. Both are expressions of spirituality as empowerment for service.

REFERENCE

1. Oxman, T. E. et al., Lack of Social Participation or Religious Strength and Comfort as Risk Factors for Death after Cardia Surgery in the Elderly, *Psychosomatic Medicine, 57*, pp. 681-689, 1995.

Reverend Tom Droege, Ph.D.
Interfaith Health Program, The Carter Center

Contents

SECTION 1:
Health Care and Spirituality: Professional Perspectives

SECTION 2:
Health Care and Spirituality: Belief System Perspectives

SECTION 3:
Health Care and Spirituality: Ethnic and Gender Perspectives

SECTION 4:
Health Care and Spirituality: Patient Perspectives

Introduction

Reverend Richard B. Gilbert

Institutions stand free of the larger society, yet are expressions of that society. Health care, as an institution, and the institutions where health care is delivered, both express and are victimized by the dynamics that both guide and distract contemporary society.

Rapid change. It has been said that modern medicine has seen more introduced to it in the last fifty years than in the whole previous human experience, and it is an acceleration of change exceeded only by what has been experienced in the last five years.

The geography of health care has changed. Large, fortress-like, "safe" institutions, once places where people "went to die," are being reconfigured, occasionally torn down, and often replaced with drive-by, convenience oriented, "stop-and-shop" centers offering everything from prescription service to surgery to psychotherapy. Diseases that yesterday meant certain death, today are treated with antibiotics and may require only a visit to a physician's office. Outpatient/same-day surgery now applies to over 60 percent of contemporary surgery schedules. Major discoveries with anti-depressants have shut down many inpatient psychiatric units and led to group homes, outpatient care, and private therapy sessions with individual counselors. It has also led to a whole new population of people living on the streets.

"Length of stay," "discharge planning," "utilization review," and "prior authorization" are the watch words of modern medicine and, sadly as some would argue, have become the new language of diagnosis and treatment. Physicians often are guided more by people in distant legislative and funding offices than the tools of medicine.

Ethics committees, unheard of only a few decades ago except for in large teaching hospitals, now are in most hospitals and also appear in hospices, home health agencies, and nursing homes. These committees, combining monitoring, decision making, education, and a screen of legal protection, reflect not only the burgeoning content of new information that needs interpretation and clarification, but the ethical values and weight that come with more and more decisions. Nothing seems simple or straightforward anymore. Many ethics committees now deal more with the morale and needs of the staff, and all of them are shadowed by this age of litigation.

Alternative medicine has become complementary medicine, including new expressions and experiences of spirituality, and they are slowly chipping away at one of the last strongholds of resistance to change: Western medicine. This has also introduced a cast of new characters, new job descriptions, and new approaches to how we provide medical care and what care we will offer.

Spirituality, the "hot" subject in conversation and publications, has gained new attention in health care. Standards for accreditation now include the language of spirituality and also emerging standards for pastoral care. Physicians and other professionals, led by the research offered at the National Institute of Healthcare Research, are investing more of their time and expertise around spiritual matters. Research is providing the data that has given evidence to what chaplains and other spiritual care providers have long known. Spiritual care, once the domain of chaplains and, in many ways, nurses, is now the responsibility of all health care providers. This is redefining the role of chaplains, the providers of pastoral care who must work harder to claim their place as the resources and teachers in spiritual matters, who now find themselves spending more of their time working with staff (training, pastoral care, and counseling) than with patients.

Our awareness of spirituality and religion, how they relate and how they differ, has also been influenced by another strong dynamic in our society and in our institutions. We are becoming more aware of cultural diversity and the diversity that is captured in gender issues, ethnic values, spiritual practices, and how people do and do not make decisions.

There are many other issues that reflect what is happening in medicine and to medicine, medical providers, and health care institutions. What has not changed is the human experience or expression which is at the heart of all that we do in medicine. We still are living with life and living while dying. We still work to provide palliative care for the dying in a society, and in institutions, that still denies our mortality and still sees death as the enemy. Some things never seem to change.

What also has not changed is the ultimate struggle of what it means to be a patient. We have added ventilators, outpatient surgery, discharges that often seem premature, and easy access clinics, but the questions remain the same: "What is happening to me?" "Why is this happening to me?" "How will I cope?" "Is there any hope?" These are the questions of life and death, the language of our patients, and, in some form, the language of those who provide for their care and explore what these issues mean for their own lives. These are also the questions of spirituality, the center of who we are, how we feel about ourselves, how we face the world around us, what/who transcends it all to bring meaning and direction, and what will be our inner strength as we are forced to cope with new experiences in the wilderness of disease, trauma, violence, and aging.

These issues become the stories we call contemporary health care delivery. They are the stories encountered daily by physicians, nurses, social workers, chaplains, therapists, technicians, dietitians, administrators, and the rest of the people who make up the health care team. These stories are people, people who demand that we listen to their story, who work with them to assess, to give meaning, and provide the caring, the appropriate care to address their needs, their stories, their whole selves. We have tried to capture these stories through the balancing of story/experience, data, research, and the details of contemporary health care.

This book is about people and their stories. It is about the response of health care delivery systems to these stories. *First*, the book seeks to be a wake-up call to health care professionals. We have been moved to the margins. The paradigm shift is ongoing. Power and control are shifting away from the medical model to those who set the standards and control the dollars. We are scurrying about to claim our professional identity and standards as the "system" pushes us further into the margins. What does it mean to be a doctor, nurse, social worker, chaplain or another professional these days? Who makes that determination? Are we really free to say or are others seeking to say it for us? So the wake-up call to say that we are in the margins, things are changing, and we must change with the process. Change still doesn't come easily.

Doctors are having to listen to more "authorities," additional "experts," and slow down to work with the team. It no longer works to sneak in, make rounds early so that you can rush through and get to the office. Fortunately it is becoming a team of allies with a common cause or concern, not just "one more thing to slow me down." Teams have meetings. Families want time. Documentation is increasing at a rapid fire pace. Nurses went into their profession in response to the sacredness of a profession committed to the care of people. Much of this "care" is now realized through meetings, charting, more charting, and as "electricians" who reluctantly spend more time responding to equipment than to people. It has led to an enormous morale issue for many nurses who state, "I don't have time to spend with people anymore." Social workers train for case management, advocacy, therapy, and intervention, and find the very name "social worker" often redefined as a discharge planner. Many social workers have been pulled off the floors, moved away from the patients, and confined to a desk and telephone to "move people through the system." More and more chaplains are losing their jobs, and those remaining do "God-on-the-run" pastoral care, while trying to keep pace with change, the rush of schedules, the relocation of patients to a variety of new campuses and delivery styles, while still trying to listen, counsel staff, work with families, train clergy, recruit volunteers, and keep up the twenty-four-hour-a-day, seven-day-a-week pace that is essential to chaplaincy. The largest single group of chaplains identified in their professional organizations is "one person departments." The only "cut" left may be the entire program. Life in the margins.

Second, in the stories and data presented by the various contributors, we are also offering the perspective that nothing has changed. We can lash out about what has happened to health care, and those messages must be raised. It does take us away from our professional/vocational responsibilities for listening, assessing, caring. We do have to rethink our priorities, how we spend our time, and how to work more effectively as a team. It does mean that we become wary of the turf battles that can easily arise in a paradigm shift, and keep ourselves focused on the patient. It means that all of us commit to the listening that is still the bottom line of health care, despite a few voices who would suggest that the bottom line is the budget. It means that nurses do nursing, and that that includes spiritual care, spiritual assessment, and working with the chaplains. It means that, while insurance companies legislate the amount of time physicians are to spend with the patient, the doctors still can ask the important questions, add the important pieces of the story to their assessment, and willingly listen to the messages of the entire team. Even when limited to the desk and the telephone, social workers have a great opportunity to claim the story of the patient and include it as the vital message in discharge planning. Chaplains may not have as many opportunities just to sit at the bedside and listen (the patients may not be there), but they still are the people called, as Holst describes in his writings, as those who walk in two kingdoms, the kingdom of God/spiritual/mystery and the kingdom of the institution.

The vocation remains the same because the stories, the people, remain the same.

Finally, as marginalized professionals forced to answer to many new authorities and expectations, it is in the margins where we do our best work. It is in the margins where we meet the patients and their families, marginalized by disease, trauma, violence, aging, emotional distress, spiritual crisis, and the many other experiences of life that bring them into our margins as we seek to enter theirs. It is there, in the margins, when we move, even momentarily, from the system to the person, where we will again recognize that there is a story, hear that story, and, working with the patients and their loved ones, work through meaning/assessment to quality care.

Even with some hoped-for chapters omitted, the book grew too large. As a result we had to delete the extensive annotated bibliography and the descriptive information on The Association of Professional Chaplains and The National Association of Catholic Chaplains. This information is available from the editor.

*   *   *

We are indebted to the many along the way who, verbally or otherwise, "said" this story needed to be told, to Stuart Cohen, Baywood Publishing Company, and to the many contributors (especially the non-clergy who spoke so eloquently about these issues). It is impossible to thank Jack Morgan sufficiently for all he means to me personally, to health care, and especially to the worlds of ethics, care of the dying, and bereavement care. To me he is the consummate friend, mentor, teacher, confessor, and priest.

Reverend Richard B. Gilbert

Transversing Purgatory

Reverend Denise A. Ryder

Dingy, dark, dreary.
Stale, dusty air
stirred by exhaust
of unknowns from above.
Slippery, slimy floors—
feet glide then grab abruptly.
Walls of rusty white,
curdling like outdated buttermilk.
Spectres seemingly slide
along the walls.
Muted voices
reverberate from afar.
Alone. Isolated.
Fear not.
You are with me.

SECTION 1:

HEALTH CARE AND SPIRITUALITY: PROFESSIONAL PERSPECTIVES

Introduction

Reverend Richard B. Gilbert

"Divide and conquer" may be an appropriate strategy in war games, but it has become an all too common dynamic in contemporary health care. Today's health care litany, "Managed care, limitations, legislation, downsizing," unfolds as we swing from pillar to post trying to respond to this rapid fire change. These are adjustments that often occur despite our inability to discern their wisdom and often they are perceived as in conflict with our professional standards and workplace goals. We experience a diminished capacity to negotiate effective change that both understands and upholds our professional and spiritual values.

Change is occasionally welcomed when we feel we have some control over the intrusion of change and its outcome. The rude awakening in health care is that change has snuck in the back door like an unwelcomed intruder, a sudden burst of wind that has knocked us off the foundations of our values and standards.

The question becomes, "Who is in charge here?" as patients continue to ask, "Will you take care of me?" We lash out in every and any direction because there is no one person or power to blame. The federal government? The legislators? Doctors? The Board of Directors? Insurance companies? Patients? God? Death? No place here to hang our hats, so we divide and conquer to protect our own interests, ambitions, and commitments.

In the midst of all of this is the patient, surrounded by loved ones and friends and cared for by an enormous array of professionals and volunteers. All have something to give us and all demand something from us. It is not we versus them, but all of us, in tandem, a team, working together for the common good of the patient and the workplace.

This section offers chapters that approach the book's themes through the perspectives of several professional disciplines. We see the unique challenges of identifying, molding, and, at times, healing the organizational culture, with special mention of the spiritual dynamics present and the role of the chaplain in identifying those needs for the patients. Cynthia Russell opens this section with a strong statement on the role of the nurse in tending to the holistic needs of patients. Chaplain Richard Stewart, retired supervisor of chaplains for the United Methodist Church and a past president of the Association of Professional Chaplains, offers an historic overview of the professional development of chaplains, serving as a foundation for an expanded discussion of who chaplains are, what they do, and how they work as team members in the care of the patients and the providers.

The historic perspective continues with a contemporary and future perspective offered by Chaplain Richard Gilbert.

While this book is not about chaplains alone, it is an important reminder from a group of professionals who often go quietly about their work and do not take the needed time to articulate their story. It is a preliminary look at the unique place for both spiritual care and pastoral care, and how they must come together for quality health care. In the final contribution, David Adams and Rick Csiernik offer a timely study that serves as their preliminary evaluation of their spiritual survey of health care professionals and a growing awareness of the spiritual needs of the professionals called upon to face working in the contemporary health care setting.

CHAPTER 1

A Nurse's Perspective

Cynthia Russell

He said to her, "Daughter, your faith has healed you. Go in peace and be freed from your suffering" [Mark 5:34].

> William was sixty-four years old and had battled his demons for nearly all of those years. Unfortunately, at this time the demons were prevailing. For some reason he told himself his mental illness was easier to oppose when he was younger. The latest wonder drug to combat schizophrenia did not stop what he referred to as "the pressure in my head." He viewed himself as "old" and felt that he would never again find relief from his agony. William had lost all hope. Yet, as I held William's hand in mine, I felt blessed to be in his presence. Tortured though it might be, William allowed me to touch his spirit, the essence of his being. As we sat together surrounded by the activity of the psychiatric unit, there was a connection. I sensed an individual of great integrity and depth, a fine and caring soul. Though the medication had not been able to quell the pain, the human connection had allowed him a few moments of peace. William reported that he felt somewhat better as he left to attend group therapy.

Far from the life and death drama of an emergency room or intensive care unit, where spiritual connectedness might be expected, the above scenario illustrates a more routine nurse-patient experience. With more than 2.2 million nurse colleagues in the United States alone, this chapter represents but one voice on the subject of spirituality and nursing. One voice, however, in a sea of voices. Nursing is one of a select group of disciplines, including medicine and the ministry, which is permitted to routinely connect with the human spirit. An almost

3

universal premise, nurses care for the physical, emotional, intellectual, social, and spiritual needs of people. These are the parts of the whole person; all interconnected and inseparable. This translates into the holistic practice of nursing.

However, in this world of advanced technology in health care, pressured by cost-containment activities, the connection of nurses with the spirit of those in our care is at risk of extinction. This is an unacceptable loss to "high-tech" clinical environments, managed care, and down-sizing. It puts not only the patient but also the essence of the nursing profession in grave peril.

This chapter will explore the link between spirituality and nursing. A framework for better understanding nursing's connection to care of the spirit is considered. Actual nurse-patient interactions will illustrate this association. The chapter concludes with a brief look at the consequences of a "spirit-less" system of nursing care and considers "spirit-enhancing" opportunities for nurses that exist in today's health care environment.

SPIRITUALITY AND NURSING

From the Latin "spiritus" or breath, spirit is described as the vital principle or animating force traditionally believed to be within living beings [1]. The term "vital" identifies the spirit as a necessary aspect of being human. "Animating force" presents the image of being filled with life. Spirit is also recognized as the essential nature of the person, the soul. It is clear from its roots: the spirit is at the central core of human existence.

Recognizing the universal presence of spirit, spirituality is a broad concept that includes values, meaning, and purpose [2]. Nagai-Jacobson and Burkhardt identify spirituality as that which gives meaning and purpose to life [3]. According to Burkhardt, spirituality is described as an unfolding mystery, harmonious interconnectedness, and inner strength [4]. Unfolding mystery deals with life's uncertainties and the discovery and struggles with finding meaning and purpose in one's life. Relatedness to self, others, and God or Higher Being reflects harmonious interconnectedness. Inner strength includes one's inner resources, consciousness, and sacredness.

Noted psychotherapist Victor Frankl refers to a person's search for meaning as the primary motivation of life [5]. Tensions may be aroused in search for life's meaning. Frankl believes that these tensions facilitate our journey toward health and are the key to our survival. Frankl credits

Nietzsche with summarizing this best as he quotes, "He who has a why to live for can bear almost any how."

Since the nurse joins all of humankind on this lifelong journey, he/she must first be open to examining his/her spirituality. This is a necessary precursor to supporting the patient's journey. Self-reflective questions of meaning and purpose, inner strengths, and inter-connections must be considered closely by the nurse. This is a dynamic process requiring the nurse to continuously reexamine his/her under-standing of life's meaning and purpose. In this process of self-exploration, the nurse is aware that religious considerations are but one component of his/her spirituality. Religious beliefs may contribute to the nurse's understanding of life's meaning, but these beliefs are not a required component of his/her spiritual sense of being.

The profession of nursing provides ample opportunity for self-reflection and analysis of life's meanings. John, a student enrolled in a psychiatric nursing course, was confronted with one such occasion. John was assigned to a young woman who made an unsuccessful suicide attempt the preceding night. Near the end of the shift, John came to me in near tears. He was struggling with this patient's intense desire to die. This was contrary to John's belief that life was a gift from God.

As God's gift, the student believed that life could not be inten-tionally ended. On analysis, John recognized that his Christian beliefs provided the foundation to this understanding. He also realized that his family gave his life meaning, something that this young woman found to be a void. Through direct confrontation, John was able to clarify and increase his awareness of his feelings about the value of his life and the lives of those in his care. He became aware that his faith in God and the support of his family provided him with inner strength and a sense of connectedness. At the young age of twenty-one, John emerged from this experience with a deeper appreciation of his spiritual self.

The nurse, because of his/her close association to deeply spiritual issues often linked to illness and suffering, is compelled to examine life's meanings and purpose, inner strengths, and interconnections. As illus-trated by the above scenario, this process necessarily begins while the nurse is still a student. Few who enter nursing realize that a career in nursing is also a part of their spiritual journey. I frequently ask students at the beginning of their studies, "Why nursing?" The most common response to this question is, "I want to be a nurse so that I can help people." Most beginning students appreciate the extensive under-standing of human functions that is essential to their preparation as a nurse. Few, however, are aware that study of the human spirit, especially their own, will be required.

While journal articles and textbooks provide the foundations for understanding the science of nursing, the anatomy of the spirit is most frequently examined in the clinical setting. Nurse educators incorporate the task of fostering spiritual awareness in students through such methods as case analysis, seminar discussions, and journal entries. Few health disciplines offer this possibility so early in professional study, nor with such earnest attention to self-exploration and awareness.

The spiritual connectedness that begins with the nursing student, continues throughout the career of the nurse. Natural developmental stages of growth, changing trends in health care, exposure to new case situations, and personal encounters with illness and suffering make it difficult for the nursing professional to be spiritually stagnant. The nurse is consistently confronted with opportunities that encourage revision or increased depth of understanding of the purposes and meaning of life, or possibly a clearer awareness of a Higher Power.

A FRAMEWORK FOR SPIRITUAL CARE

The nurse, in touch with his/her spirituality, can facilitate the spiritual connectedness of patients and their families. How is this possible? In times of illness and suffering patients are more acutely aware of their vulnerability. Defense processes like denial of human mortality and rationalization of symptoms are difficult to maintain during episodes of distress. Individuals have the opportunity to more closely examine their purpose and meaning of life, recognize inner strengths, and become more aware of interconnections at risk periods in their lives.

Wherever the patient finds himself/herself, whether in the acute care hospital, nursing home, or at home, nurses are usually present. Typically this presence is for an extended time, such as an eight- or twelve-hour shift or regularly scheduled home visits. Other health care professionals will be engaged in the care of the patient, but it is nursing's unique place in the health care system to provide for twenty-four-hour coverage. Of course this is not the responsibility of one nurse, but many. However, nursing as a discipline strives toward the provision of continuity of care. At its best, nursing care should be seamless and comprehensive.

Mere presence does not explain the nurse's role in the engagement of patients on a spiritual level. An essential ingredient is the establishment of a trusting relationship between the nurse and the patient. Not only is the nurse present, but she/he remains with the patient in oft-times challenging circumstances. In times of illness and suffering, societal rules fade and our public facade is dropped. The nurse is allowed to move into and out of the personal, sacred space of the patient. A few examples will help to illustrate this point. The nurse will wash the body of the patient who is unable to clean himself/herself. The nurse will feed the patient too weak to lift the spoon. The nurse will tend to matters of elimination. These are deeply personal acts. The nurse sees the patient unshaven or without make-up. The nurse holds the emisis basin for the cancer patient sickened by the chemotherapy medications infusing into his/her body. The nurse is frequently there at time of death to comfort the grieving family members. In each of these examples the nurse, by means of the trusting relationship, moves beyond the customary social space and into a spiritual space.

A personal experience comes to mind as I reflect on the power of the nurse-patient relationship to quickly transcend social boundaries and move into a sacred and spiritual place. I had arranged to meet with the wife of a patient with moderately advanced Alzheimer's disease in their home. Though we had never met, she greeted me at her door with a kiss and held me close. Even today, I can recall the powerful connection of our spiritual selves. Over the next three hours, she shared her inner-most thoughts and experiences in caring for her husband. She described that caring for her husband gave purpose and meaning to her life. She felt connected to her God and to her church home. She describe how her relationships with her children had been strengthened over times following her husband's diagnosis. We laughed and we cried. When I left, she expressed her joy at having an opportunity to share from deep within herself.

I know that it was not specifically Nurse Cynthia Russell that was given entry into her sacred space. We were strangers. Rather, I represented the caring presence of "the nurse" and was allowed to share this time and space as she poured out her life's story. I entered her home partnered with the nurses that preceded me and with those to follow. Before asking one question or sharing a thought, this caregiver invited me to join her spiritual plane. She exposed her spiritual self through her thoughts and actions as the interview progressed. She described how she suffered loosing her loving husband of nearly fifty years to this cruel disease without cure. Despite all the hardships his illness created, she identified that it gave her life meaning. In her sorrow, she also found peace of purpose.

Donley, using Johnstone's framework of understanding human suffering, eloquently describes three distinct approaches to suffering [6]. These include compassionate accompaniment or being with the suffering person, giving meaning or bringing an interpretation to the responses and causes of suffering, and action to alleviate suffering and/or its causes. It could be convincingly argued that the nurse might be involved in all of these approaches, along with members of the clergy, family, physicians, and other health-care providers. As I described in the preceding section, the nurse often engages in compassionate accompaniment.

While the nurse is less likely to interpret the causes of suffering, he/she frequently implements actions to reduce or alleviate the suffering. This is especially true of suffering expressed as pain. There are numerous interventions performed by the nurse to reduce or alleviate suffering, but perhaps none more pertinent than the administration of pain-relieving medications. Though the physician often prescribes the medications, it is the nurse who presents them to the patient. Medications are dispensed on either a regular schedule or on an as-needed basis. In the case of the on demand medications, the nurse is closely connected to the patient's here-and-now experience of suffering.

In monitoring the effects of the medication, the nurse is often at the patient's side as he/she experiences pain relief. Providing that the patient is not heavily sedated by the medication, these periods of relief are often deeply reflective times for the patient. Spiritual connectedness can be facilitated by the attentive nurse, willing to listen and support the patient.

Besides medications, nursing has a tradition of using non-invasive, non-chemical methods to relieve pain and suffering and promote spiritual health. Bauer and Barron identify numerous spiritual-care nursing interventions including offering to pray with patients, inspiring patient's to be hopeful, respecting the patient's religious articles and rituals, preparing the environment to promote spiritual matters, arranging for the clergy to visit, and alerting patients of spiritual services and programming [7].

Other interventions might include the use of massage, therapeutic touch, proper body positioning, guided imagery, and environmental adjustments to temperature, lighting, odors, and noise. These multi-dimensional comfort measures are targeted at supporting the patient in a holistic manner as he/she heals.

A SPIRITLESS SYSTEM: CONTRIBUTING FACTORS

The discussion of spirituality and nursing up to this point has been from a very positive perspective. It is also important to reflect on negative influences and considerations in today's health care arena. This could be referred to as the spiritless system of care. In this section several factors that contribute to a loss of spirituality are examined.

These factors include nurses who have in effect "shut down" their spiritual connectedness both personally and professionally, the movement toward managed care and down-sizing, and the increased reliance on technology and the allopathic approach to care. In many ways it is difficult to separate these factors since they are often interrelated. However, for the sake of this discussion I have examined each one independently.

As mentioned earlier in this chapter, the nurse must be aware of the significance of spirituality in the total well-being of patients, both in times of sickness and health. The nurse or student nurse must be sensitive to his/her own spiritual issues to facilitate spiritual connectedness with those receiving care. The nurse can develop a spiritual block or barrier, and in effect "shut down" his/her spiritual self-awareness. As with all human beings, nurses are at risk of closing down spiritually as a response to emotionally charged material from childhood, an abusive home situation, addictive behaviors, depression, and the like. No one is immune to this response. Personal issues of the nurse are carried into the work place. The nurse who is numb to her own spiritual issues is not in a position to foster the spiritual growth of others. Only when the nurse is willing to confront his/her own spiritual issues will he/she be fully available to the patients under his/her care.

The day-to-day exposure to the pain and suffering of patients can have a numbing effect on the nurse. Even as it is a gift that the nurse is permitted to move into the spiritual realm of care, it can also be extremely difficult. The act of the spiritual "shut down" can occur as a self-protective device used by the nurse to maintain his/her ability to go to work each day. This can occur when one patient's suffering or pain makes the nurse feel too vulnerable. It could be the result of a cumulative effect of a number of patients. The numbing of the nurse can be brief and transitory or it could continue indefinitely and become a terminal state. Often the nurse is unaware of what has happened to his/her ability to connect on spiritual issues. The care for the physical, emotional, social, and intellectual needs of the patient continue. Something, however, is missing in the holistic care of the patient. The patient may be aware of this distance, recognizing that he/she cannot enter into a spiritual exploration of the meaning and purpose of their experience with the nurse. If an attempt is made by the patient, the nurse avoids or ignores the request for spiritual support. The nurse does this as a means of self-preservation.

From my experience at the bedside of pediatric patients and their families, I recall inviting a spiritual "shut down" to occur. In a period of two days I cared for the family of an eighteen-month-old child dying of cancer, a child with a rare degenerative disease which had reversed her functional ability from a healthy five year old to five months, an eleven-month-old baby who suffered a severe concussion along with several broken bones at the hands of his father, and a two-year-old child whose feet were amputated at the ankles following an accident with a lighted stove.

As could be imagined, I along with the other care providers and families could not dismiss the questions of "why" and "for what purpose." I prayed to God for understanding and strength, though I would have been thankful for a spiritual anesthetic. I rejoiced when my shifts were complete. It was difficult to find peace even at home. Away from the bedside, the questions of purpose and meaning continued to plague me. I do recall that I held my six-month-old son and husband especially close during those days. This was a spiritually challenging time for me. The children and their families taught me a great deal about putting faith in God for unanswerable questions, summoning inner strength, and relying on interconnections for stability. Another lesson garnered from this experience was how vulnerable nurses and all care providers can be to spiritual numbing. A spiritual "shut down" can occur at any time, to any nurse, and last for an indefinite period of time.

While the media abounds with discussions of changes that have occurred in today's managed care environment, few have discussed the affects such changes have had on the spiritual aspects of care. A primary goal of the managed care movement is to promote health and wellness while decreasing consumer use of expensive interventions and treatments. When hospitalization is required, the aim is to reduce the time in the hospital to the shortest possible length. Shortened hospital stays and early discharges diminish the total time available to the nurse to explore spiritual issues with a patient. The time that is available is further complicated by other important efforts of the care process. Laboratory tests and imaging procedures might take the patient away from his/her room for extended periods of time. Rehabilitation activities, such as physical, occupational, and speech therapy, begin almost immediately with hospitalization. In addition, time must be devoted to the teaching-learning needs of patients to be discharged to the home. The patient and his/her family are expected to be involved in learning the necessary techniques and methods of care to support treatment in the home. Unstructured time is reduced to the barest minimum in an environment that is focused on early discharge. In the past, this unstructured time was the nurse's window of opportunity to gain entry into the patient's spiritual fears and concerns. Today's nurse must take advantage of any situation that might allow for spiritual exploration because another opportunity may not present itself before discharge.

The down-sizing experienced in many acute care facilities, while closely related to the move to managed care, brings additional concerns. The shift to employ fewer professional nurses and more unlicensed assistive personnel is a reality in most hospitals. Nurses must delegate to the support personnel many direct care activities previously found only in the nursing domain. While these assistants may be competent to complete specific tasks of patient care, they often do not have the educational background nor the preparation to met the holistic needs of the patient. This is particularly true for the spiritual aspects of care. Without the professional nurse at the bedside, the spiritual needs of the suffering may go undetected and untreated.

One final element of a "spiritless" system of care is medicine's heavy use of life-supporting and sustaining technology. The miracle of these scientific advances has come at some cost. First, nursing care is often relegated to attending to the machines that support the patient's life. The human being beneath the lines, tubes, monitors, and regulators can begin to fade into the mechanistic surroundings. The nurse must guard against viewing the patient as a part of the technology. The spiritual concerns of the patient can become lost as the nurse attends to the physical aspects of care.

Second, today's advances in medicine can give the illusion that death can be avoided. Physicians, nurses, patients, and families can build a faith around the technology of care leaving little room for the spiritual component of illness. The issues of the spiritual realm can be excluded in preference of this form of denial that relies on hope and scientific precedence. The belief in the healing power of allopathic medicine can be maintained even into the dying process, leaving little opportunity for the patient and his/her family to deal with concerns of the spirit.

SPIRIT-ENHANCING OPPORTUNITIES IN NURSING

This chapter concludes with a brief discussion of some spirit-enhancing opportunities and approaches to nursing in today's health care environment. The comments to follow are directed at nursing care in general versus nursing specialties such as parish or hospice nursing. Certainly some branches of nursing have more experience and expertise in matters of the spirit.

As a consequence of shorter hospital stays and the increased reliance on ambulatory care centers, nursing care has migrated into the community and home. With the rebirth of in-home nursing care comes the opportunity for nurses to attend to patient needs in the domain of the patient. This environment can be extremely conducive to supporting a patient's spirituality. Away from the sterile hospital room with its constant noise, bright lights, and frequent interruptions, the patient at home can stay connected with people, pets, and personal belongings that give life meaning and purpose. The privacy often afforded in the home setting is frequently more supportive of spiritual explorations as well.

One patient with cancer described the spiritual space that she found at home this way: "I can look out my window to my backyard to the birds that flutter between the bird feeders and I am transported to my scared, safe place. It is here that I find relief from the anxiety and pain of this disease." The nurse in the community must be sensitive to these increased opportunities to discuss spiritual matters such as meaning and purpose, inner strength, and interconnections. Out of these discussions the nurse can obtain a better understanding of the individual patient. Beyond the therapeutic qualities inherent in discussions of spiritual concerns, the nurse can gain powerful insight into patient-centered care. For example, I was able to integrate the scared space of the backyard with the flutter of the birds into the guided imagery exercise developed in collaboration with the patient quoted above. A personalized tape recording became a central part of this patient's treatment regimen, along with standard oncology treatment.

In-home care also offers the possibility of developing an ongoing relationship between the patient and his/her family and the nurse. With the chronic nature of many of today's health-care concerns, the nurse might be involved with the patient for extended periods. Efforts should be made to maintain stable patient assignments. Over time, an increased level of comfort could be expected to develop between the patient and nurse that could foster the patient's willingness to talk about the intimate issues of the spirit. Also, the nurse might expand his/her plan of care to emphasize care of the patient's spirit over the course of treatment.

Qualitative and quantitative research studies, within the discipline of nursing and beyond, are published that address the significance of spiritual factors in health and healing. Nurses must be aware of this research and consider its implications for nursing practice. As an applied science, nurse researchers should be encouraged to engage in the scientific exploration of spiritual aspects of care with greater frequency.

Finally, I would challenge nurses to capitalize on society's movement toward spiritual matters. In the decade of the '90s, the popularity of authors addressing spiritual concerns, such as Thomas Moore, Caroline Myss, Joan Borysenko, and Deepak Chopra, provides evidence of the public's desire to examine spiritual issues. Without evaluating the theses of these authors, their fashionablity speaks to a society's search for spiritual connectedness. This would be especially true for those individuals confronting illness and suffering, with their questions of meaning and purpose, inner strength, and interconnections. Though not generalizing to all patients, nurses should view this indicator that suggests spiritual care is valued by the patient and his/her family. This reinforces the central premise that every nurse-patient situation should include the spiritual component as part of a holistic plan of nursing care.

REFERENCES

1. *The American Heritage Dictionary,* 2nd Edition, Houghton Mifflin, Boston, 1985.
2. B. M. Dossey, The Transpersonal Self and States of Consciousness, in *Holistic Health Promotion: A Guide for Practice,* B. Dossey, L. Keegan, L. Kolkmeier, and C. Guzzetta (eds.), Aspen, Rockville, Maryland, pp. 23-35, 1989.
3. M. G. Nagai-Jacobson and M. A. Burkhardt, Spirituality: Cornerstone of Holistic Nursing Practice, *Holistic Nursing Practice, 3*:3, pp. 18-26, 1989.
4. M. A. Burkhardt, Spirituality: An Analysis of the Concept, *Holistic Nursing Practice, 3*:3, pp. 69-77, 1989.
5. V. E. Frankl, *Man's Search for Meaning,* Beacon Press, Boston, 1959.
6. R. Donley, Spiritual Dimensions of Health Care, Nursing's Mission, *Nursing & Health Care, 12*:4, pp. 178-183, 1991.
7. T. Bauer and C. Barron, Nursing Interventions for Spiritual Care, *Journal of Holistic Nursing, 13*:3, pp. 268-279, 1995.

CHAPTER 2

A Chaplain's Perspective:
The Early Years

Reverend Richard Stewart

While it is true that hospital stays may bring good news as well as bad, in most cases, by nature, one's life is impacted by hospitalization (inpatient and outpatient) in such a manner that stress, danger, challenge, or fear are often part of the equation. Physicians admit patients usually for one cause, and that cause can pose a real problem for the patient, and for the patient's family members. In some cases the cause and the hospitalization can pose a real problem for the medical staff and for those who tend the patient and his or her family members.

In a long-ago moment in our country's history, persons went to the hospital primarily for emergencies and to die. The hospital often was the last defense against death. That defense was often breached.

Infections, conditions less than sanitary, severe wounds and injuries, old age, weak and infirmed bodies all combined to make the hospital almost feared as a place in which persons might place their loved ones.

War, the greatest killer of all, had the amazing effect of leading to procedures and medicines and treatments on the battlefield which translated to cures and treatment modalities in the peace-time hospital. Vietnam, with the dust off helicopter and the MASH (Mobile Army Surgical Hospital), saw the advent of in-the-field medical care unequaled in the history of warfare. Any American soldier in any skirmish in Vietnam was always within minutes of medical care, should it be required. Many soldiers who would have died before the introduction of the dust off helicopter found themselves receiving life-saving medical

15

care days earlier than would have been possible previously. The wait between the infliction of severe bodily trauma and the introduction of supreme medical intervention had been miraculously narrowed to a relatively few minutes. Soldiers engaged in battle knew that if they could survive the penetration of the wound-inflicting missile, they had a good chance of surviving. The helicopter whisked them to medicines which did much to relieve the trauma and to move them toward a much more rapid healing process than our forebears could have ever imagined.

Our sisters and brothers in medicine have had no difficulty in translating what they learned on the battlefield and introducing it into the civilian community. Cosmetic surgeries, blood transfusion, head and neck surgeries, the emergency room with its triage system, the EMT, all of them ideas honed to near-perfection on the battlefield experience are now incorporated into the modern day hospital, or themselves replaced with even more creative procedures. So smoothly has this been done that many current medical students may have lost the appreciation of modern medicine's benefits from the horrors of war.

It will surprise many of those students to learn that right there in the middle of the conflict of war was a representative of the religious community, a military chaplain. Everywhere the soldier went into combat, the chaplain came and brought the representative presence of Almighty God into the midst of the demonic. These were chaplains of many faiths and denominations, for the soldier was of all faith systems and denominations, and of no particular belief system.

The chaplain was also the pastor for those who professed no faith, and in some instances insisted that they desired no religious expression at all. This was respected, of course. Many such soldiers still had great respect for the chaplain, one who was exposed to the same dangers as were the soldier, but who was committed to being present without taking up arms to protect the chaplain's own life.

Through Clinical Pastoral Education (C.P.E.) the worlds of chaplaincy in the hospital and chaplaincy in the military began to merge, as more and more military chaplains found themselves taking training in civilian institutions. These military chaplains volunteered to have themselves removed from the military "track" (necessary to promotion and a successful military career) in order to take C.P.E. In some cases some of these chaplains went on to become C.P.E. supervisors.

Civilian C.P.E. students and supervisors were often pleasantly surprised at the breadth of the military chaplain's experiences, and the chaplain's ability to deal with authority issues, while daily living in a world in which authority issues had to be easily dealt with and incorporated into the chaplain's being. Were that not the case, the chaplain would have long since been discontinued as a contributor to health care.

As the differences between the two types of chaplains began to disappear, their commonality began to emerge. Whether sharing in the concern and pain of a colleague's loss of a loved one, or in the elation of a colleague's celebration at getting through to a patient who had been so threatened by a judgmental God that the patient had locked herself into an impossible position of blaming her child's illness on her own unworthiness and sin. Through verbatims and Interpersonal Relations (I.P.R.) sessions barriers tumbled and friendships developed. The medical staff and the nursing staff were the direct beneficiaries of a chaplaincy that produced mature, competent, capable representatives of the church and synagogue. As these chaplains became more seasoned in their judgment and competent in their expression, the inter-disciplinary team found worthy compatriots, persons whom they trusted and valued.

While there was not a great flood of these chaplains, those who interrelated with each other shared understandings and experiences which made each better. The military chaplain, who had been exposed to death and dying in ways almost impossible to fathom (death by sudden and extreme violence inflicted through bombings and rockets), now found death and the threat of death considerably different from previous journeys. While death and violence came, it now came at a much different pace, and the continued bombardment of its effect was lessened by the lessening of the numbers. Even in the big city hospital and large emergency room (except the hectic weekend and holiday nights), this pace was less terrifying. While in the big city trauma room care and concern has to be expressed, for the most part the physical danger of the war itself is not present in the room.

Essential to an expression of the place of the chaplain in the medical hospital is the full realization that always and utterly the concern of the patient comes first. Chaplains, as do all of the members of the interdisciplinary team, have the care of the patient as primary and essential. Because of the nature of the patient's illness or injury, the patient gives away most of whatever power they may have had when they came into the institution. The patient has no choice on when going to bed, or when arising. There are precious few choices on nutrients and fluids. Visitors are regulated (generally not based on patient wishes) by the decisions of others.

The patient gives this control with the expectation that the result will be health and well-being, followed by discharge to home. This would seem to be a fair bargain. It obviously does not always work out that way. Sometimes in the helplessness experienced by patients, the reality is that what was bargained for will not be the reality.

Physicians who make the determinations on treatment, admission, and discharge often exercise this freedom without any expression of opposition from the patient.

The chaplain is a member of the interdisciplinary team. The chaplain is a specialist, yet often viewed as the last generalist left. He or she is usually professionally trained and certified for ministry in this setting, and can still be viewed as the last "safe place" for patients, and, yes, for staff members.

The chaplain is well versed in spiritual matters, but understands the difference between spiritual care, which is the commitment of all concerned with the well-being of a patient, and pastoral care, bringing special insights, experiences, resources, and strengths to the care of the patient. The chaplain articulates this role through constant example, through a steady presence, and through ongoing education and clarification. The chaplain travels across the many disciplines as pastor of the entire institution, but respects the boundaries that emerge within the team. Through case conferences, consultations, discharge planning, and individual contact, the chaplain gives input on the patient's spiritual outlook, moral and morale problems, and the endless struggle to find meaning and hope.

The chaplain respects confidentiality. If circumstances threaten that confidentiality, the chaplain's Religious Endorsing Body is prepared to advise the chaplain and the institution on these issues and dynamics.

The Religious Endorsing Body is the faith group's official endorsing agency, and is entitled to speak for the faith group on matters involving the deployment and selection of its chaplains. It involves the establishment of requirements and continuing relationship between the individual chaplain and the church or faith group represented. Minimum training involves units of Clinical Pastoral Education and certification by The Association of Professional Chaplains and/or The National Association of Catholic Chaplains. Because the chaplain must be supported by a faith group, each pastoral care provider must continue in good relationship with that endorsing body.

Two brief examples on how the chaplain impacts on the healing processes and well-being of patients follow. These are stories and they are not uncommon to the life and work of the chaplain. The first is a woman who is presented with medical information that strongly suggest that she consider terminating her pregnancy. It is clear that, at least at the outset, the patient's religious training prohibits these kinds of decisions or alternatives. The chaplain is present to protect the rights and beliefs of the patient should they be brought into question, and also to help her explore the spiritual, emotional, and grief issues that may be present. The chaplain does this regardless of his or her own preferences on this or any other ethical issue.

The second story is that of a C.P.E. student who was serving in a Neonatal Intensive Care Unit of a large teaching hospital. The small unit had room for eight babies. The decision to select out prospective neonates fell to the medical staff of that unit. One day the chief of that service polled his colleagues on selecting who would enter or leave the unit in the crunch of census problems. The decision was reckoning not with beds and numbers, but with deciding which baby would die and which baby might have a chance to live. Each person was asked his or her opinion; finally the doctor asked, "Chaplain, how do you vote?"

That story affirms the place of pastoral care within the team, and the invitation chaplains receive to be present in the very life of the institution and in the daily struggles and obstacles experienced by patients and by staff. It is not uncommon that chaplains, on a given day, will spend more time with staff than with patients. The weight of change in health care is staggering. Ethical issues deliberated and debated are never easy, cutting to the essence of life's meaning, which includes the spiritual. In many institutions employees struggle to stay patient-focused when they know that, at any time, the next "pink slip" will be theirs. This is life in the contemporary hospital, and it is the "parish" of our hospital chaplains. It also begs the question of why, in the name of cost effectiveness and profit, chaplains are often the first cut. What is this saying about the "health" of health care?

Chaplaincy is often a silent presence. Chaplains historically have sacrificed the invitations to write their experiences and tell their stories, opting instead to use that time for a pastoral care of presence. Some good writing does exist, and we conclude with two quotes about who chaplains are and what they do. In his book *The Hospital Chaplain*, Kenneth Mitchell offers the following observation, edited to reflect a more inclusive perspective:

> A chaplain is a *person* with a foot in two worlds: the world of faith and the world of modern medicine:
> Not a doctor, but often asked to "explain" an operation.
> Not a priest, but sometimes a baptizer of Catholic babies.
> Not a social worker, but often a family counselor.
> Not a professor, but on and off a teacher of young doctors.
> Not a parish pastor, but usually a pastoral counselor.
> In a society where medicine is more and more complex and impersonal, a *person* who sometimes can make the hospital seem more human.
> Sometimes just a *person* who listens over coffee to the bitching of a scared and exhausted young intern.

A *person* whose prayers are seldom uttered in the quiet of a church, but more often on the run, or down the hall, or as *he/she* hangs up the phone.

A *person* who can't ignore the special claims of *his/her* own *religious community,* who must wrestle with his own faith (and faithfulness), but . . .

A *person* who may have to minister to Baptists, Pentecostalists, Jews, Catholics, Presbyterians, and help them tussle with their own beliefs in the midst of crisis.

An impossible job?

Maybe that's why *he/she* does it [1, p. 16].

Or this more contemporary look, from *Spiritual Care of Dying and Bereaved People*, by Penelope Wilcock.

A considerable amount of a chaplain's time is spent in simply hanging loose with patients and staff, talking and laughing, over inconsequential things, and time spent like this is not wasted. It is thus that ground is established so that when a patient or family member or member of staff needs to talk, a friendship has been established, a foundation for trust. Also, as faculties diminish with illness, and maybe speech goes, the chaplain will know the idiosyncrasies and personal characteristics which enable this person to continue as a complete individual, living, not dying, to the very end [2, p.16].

and,

This ability to remain poised, centered, collected as a listener is an important skill for the spiritual carer; for spiritual care embraces another dimension than the psychological (though undoubtedly psychology enters the picture).

When we listen, we can be a bridge, a touching place, a way back into spiritual connectedness for the one who is torn apart by grief or fear. If we do not allow ourselves to be dragged here and there by the patient's experiences and responses, but in simplicity remain present, centered, then we may become like a rock in a turbulent river; an earthed solidity, a connection with the ground of being, a place of respite [2, p. 42].

REFERENCES

1. K. Mitchell, *The Hospital Chaplain,* Westminster Press, Philadelphia, 1972.
2. P. Wilcock, *Spiritual Care of Dying and Bereaved People,* Morehouse Publishing, Harrisburg, 1997.

CHAPTER 3

A Chaplain's Perspective:
The Challenge for Today

Reverend Richard B. Gilbert

The late Dr. Granger Westberg, a pioneer in contemporary hospital chaplaincy, who was present in the earliest days of modern chaplaincy in the 1940s, and the formation of the then College of Chaplains, often said that we have "come a long way" from the early days of chaplaincy.

Westberg describes how he "earned" his first job, competing with the notion that chaplains were supposed to be old, gentle, generally not in the way men (in those days) who just went room to room to see if anyone wanted to talk. We now have thousands of chaplains who are health care professionals, most Board Certified Chaplains, who bring with them the extensive training that they would normally have as ministers (and now many lay ministers), plus considerable additional training, heart wrenching process and certification committees (an experience seldom experienced by other professionals), clinical residencies in approved institutions and with certified supervisors, rigorous continuing education requirements, and the additional endorsement standards of their own denomination or religious beliefs. The Association of Professional Chaplains, a new merged community built on the history of The College of Chaplains, has certified members who are Roman Catholic, Orthodox, Protestant, Jewish, Islamic, and some who are more "New Age," non-denominational and, in some cases, non-descript. Joined by the many members from The National Association of Catholic Chaplains, and several smaller groups representing particular workplace settings, bring their integrity, values, and commitments, not to place on the patients (which is inappropriate and abusive), but as an arena of safety and sanctuary that allows the patient, family member, or staff person to explore his or her own issues, beliefs, values, and wounds.

Integration has become the watchword for health care. This means the integration of the whole person (including spirituality and religion) and the integration of the whole team. Chaplains are now even more actively involved and present in the team approach to the delivery of care. Chaplains participate in team meetings, Ethics Committees, Critical Incident Stress Management, discharge planning, and other roles of leadership and decision making in the institution. Chaplains are finding themselves, like other professionals, pushed further and further from people, parked in front of a computer or paper chart to document, attending more meetings, covering more ground, and still generally with very minimal staffs and resources stretched beyond recognition. The largest group of professional chaplains still is the one person department. It is almost "miraculous" how chaplains, with very small budgets, manage to carve out a twenty-four-hour, seven-day coverage that includes volunteer clergy, lay volunteers, and others to fill in the schedules so that weary chaplains can have some rest while the needs of the patients are addressed.

Chaplains are engaged in turf battles. Because everyone is expected to demonstrate some expertise in spiritual matters in their health care work, and since chaplains are generally reluctant to write, do research, and otherwise broadcast their stories, it has become easy, in this "bottom line" mentality of health care administration, to ask why we need chaplains. Some administrators and boards do not know what chaplains do, and many chaplains have not discerned their need to market if the work of pastoral care is to continue in health care. Chaplains are stating statistically, and through other approaches, their value to the "soul" of the institution, in supporting the leadership of the institution, working with staff, including tending to their spiritual and emotional needs, outreach in the community, contributing complementary forms of care through bereavement care, home visits for pastoral care and pastoral psychotherapy, to give new awareness about their place on the team. Standards for certification, endorsement, and continuing education are at their highest. Chaplains are learning that they must continue to change while maintaining the timeless questions and issues identified in the introduction to this book.

THE TASKS OF CHAPLAINS

Who are we as chaplains? Others might ask, "What do chaplains do?" Rabbi Jeffery Silberman, himself a contributor to this book, spoke powerfully on this issue at the Kansas City convention of The Association of Professional Chaplains, Spring 1999. Copies of this recorded speech are available from The Association of Professional Chaplains [1].

In his address he spoke of what the chaplains do and what they bring to the delivery of care through the three typical styles of ministry known to all of us, *rabbi, priest, minister*, the several hats worn by all chaplains. This essay suggests that a fourth needs to be added, *prophet*. Chaplains are rabbis. Rabbis teach. It is the work of the chaplain to teach, to bring the wisdom of the ages and the teachings of a patient's particular beliefs and practices to each diagnosis, each ethical dilemma, and to how patients will or will not cope. What a person's beliefs "teach" about life, about creation, about death may well determine what a patient opts to do or not to do with chemotherapy, with a pregnancy that may require interruption, organ transplants, how a person's body is to be treated at the time of a death, and how we choose to make our spiritual connections. The chaplain affirms and clarifies these teachings to the patient, but also on behalf of the patient to the team. For a team to proceed with hearing and respecting these teachings is to be as abusive of the patient as is the disease they are trying to treat. Chaplains teach.

Chaplains are *priests*, tending to the ritual needs of the patients. The chapter contributed by Fr. Joseph Driscoll outlines the priestly role expected by many Roman Catholic patients. Rituals are the practices that we follow to clarify what has happened, give meaning to it, and to find the inner strength that we need to cope. Chaplains are the specialists in rituals, rituals that may include baptism, communion, and anointing, can be experienced with prayer and readings, could include incense (despite fire regulations) and candles, ritual dancing and singing, crystals, herbs, dietary needs, and more. These are the "tools of the trade" for the believer and they are the care of the chaplain in seeing that they are respected (diversity), facilitated, and incorporated into the care of the patient. The chaplain, a religious specialist, becomes the generalist, networking with the religious (and other) resources in the community so that the specific or particular needs of the patients are met. Bread and wine work for some, and for others they are an insult. I have witnessed dances, singing, drama, circles of prayer, and also things that, for me, appear to be magical and rooted in superstition. My background may prefer specific rituals, but my background and needs are not imposed on the patient. So we do hear about rituals that may seem contrary to the contemporary scene, but they are at the heart of the patient's inner strength and ability to cope.

The chaplain is a *minister*, a specialist in pastoral care. The chaplain represents sanctuary, a point of connection and safety, sought after by the patient. The patient may not believe in God, but still has the right to touch his or her own spirituality or beliefs for coping. Institutions can become abusive as we listen less to the story and more to the pressures of clock and regulation. The chaplain is to be a generalist, a story teller and a story listener, one essentially with no agenda or plan of action or treatment, who provides a non-judgmental safety or sanctuary that allows the patient space and place to explore issues, feelings, beliefs, and values.

Some limit "sanctuary" to a specific place. We have chapels or, in this age of political correctness, meditation rooms. Those are spaces set aside from the world of medicine to be safe, free, and find a measure of rest. Sanctuaries are locational, symbolical, and relational. For some, the chapel, church, or synagogue is the place to go to make a connection. For others it is in the rituals of prayer, sacraments, conversation with another believer, or the practices of a specific religious community. Crosses, chalices, Bibles, and other sacred books, jewelry, candles, the symbolic reminders of sanctuary or safety. For others it is measured in people, often clergy or other representatives of chaplaincy/pastoral care, but often the doctor, the nurse, the social worker, or another person who, willingly or by default, become that moment or connection of sanctuary for the individual.

Chaplains are also *prophetic*. Prophets often are thought to be the people who connect us with the past. The Old Testament speaks of many prophets who reminded Israel of their covenant, their identity, their past. Many think of prophets as futuristic, speaking of the tomorrow for a religion, an institution, or an individual. Prophets use the messages of the past, and can point to the future, but are messengers of the present. What does a person's belief system have to say to the "now" in their story? That is the work of the prophet.

Chaplains bring the larger context of a belief system to the patient's bedside, to the cart they lay on outside an x-ray room, in a holding area, in an ambulance. It is to bring the global to the local, the distant to the intimate.

Chaplains are described as representatives of the religious community to the health care institution and vice versa. This is also true of the chaplain in relating the patient, and the beliefs and practices of that patient, to the larger medical community and the mission and values of the institution. The prophetic voice must bring the cultural, cultic, and community voices of the patient to the attention of the institution.

In his book *Christianity and Civil Society,* Robert Wuthnow presented a number of statistics that may be familiar to most of us [2]. On page 18 he reports from various sources that 69 percent of Americans are members of a church or synagogue and 94 percent believe in God. On page 75 came a very surprising statistical notation. He reports that there are now some 1,600 denominations in the United States and 44 percent of them are "non-Christian." While Christianity, in various expressions and with a diversity of commitment, continues to be the "majority religion" in the United States, we cannot ignore the religious diversity that is present in our society. We are no longer all Western European Christians in our thinking, values, and priorities. Donald Irish et al., in *Ethnic Variations in Dying, Death, and Grief: Diversity in Universality,* cite several instances in which Western medicine has violated the religious practices of patients from Eastern religions because they were expected to accommodate themselves to Western beliefs [3]. Physicians (and others) would not take the time to understand that these Eastern beliefs include specific requirements at the time of the death which, if not followed, have condemnatory outcomes for those who believe in reincarnation. The prophetic voice is an advocate for the patient to the institution. There is no one voice, ritual, or practice that exists, and it is an abuse of the patient to expect the patient to fit into the religious garb that we prescribe for them.

The *USA Today* issue of September 7, 1999, had a cover story on the cultural statistics and change in the United States from recent census data. Under the headline "Blended Races Making a True Melting Pot," we were reminded that more Americans in the next century will be from minority groups. The column suggests that the number of people claiming mixed ancestry will triple to 21 percent. The Caucasian population will decline from 72 percent (1999) to 62 percent and, by 2005, the largest minority group will be people of Hispanic origin, soon to be 17 percent of the population. The black population will increase by 31 percent, remaining at 13 percent of the population. The group with the fast growth rate, 102 percent, will be people of Pacific and Asian descent. These statistics have very strong implications for denominations if they are to have religious leaders that can relate to the minority groups in their congregations. For health care, it is the realization that diversity is here to stay and will become the norm. The prophet must continue to speak for diversity to institutions that still speak "different" rather than "diverse."

The July/August 1999 issue of *The Door*, reported that there are 537 active hate groups in the United States, Florida and California bearing the heaviest concentration of groups [4]. Groups identified were the Ku Klux Klan, Neo-Nazi, Skinhead, Identity, Black Separatist, and then a non-descript "other." Most of these groups are anti-Semitic, anti-Black, and anti most other things that stand in the way of their perceived rights, beliefs, and practices. We can protest these groups and lump them under a sociological label or grouping. The prophet, the chaplain, often with people abhorrent to him or her, must also keep before the institution that these hate groups are *religious* in their structure, as determined by the believer. They have the religious ingredients of cult (ritual), creed (beliefs), and community, a common set of believers and prescribed practices for that community. Many profess no belief in God, but function as a religion that is as strongly influential over that individual in your clinic or surgery suite as someone with religious practices that leave you more comfortable. How do we represent racists who deny, often quite physically, the richness of diversity that we profess for the institution?

CONTRIBUTIONS OF THE CHAPLAIN

Chaplains are specialists who function as generalists. They keep changing hats to accommodate the needs of the work place. Some teach, others counsel, many make home visits, others develop policies, and some do a little of all of that . . . and more. Chaplains dare not claim exclusive right or privilege to the work of spiritual and religious care, but they do bring unique contributions to the team.

Informant on Definitions and Traditions

What is appropriate care for an Islamic woman who dies? What are the dietary needs of an orthodox Jew? Are flowers appropriate for all funerals? What does a person mean when they say, "I want to be anointed?" Why do some patients refuse to make decisions without first consulting their religious leaders? Diversity is as rich in religious practice and affiliation as in ethnic origins and culture. Even within denominations there is diversity. Some denominations have a wide range of beliefs and practices, some at great or extreme distance from others, yet they all claim the same religious preference. With 1600 denominations functioning in the United States, it is hard enough for chaplains to stay informed. It is the responsibility of the chaplain to have access to that information and to help the entire team access definitions and traditions as professed and preferred by the patient.

Access to Resources and Rituals

The pastoral care/spiritual care department monitors the religious community that feeds into the hospital. Usually this means that clergy and other visitation ministers (ordained and lay) are required to register at the hospital before accessing patients. It is a way of protecting the patient, but also protecting the right of the minister to do his or her work. It also provides a network of people, beliefs, and resources that the chaplain is in a position to access for the believer/patient. Not all religious communities are located in every community, but the chaplain helps network the needs with those best able to tend to those needs.

Helps Identify Spiritual and Religious "Filters"

We all experience filters in life. We often fail to grasp the power of spirituality and religion as filters. If, for example, we believe that God is in control of all things and determines or designs all that happens to us, the newly diagnosed cancer patient may well have some spiritual work to do. Some simply surrender to that teaching, "God has a reason for me to have this cancer." Others find any notion of such an abusive God repugnant to their beliefs that they may now be dealing not only with a diagnosis, but a redefining of who God is and will be in their lives. That is a spiritual crisis. It is easy to say that that is "bad theology," but, in doing so, we become the judge, and thus, another abuser. Spirituality and religion are heavily filtered, but also filter very heavily. It is the pastoral care team that helps the full team recognize the place for spirituality and religion in the treatment of the whole person, and how to recognize when spirituality or religion become a problem rather than a pathway or solution.

Participates in the Diagnosis and Treatment of the Patient

Many chaplains often feel more comfortable working around the medical team then within medical labels and definitions, but chaplains are part of the team. The spiritual perspective needs to be part of the diagnostic tools along with blood counts, x-rays, lab reports, or other data determined by the physician. Chaplains work within the team to develop a common strategy for patient care. Chaplains also walk the halls, make their own introductions, and provide an additional access to help and safety as claimed by patients, visitors, and staff.

Stands Apart or at a Distance, Seeing the Larger Picture, Asking Different Questions

The chaplain serves as a prophetic voice, often asking "why," and brings different yardsticks to the work of the team. In a sense, the spiritual caregiver is the one who must call a "time out" and ask, "Why are we doing this? Is it in the best interest of the patient?"

Serves

The chaplain serves as prophet, priest, rabbi, and minister to the patient, the visitor, the staff, and the institution.

Assist Other Professionals in Identifying and Tending to Their Own Needs and Issues

Despite the high cost of technology and the commitments to medical care throughout the institution, the best "product" that the institution offers is people. You cannot work in health care without assessing the impact of that stress on your own life, coupled with the stress of your private life that follows you into the institution. Professionals soon find themselves asking the same "why" questions about life, faith, death as do the patients. Many chaplains report that they are now spending more of their time on the "health" of employees and the institution than with patients.

Assist with Discharge Planning, Referral, Networking, Aftercare, and Marketing

Pastoral caregivers also know the community and can assist in the discharge of patients to other caregivers, including individual clergy or other religious leaders, institutions, private counseling sessions, and other support services. Chaplains help develop bereavement and other aftercare programs, and also, from the marketing perspective, represent the hospital or other institution when they conduct weddings and funerals and provide ministry to various congregations and religious communities.

THE CHAPLAIN AND SPIRITUAL ASSESSMENT

There are a number of resources that offer different assessment tools. We would recommend the work of George Fichett [5] and the *Palliative Care Manual* from Aspen Publishing [6]. Both items are in the references. In this section we want to offer the essentials or framework of spiritual assessment. The challenge and gift is for each team or setting to develop the general tool that will work best in your setting, with the expertise that your team brings to the task, and that best expresses the beliefs, practices, burdens, and needs of your patients.

To assess is to give meaning. It can include data, diagnosis, treatment plans, definitions (as offered by the patient), ethical concerns (if offered), religious criteria (if appropriate), but it is ultimately about bringing the team (caregivers) and the patient together in a manner that affirms the patient, validates his or her beliefs and wishes, and confirms that the team has heard this and is committed to it.

As you develop your spiritual assessment tool and your approach to spiritual listening, here is a reminder of the goals or desired outcomes for spiritual assessment:

- To understand a person's beliefs about involvement with God and religious practice;
- to determine the extent to which a person's religious practices and spiritual understandings serve as a resource for faith and life;
- to assess whether a person's resources for hope and strength are founded on reality;
- to give a person an opportunity to accept spiritual support [7, p. 5:11].

Religious data might include a congregational or denominational preference, beliefs or teachings that influence how we do or do not make decisions, rituals that are appropriate to the health setting, and sacramental and other tools of ministry that will bring insight, comfort, and support to the patient. Spiritual assessment includes the four essential criteria of spirituality: how I feel about myself; how I relate to the world around me; how my self, the world, and my social network relate to what brings me into this health predicament; and what/who transcends all of this to give meaning, validation, direction, and hope. Words common to spiritual assessment and concern include hope, hopeless, despair, peace, guilt, forgiveness, fear, courage, etc.

The chapter by Chaplain Burton, in which he shares the story of his singing a hymn with a frightened patient in the middle of the night, is an example of an assessment that was not written (though needed to be documented), but was expressed, experienced, and affirmed. Patients want to know:

- Will I be okay?
- What's happening to me?
- Why is this happening to me?
- Does God (or other beliefs/relationships) know I am here?
- Will you take care of my pain?
- Will you respect my wishes?
- Will you stay with me?
- Is there hope?

These criteria can be developed by the team as guides to capture what the patient is expressing, verbally, emotionally, in body language, in the silences, through rituals as we hear the full story offered by the patient. Some teams list blank spaces in which caregivers give feedback. Others rank them and rate them numerically. Each team must develop the best model for them, realizing it will require constant revision. As always, we adjust the assessment tool to the patient; we do not fit the patient into the assessment tool.

In gathering information, these are some of the concerns that need to be addressed. Some information will emerge from conversation, other data will come as the team shares the broader picture about a patient, and, in some cases, you simply ask.

- When you are feeling discouraged or hopeless, what keeps you going? What are your sources for courage and energy?
- Where have you found strength in past experiences of loss, health crisis, trauma, or emotional struggle?
- What is hope for you? Where have you "found" it in the past? Are you able to find it now? How can I help you? Is there someone else who can help you?
- Who do you look up to? Who inspires you? Is inspiration available to you?
- What does dying (if appropriate) mean to you?
- What does suffering mean to you?
- What does "religious community" mean to you?
- What does "religious leader" mean to you?

The last two items need some clarification. Contemporary trends find more people claiming a spiritual preference and practice, but often without any community commitment or experience. For them, the experience of a health crisis will be heightened by a new awareness of isolation, abandonment, or lack of community. For others, burdens of guilt or shame (sometimes produced by their religious community) might create a need for them to isolate from their community. In some cases, the feelings depart from the facts, and there is a need for reconciliation that may only come with the involvement of community. For others, there are serious grief issues. Some have not received support in previous loss or life experiences and now undergo re-grieving. For others, especially the elderly who cannot participate in community activities as they have in the past, this is another reminder of loss in their life.

In the *UNIPAC Two* publication of The American Academy of Hospice and Palliative Medicine we have a different perspective on the inquiries we might present to a patient in order to accommodate our listening to their story. It is part of the assessment questionnaire for evaluating for psychological and spiritual pain.

- What are some of the ways this illness has affected your life?
- What are some of your main concerns, worries, and fears about the future?
- Have you been sad? Frightened?

- How has this illness affected you physically? Emotionally? Spiritually?
- What do you miss most as a result of this illness?
- What are some of the things you wish you could talk about? Who do you wish you could talk to?
- What are some of your family's biggest concerns, worries, fears? How do you deal with their concerns?
- In the past, what has given you the strength to cope with difficult decisions?
- Has your illness made you think about religion or spiritual issues? What are some of those issues?
- How can [we/I] help you with your religious and/or spiritual concerns and practices [8, p. 27].

Illness, trauma, and loss present their own wilderness experiences: the experience of loss of boundaries, loss of direction, loss of the familiar. It can be manifest in mood swings, changes in behavior, and an inability to connect with spiritual/religious connections. Spirituality and/or religion can themselves be a wilderness experience because, if they are healthy, are themselves an unfinished journey. An unfinished journey can often appear conflictual when one is in a wilderness.

It is important to help the patient/client find safety (sanctuary) in wilderness and to articulate what they are experiencing, feeling, and pondering. In these discussions it may be necessary to clarify that wilderness is challenging, but is neutral. In other words, it is not necessarily bad. Another way of approaching it is to distinguish that which is wilderness, part of the journey experience, from that which is abusive. Spiritual abuse is real; so is religious abuse. Sometimes they come from the misreading of the signs (or lack of signs) in our wilderness. At other times they emerge from poor or faulty definitions, unrealistic expectations of yourself, or from the wearisome "side effects" of the disease process.

Spiritual abuse generally emerges from outside sources, things or people beyond ourselves. It can be the busy pace of the professionals (including ourselves) who unintentionally appear abusive because we discount a person's spiritual issues or will not take the time to listen. It can come from the family, especially family (or friends) that impose their own expectations and practices on the patient. Sadly, much of the abuse comes from our religious communities, religious leaders and the abusive teachings, practices, and rituals that they impose.

What often is experienced as the most offensive spiritual abuse is that which we identify as received from God or the divine as we define transcendence. It usually emerges from our past definitions or expectations with God, which may not be healthy, and the lack of health heightens the unhealthy within others. Healthy spirituality affirms, listen, guides, and forgives. Healthy spirituality is about affirmation, hope, and peace. Glaser offers this definition of spiritual abuse.

> Spiritual abuse is the wounding, shaming, and degrading of someone's spiritual worth by a perpetrator intent on taking control. Spiritual abuse is any attack (subtle or blatant, unintended or intentional) on our beloved and sacred worth as children of God. . . . Spiritual abuse is far more pervasive and permissible than other forms of abuse because it is perceived as "ordained by God" [9, p. 27].

The recognition of spiritual abuse is particularly challenging for us. Apart from the obvious reasons that it takes time (a commodity in short supply, as we often suggest), the recognition of spiritual abuse and neglect can touch the raw nerve of our sense of injustice for our patients as well as our own spiritual or religious issues and shadows. We dare not run and hide from these issues, but should work collaboratively with the chaplain. Listening is still the gift in the midst of spiritual abuse. Non-judgmental care is noticeably contradictory to the abuse the victim receives elsewhere. Because abuse can often produce co-dependent needs and behaviors, it is important to monitor our responses and behaviors so that we do not feed into their inappropriateness. This must be expressed carefully.

Any sense of rejection or disapproval with co-dependents fits like a harsh judgment or abandonment. It is even worse if it is perceived that this rejection is in the name of spirituality, religion, or God. Avoid simple answers or any answers to questions that are really more about grabbing your attention. Do not belittle their issues or disease with pat answers or theological jargon. Watch out for the cliches. "It's God's will" may sound wise, theologically, but it can be "heard" as additional judgment. Work with the patient by walking with the patient.

There can be symptoms of spiritual abuse expressed by the patient. The American Association of Hospice and Palliative Medicine (AAHPM) identifies several that should be notations on your assessment form to be considered as you listen to their story.

- physical pain not controlled by usual means
- torment and anguish
- complicated reactions to loss
- pervasive, existential guilt
- fear and dread
- noncompliance with care plan
- diminished quality of life

- sense of abandonment and betrayal
- isolation and withdrawal from support communities
- breakdown of relationships [8, pp. 91-92].

The source also identifies "spiritual pain related to general issues of meaning," as noted below:

- Expression of life's meaninglessness and loss of faith;
- questioning the adequacy of present belief system, world view or philosophy, whether religious or non-religious;
- expressions of desire for a belief system, world view, or philosophy to help cope with spiritual pain;
- presence of unresolved religious issues, e.g., "If only I had enough faith, I would be cured";
- guilt associated with religious beliefs;
- isolation from religious/spiritual communities with similar beliefs [8, p. 92].

In her very helpful grief resource book for and about teens, Donna O'Toole offers these symptomatic approaches to spiritual reactions to loss:

- Feeling lost and empty;
- feeling forsaken, abandoned, judged or condemned by God;
- questioning a reason to go on living;
- extreme pessimism or optimism;
- needing to give or receive forgiveness;
- needing to give or receive punishment;
- feeling spiritually connected to what/who was lost [10, p. 12].

"Religious leader" often comes with wounds, experiences of manipulation or abuse, or simply areas of relationship that have not previously been explored. Wesley Carr reminds us that people often project onto their religious leaders the pictures they have of God [11, p. 234]. If their relationship with God is troubled, then these troubled waters may carry over into their relationship with a religious leader. Some limit needlessly the resource the leader can bring to a crisis. Others project considerable authority on the religious leader and will make no decisions without consulting this leader. To ask questions about religious leaders is to ask questions about relationship, and also to encroach on possible stories of abuse, manipulation, neglect, or loss.

THE CHAPLAIN AND THE WORK PLACE

As contemporary society and spirituality come together, we are redefining what spirituality is, how we claim and experience it, and how it fits or doesn't fit into the many aspects of our life and living. This has seen a new interest in the spiritual dimensions of work and what some would consider the "soul" of the work place.

Chaplains have a long investment in work place and business chaplaincies. There is a network within the Association of Professional Chaplains and there also is a professional organization for these chaplains [12]. The funeral industry is giving consideration to funeral home chaplains. Chaplains are taking an active role in the Employee Assistance Program (EAP) and other counseling programs and centers.

For the health care setting, what becomes the "soul" of the hospital, clinic, hospice, etc., and, as many now express, with all that is happening in and to health care, is there a soul? Two quotes from Briskin's work on spirituality and the workplace focus for us.

> No one who works today needs to be told that change in and out of the work place is accelerating beyond our ability to grasp the implications of those changes. The future is uncertain. And during uncertain times, we search for what is truest about ourselves and what is most desirable about our relations with others [13, p. xiii].

(and)

> I do not believe the answer lies in a program, a technique, or a mystical belief system. To listen to the soul's voice is to become more mindful, to pay attention to what is happening inside us and around us. The gathering of our attention awakens the energies of soul, and the patience to follow what we notice releases these energies within us [13, p. xv].

In this age of managed care, when jobs (and values) are being redefined more frequently, and more frequently by people and voices outside our control, we are seeing an impact on health care professionals that is proving very costly to the industry. Good employees are leaving, finding other work places that seem to respect their professional "soul." We commit to people, and find ourselves moving or being moved further from them. That is a spiritual crisis. The stresses of our lives and families accompany us into the already stressful work place. This leads to additional tension, burnout, conflict, addictive and abusive behaviors.

Even if we must justify all that we do based on the "bottom line" of cost, chaplains and others must continue to articulate that our biggest "expense," and best "product," is the labor force. This is a labor force that must be healthy if it is to provide healthy care to the sick and troubled. It means that the work place that is healthy respects the institution's soul and the soul of the worker, and provides quality alternatives, often offered through the chaplain's office, for individual and family counseling.

In many ways, and sadly so, health care has changed to a point where it may never be the same again. It still can be healthy or healthier, and that will be realized and respected as we commit to a healthy work place.

REFERENCES

1. The Association of Professional Chaplains, 1701 E. Woodfield, Suite 311, Schaumburg, IL 60173. 847.240.1014.
2. R. Wuthnow, *Christianity and Civil Society,* Trinity Press International, Philadelphia, 1996.
3. D. Irish et al., *Ethnic Variations in Dying, Death and Grief: Diversity in Universality,* Taylor & Francis, Bristol, Pennsylvania, Chapter 6, 1993.
4. B. Garrison, "*Door* Interview: Mark Potok," *The Door, 165,* pp. 15-21, July/August 1999.
5. G. Fitchett, *Assessing Spiritual Needs: A Guide for Caregivers,* Augsburg, Minneapolis, 1993.
6. Aspen Reference Group, *Palliative Care: Patient and Family Counseling Manual,* Aspen, Gaithersburg, Maryland, 1996 (with annual supplements).
7. R. Gilbert, *Spiritual Assessment* in Aspen Reference Group, *Palliative Care: Patient and Family Counseling Manual,* Aspen, Gaithersburg, Maryland, 1996.
8. P. Storey and C. F. Knight, *UNIPAC Two: Alleviating Psychological and Spiritual Pain in the Terminally Ill,* The American Academy of Hospice and Palliative Care, Gainesville, Florida, 1997.
9. C. Glaser, *Coming Out as Sacrament,* Westminster John Knox Press, Louisville, 1998.
10. D. O'Toole, *Facing Change: Falling Apart and Coming Together Again in the Teen Years,* Mountain Rainbow Publications, Burnsville, 1995.
11. W. Carr, *Handbook of Pastoral Studies.* NLPC Resources, London, United Kingdom, 1997.
12. National Institute of Business and Industrial Chaplains (NIBIC), Institute of Worklife Ministry, 7100 Regency Square Blvd., Houston, TX 77036-3202. 713.266.2456.
13. A. Briskin, *The Stirring of Soul in the Workplace,* Jossey-Bass, San Francisco, 1996.

CHAPTER 4
A Beginning Examination of the Spirituality of Health Care Professionals

David W. Adams and
Rick Csiernik

Wellness has become an increasingly discussed idea in the health field, the work place, and the media. While the common conceptualization of wellness often begins and ends with physical health, wellness is a significantly broader construct. The origins for the contemporary definition of this concept are credited to Halbert Dunn, a physician, whose book *High-Level Wellness* [1] was initially premised upon the World Health Organization's definition of health:

> Health is a state of complete physical, mental and social well-being, and not merely the absence of disease and infirmity [2, p. 1].

For Dunn, a complete state of well-being involved wellness of the mind, the body, and the environment including family, community life, and a compatible work interest. Wellness also included a way of living that maximized one's potential, adapting to the challenges of the changing environment, and entailing a sense of social responsibility. Dunn postulated that being well does not merely constitute a state where one is not ill, or "unsick," a position that was echoed by Donald Ardell [3]. Ardell envisioned wellness as the inseparable integration of the mind, the body, and the spirit [3]. For Sefton and her colleagues the concept of wellness, or optimal health, involves an interdependent balance among five areas: physical, emotional, intellectual, social, and spiritual health [4]. Of these five areas, spiritual health and the concept of spirituality in general is the component of wellness that many health professionals attend to least. Perhaps, this lack of attention results from spirituality being perceived as too ethereal and lacking a basis in the practicalities of modern health care and in the personal lives of health care professionals. Perhaps, inattention results from spirituality being viewed as too esoteric, too closely linked with organised religions and hence falling solely in the domain of the clergy [5]. DeVeber, a pediatric haematologist and oncologist, points out that until recently, personal discomfort or lack of expertise in spiritual matters, or both, have contributed to token inclusion or complete exclusion of spiritual concerns in the curricula of health professionals, and of physicians in particular [6]. What has been unclear, uncomfortable, or misunderstood has also, in the minds of the authors, lead to uncertainty for health professionals regarding the components of spiritual health. This uncertainty constitutes a fundamental reason for undertaking a pilot examination of the spirituality of health professionals that is discussed later in this chapter. At this point, it is worth noting that themes associated with spiritual health include meditation, love, charity, purpose, and self-actualization [7]. Spiritual health is not just a component of the wellness of the patients that health professionals serve, it is also an integral part of their own well-being.

SPIRITUALITY

Spirituality is known to involve a wide range of components, including: prayer, divinity, awe, wonder, the sacred, solitude, nature, one's soul, healing, inspiration, faith, wonder, transcendence, Tao, inspiration, hope, love, and healing. A multitude of questions arise when one dares introduce the concept of spirituality in an assessment of health or wellness. When beginning to struggle with the role of spirituality in caring for ourselves and our patients, we are led to the question: How do we define spirituality? How does spirituality develop and what does spiritual care involve? Who is responsible for spirituality in the health care process? What factors impinge on spirituality and spiritual care for both ourselves and our patients?

The International Work Group on Death, Dying and Bereavement (I.W.G.) defines spirituality as follows:

> Spirituality is concerned with the transcendental, inspirational and existential way to live one's life, as well as in a fundamental and profound sense, with the person as a human being [8, p. 33].

For Morgan, spirituality is rooted in our need and ability to think and to will. It is linked with our individuality, our unique sense of self, and our solitude. This self-directed, yet finite conception is a core feature that differentiates humans from other life. Spirituality involves our quest for meaning; the ultimate question of our existence [9, 10].

Twycross suggests that spirituality is much broader than what is presented through organized religions. It is a factor in the nature of cognition and human willing linked to several significant factors:

- our ability to reflect on ourselves;
- our culture;
- the ideas by which we live; and
- our interpretations of fact and human created ideas [11].

Spirituality is a component of our personalities that integrates all other aspects of personhood. Stiles claims that spirituality is a hidden but energizing dimension that provides insight and new understanding of the human experience. To be spiritual is to know oneself and also to know others. Spiritual insight and growth as a caring perspective adds personal meaning to caregiving by professionals [12]. Spirituality may be considered to be an integral part of healing and may be revitalizing for both patients and their family members.

Spirituality, in its broadest sense, independent of matter, and associated with one's ability to interpret fact and human constructs can be readily associated with rejoicing, suffering, or grieving. Our sense of spirituality and its importance tends to be heightened by crises, particularly medical crises which force us to examine our mortality, even if momentarily [10]. The development of spirituality stems from formal schooling, our ongoing quest for positive self-regard, and our comfort with and our exploration of the world as we know it. Spiritual development determines who we wish to be and shapes our obligations to a larger whole [9, 13].

Spiritual development has been cited as entailing unconditional love while assuming responsibility for one's actions [14]. Highfield states that spirituality involves self-acceptance and self-trust and significant relationships with others including a supreme other characterized by unconditional love, trust, and forgiveness. Lastly, a basic spiritual need is hope: imagining and participating in the achievement and enhancement of a positive future [15].

As we face another millennium, ties to organized religions are weakening due to the infiltration of the media into homes, a multitude of leisure activities, and seven-day-work-week commercialism. Likewise, the role of spirituality is also being questioned. Ever increasing technological change, along with managed health care and its equivalents, are placing increasing emphasis upon expedience and a cost-benefit utilitarian business mentality in all facets of caring and healing. Personal and career uncertainties are fueled by an emphasis on more work with fewer resources and rewards and multi-skilling. These new demands clash with our training, experience, knowledge, and skills as well as the personal principles we derive from spirituality. The intense stress that results can undermine our desire to care for our spiritual needs, to help others to live well, and in some areas of health care, to help others die well.

SPIRITUAL SUPPORT

Clearly, spiritual support differs from psychosocial support. It consists of more personal involvements with patients at the deepest level [16]. Spiritual support may include compassion, courage, humility, maturity, and a sense of values grounded in religious and cultural experience and what may be termed natural wisdom. Spiritual support involves acceptance of the unknown and the pain of others [17-19]. It is recognition of our own vulnerability and of the uselessness, meaninglessness, hopelessness, and sense of abandonment that a lack of spiritual support brings in patients and their caregivers [20, 21]. It is "walking in the shadow of death with the patient" [22, p. 178] and it forces us to walk "on holy ground" [16, p. 93]. Spirituality is a vital part of the wellness of our patients and of ourselves and is an area that we do not tend to overtly consider when we examine how we care for others and promote healing.

METHODOLOGY

This pilot study was an exploratory examination of spirituality among health care professionals. Professionals working within a formal institutional health care setting, in a community-based agency, or in a private practice were all eligible for inclusion. Along with physicians and nurses, psychologists, occupational therapists, physiotherapists, social workers, and clergy were included in the study. For purposes of this research, practitioners, apart from clergy, who were not nurses or physicians were classified as "Other Health Care Professionals"(OHCP). Questionnaires returned by the clergy and by students were excluded from the analysis which follows.[1]

This preliminary study employed an eight-page descriptive questionnaire in four parts, constructed specifically for this investigation and pre-tested with a cohort of fifteen professionals from health and health related settings. Part A consisted of six closed-ended demographic questions. Part B made inquiries concerning the respondents' spirituality

---

[1] Data on clergy will be presented in a subsequent chapter while the student questionnaire will form the basis of a future study of students' spirituality.

through fourteen open-ended questions. Part C asked two closed-ended questions relating to how participants helped patients meet their spiritual needs, while the last two pages, Part D, made inquires about how respondents helped their co-workers meet their spiritual needs. The questionnaires were distributed to a group of approximately 530 persons, the majority of whom were professionals from health care and health care related settings attending a conference on death and dying in London, Ontario, and to a random selection of 290 health care providers within the Regional Municipality of Hamilton-Wentworth in Ontario. A total of 155 of 820 questionnaires were returned, for a response rate of 18.8 percent. Of these, seventeen questionnaires were completed by clergy and eight by students, leaving a total of 129 questionnaires to analyze for this chapter. Thus, the results that follow provide us with only a beginning glimpse into the issue of spirituality among health care professionals.

RESULTS

Population

Just over one-third (45) of the 129 respondents were nurses. Twenty-two (17.1%) respondents identified themselves as physicians, while the remaining sixty-two individuals (48.0%) were other health care practitioners most of whom would be categorized as health care or health care related professionals (OHCP). Nurses (93.2%) and other health care professionals (85.5%) were predominately female, while the majority of physicians who replied were male. This ratio is reflective of the gender mix in the majority of Canadian health care settings (Table 1). Approximately two-thirds of the survey participants identified themselves as being Christian, while twenty-three persons (17.7%) reported no religious affiliation (Table 2).

Spirituality

Over 40 percent ($n = 53$) of respondents attended religious services more than once per month, while nearly one-quarter ($n = 30$) reported no attendance in the past year. This latter finding was primarily due to the responses of physicians, half of whom reported no attendance at religious services in the year prior to the survey (Table 3).

The conceptualization of spirituality yielded a raft of meanings, with relation to one's inner self and caring for others being the most frequent replies ($n = 56$). The existence of a supreme being was cited by just over one-third of respondents ($n = 46$). This facet of spirituality was

Table 1. Sex of Respondents

	Nurse	Physician	OHCP	Total
Male	2 (4.4%)	14 (63.6%)	7 (11.3%)	23 (17.8%)
Female	42 (93.2%)	4 (18.2%)	53 (85.5%)	99 (76.7%)
No Response	1 (2.2%)	4 (18.2%)	2 (3.2%)	7 (5.4%)
Total (n)	45 (100.0%)	22 (100.0%)	62 (100.0%)	129 (100.0%)

Table 2. Religious Faith of Respondents

	Nurse (n = 45)	Physician (n = 22)	OHCP (n = 62)	Total (n = 129)
Protestant	22 (48.9%)	9 (40.9%)	29 (46.8%)	60 (46.5%)
Roman Catholic	10 (22.2%)	5 (22.7%)	7 (11.3%)	22 (17.1%)
Jewish	3 (6.7%)	1 (4.5%)	1 (1.6%)	5 (3.9%)
Unitarian	1 (2.2%)	0 (0.0%)	5 (8.1%)	6 (4.7%)
Atheist/Agnostic	0 (0.0%)	1 (4.5%)	1 (1.6%)	2 (1.6%)
None	7 (15.6%)	4 (18.2%)	12 (19.3%)	23 (17.7%)
Other	2 (4.4%)	1 (4.5%)	7 (11.3%)	10 (7.7%)
No Response	0 (0.0%)	1 (4.5%)	0 (0.0%)	1 (0.8%)

Table 3. Attendance at Religious Services

	Nurse (n = 45)	Physician (n = 22)	OHCP (n = 62)	Total (n = 129)
More than 1/month	22 (48.9%)	4 (18.2%)	27 (43.5%)	53 (41.1%)
1/month	2 (4.4%)	3 (13.6%)	4 (6.5%)	9 (7.0%)
1/quarter	3 (6.7%)	1 (4.5%)	5 (8.1%)	9 (7.0%)
Sacred holiday-1/year	4 (8.9%)	2 (9.1%)	3 (4.8%)	9 (7.0%)
Never	6 (13.3%)	11 (50.0%)	12 (19.4%)	30 (23.1%)
Other	8 (17.9%)	1 (4.5%)	11 (17.7%)	19 (14.8%)

of much more significance to nurses than to physicians. Only seven persons did not reply to this question. Of these, four were physicians (Table 4).

Respondents were next asked to rate in sequence the importance of spirituality in their lives, the importance of having their spiritual needs met, and the importance of meeting their patients' and colleagues' spiritual needs. A 5-point Likert scale was utilized, with "1"

Table 4. Conceptualization of Spirituality

	Nurse (n = 45)	Physician (n = 22)	OHCP (n = 62)	Total (n = 129)
Relates to Inner Self	20 (44.4%)	8 (36.3%)	28 (45.2%)	56 (43.4%)
Caring for Others	22 (48.8%)	9 (40.9%)	25 (40.3%)	56 (43.4%)
Supreme Being	21 (46.6%)	4 (18.8%)	21 (33.9%)	46 (35.6%)
Search for Meaning	11 (24.4%)	4 (18.8%)	12 (19.4%)	27 (20.9%)
Soul/Transcendence	4 (8.8%)	0 (0.0%)	6 (9.7%)	10 (7.8%)
Creativity/Art	1 (2.2%)	0 (0.0%)	1 (1.6%)	2 (1.5%)
No Response	1 (2.2%)	4 (18.8%)	2 (3.2%)	7 (5.4%)
Avg. No. of Responses	1.8	1.4	1.6	1.6

representing little importance and "5" being extremely important. Nurses rated the role of spirituality consistently higher than Other Health Care Professionals and physicians. Nurses rated the importance of spirituality in their lives as 4.7 while Other Health Care Professionals rated it 4.6. Both ratings were nearly a full point higher than that of physicians (3.8). Similarly, nurses rated the importance of having their own spiritual needs met at nearly "5," substantially higher than the other two groups (Table 5).

Almost all respondents (93.8%) expressed personal comfort with their spirituality (Table 6). Approximately one-quarter replied that they simply felt secure in their current beliefs (28.9%), while thirty-two (26.4%) stated that spirituality helped them in their problem solving. The belief in a higher power provided comfort for thirty (24.8%) persons. Interestingly, over 40 percent (n = 9) of the physicians did not respond to this question while those who did averaged 2.5 reasons (Table 7).

Not surprisingly, the majority (61.2%) of health care professionals surveyed stated that they met their spiritual needs through religious practices. Other frequent responses included through interpersonal communication (34.1%), through contact with nature (25.6%), by caring for others (24.8%), and by indulging in passive diversions (20.9%) (Table 8). The most prominent method through which physicians met their spiritual needs was by caring for others, a factor that was rated fourth by nurses and fifth by Other Health Care Professionals.

When asked what strengthened their spirituality most, the predominant response from the total sample was through religious experiences (42.6%) followed by human relationships (38.8%) (Table 9). When asked what life event changed their spirituality the most, there were few responses. One-third of the nurses, 38.7 percent of the Other Health Care Providers, and half of the physicians chose not to respond.

Table 5. Role of Spirituality

	Nurse (n = 45)	Physician (n = 22)	OHCP (n = 62)	Total (n = 129)
Importance of Spirituality in my life	4.7	3.8	4.6	4.5
Importance of having my Spiritual needs met	4.9	3.8	4	4.3
Importance of meeting the Spiritual needs of patients	4	3.6	3.8	3.8
Importance of helping colleagues meet Spiritual needs	3.4	3	3.3	3.3

Table 6. Comfort with Personal Spirituality

	Nurse (n = 45)	Physician (n = 22)	OHCP (n = 62)	Total (n = 129)
Yes	43 (95.6%)	21 (95.5%)	57 (92.0%)	121 (93.8%)
No	2 (4.4%)	0 (0.0%)	4 (6.5%)	6 (4.7%)
Undecided	0 (0.0%)	1 (4.5%)	1 (1.5%)	2 (1.5%)

Table 7. Reasons for Comfort with Spirituality

	Nurse (n = 43)	Physician (n = 21)	OHCP (n = 57)	Total (n = 123)
Personal Inner Self	22 (51.2%)	8 (38.1%)	25 (43.9%)	55 (45.5%)
Feel Secure in Beliefs	16 (37.2%)	5 (23.8%)	14 (24.6%)	35 (28.9%)
Helps Solve Problems	9 (20.9%)	7 (33.3%)	16 (28.1%)	32 (26.4%)
Belief in Higher Power	16 (37.2%)	2 (9.5%)	12 (21.0%)	30 (24.8%)
Allows to Care for Others	8 (18.6%)	6 (28.6%)	4 (7.0%)	18 (14.9%)
Connection to World	1 (2.3%)	2 (9.5%)	2 (3.5%)	5 (4.1%)
Connection to Soul	1 (2.3%)	0 (0.0%)	1 (1.8%)	2 (1.7%)
No Response	11 (25.6%)	9 (42.4%)	10 (17.5%)	30 (24.7%)
Avg. No. of Responses	2.6	2.5	1.6	1.9

Table 8. How Personal Spiritual Needs are Met

	Nurse (n = 45)	Physician (n = 22)	OHCP (n = 62)	Total (n = 129)
Religious Practice	30 (66.7%)	7 (31.8%)	42 (67.7%)	79 (61.2%)
Interpersonal Communication	13 (28.8%)	7 (31.8%)	24 (38.7%)	44 (34.1%)
Through Nature	13 (28.8%)	3 (13.6%)	17 (27.4%)	33 (25.6%)
Caring for Others	12 (26.6%)	9 (40.9%)	11 (17.7%)	32 (24.8%)
Passive Diversion	9 (20.0%)	3 (13.6%)	15 (24.2%)	27 (20.9%)
Creative Diversions	6 (13.3%)	1 (4.5%)	8 (12.9%)	15 (11.6%)
Living by One's Values	6 (13.3%)	3 (13.6%)	3 (4.8%)	12 (9.3%)
Physical Exercise/ Recreation	3 (6.6%)	1 (4.5%)	8 (12.9%)	12 (9.3%)
Positive Thinking and Acts	3 (6.6%)	2 (9.1%)	2 (3.2%)	7 (5.4%)
No Response	1 (2.2%)	3 (13.6%)	3 (4.8%)	7 (5.4%)
Avg. No. Responses	2.2	1.7	2.2	2.1

The next most frequent response related to experiences with death and loss of relationships, although the only group to reply at a rate more than 25 percent were nurses (Table 10).

Factors that survey participants most frequently claimed prevented them from meeting their spiritual needs were a lack of self-discipline (53.5%), fatigue and stress (30.2%), and relationship problems (20.1%). However, 17.0 percent (n = 22) again offered no response (Table 11).

DISCUSSION

As caregivers, each of us is steeped in beliefs transmitted by family, peers, and mentors during our upbringing. We are also subject to a sorting out process that accompanies our cognitive maturing influenced

Table 9. Spirituality Strengthened Most By:

	Nurse (n = 45)	Physician (n = 22)	OHCP (n = 62)	Total (n = 129)
Religious Experience	20 (44.4%)	7 (31.8%)	28 (45.2%)	55 (42.6%)
Relationships	16 (35.6%)	8 (36.6%)	26 (41.9%)	50 (38.8%)
Time Alone	8 (17.7%)	3 (13.6%)	12 (19.4%)	23 (17.8%)
Nature	7 (15.5%)	3 (13.6%)	11 (17.7%)	21 (16.3%)
Creative Expressions	6 (13.3%)	1 (4.5%)	9 (14.5%)	16 (12.4%)
Co-Workers/Work	4 (8.8%)	4 (18.1%)	5 (8.1%)	13 (10.1%)
Caring for Others	4 (8.8%)	2 (9.1%)	5 (8.1%)	11 (8.5%)
Positive Feelings	1 (2.2%)	1 (4.5%)	7 (11.3%)	9 (7.0%)
Problem Solving	1 (2.2%)	0 (0.0%)	5 (8.1%)	6 (4.7%)
Life Purpose	0 (0.0%)	2 (9.1%)	2 (3.2%)	4 (3.1%)
No Response	4 (8.8%)	6 (27.3%)	5 (8.1%)	15 (11.6%)
Avg. No. Responses	1.6	1.9	1.8	1.8

Table 10. Life Events that Changed Spirituality

	Nurse (n = 45)	Physician (n = 22)	OHCP (n = 62)	Total (n = 129)
Death/Lost Relationship	13 (28.9%)	3 (13.6%)	9 (14.5%)	25 (19.4%)
Aging	8 (18.2%)	1 (4.5%)	2 (3.2%)	11 (8.5%)
Religious Experience	2 (4.5%)	0 (0.0%)	9 (14.5%)	11 (8.5%)
General Life Events	2 (4.5%)	1 (4.5%)	4 (6.5%)	7 (5.4%)
Personal Illness	2 (4.5%)	1 (4.5%)	3 (4.8%)	6 (4.7%)
Positive Relationship	0 (0.0%)	1 (4.5%)	5 (8.1%)	6 (4.7%)
Family Responsibility	3 (6.9%)	0 (0.0%)	1 (1.6%)	4 (3.1%)
Other	0 (0.0%)	4 (18.2%)	5 (8.1%)	9 (7.0%)
No Response	15 (33.3%)	11 (50.0%)	24 (38.7%)	50 (38.8%)

by our personal, physical, and intellectual capabilities and development, life events, opportunities, and support systems. What is too often ignored or over mystified is the function of spirituality in our professional roles.

In a limited sample with an exploratory focus it is difficult to make accurate inferences. However, the following points, although largely speculative, are worth considering and may merit further exploration.

1. Although there was a high level of comfort with spiritual beliefs and practices, respondents seemed less able or less willing to articulate

Table 11. Factors Preventing the Meeting of Spiritual Needs

	Nurse (n = 45)	Physician (n = 22)	OHCP (n = 62)	Total (n = 129)
Lack of Self-Discipline	29 (64.4%)	8 (36.6%)	32 (51.6%)	69 (53.5%)
Fatigue/Stress	15 (33.3%)	8 (36.6%)	39 (30.2%)	39 (30.2%)
Relationship Problems	10 (22.2%)	0 (0.0%)	26 (20.1%)	26 (20.1%)
Intense Emotions	3 (6.7%)	2 (9.1%)	4 (6.5%)	9 (7.0%)
Problems with Organized Religion	4 (8.8%)	0 (0.0%)	4 (6.5%)	8 (6.2%)
Materialism	3 (6.7%)	1 (4.5%)	3 (4.8%)	7 (5.4%)
Isolation	1 (2.2%)	0 (0.0%)	4 (6.5%)	5 (3.9%)
No Response	6 (13.3%)	9 (40.9%)	7 (11.3%)	22 (17.0%)
Avg. No. of Responses	1.7	1.5	1.4	1.5

their rationale than one might anticipate. This seemed particularly true for the small number of physicians in the study.

2. Even though the majority of respondents suggested that they met their spiritual needs through religious practices, only one-third made reference to the influence of a supreme force or being when discussing their comfort with their personal spirituality.

3. Both intrinsic factors, such as finding peace and tranquillity through nature and attention to personal needs through passive discussion, and extrinsic factors, such as talking with and helping others, were included in meeting spiritual needs of respondents. The physicians' reliance on caring for others as their primary method for meeting spiritual needs warrants further exploration. It could be suggested that physicians may be less introspective and more practical in interpreting and meeting spiritual needs than other health professionals.

4. Although religious practices ranked high in the meeting of spiritual needs, only two in five respondents attended religious services at least once per month. In the *Montreal Pediatric Palliative Care Assessment Committee Report*, the researchers found that the religious and spiritual needs of patients and families were respected by health care providers, though religious practices for most professionals were

not a high personal priority [5]. McDermott states that a societal weakening of ties to organized religion may be associated with: 1) the belief that organized religions interfere with a person's right to develop a personal spiritual philosophy, and 2) that intellectual autonomy may lead individuals to develop their own religious beliefs independent of organized religions [23]. Mangalwadi, a Christian evangelist, supports McDermott's views and adds that "intellectual disarmament" may also be a factor as reason may be abandoned in favor of experience [24, p. C8]. It could be surmised that the 60 percent of health care professionals who do not attend religious services regularly do not depend on formal religious systems to meet their spiritual needs. Perhaps it is applied spirituality rather than religious practices that take precedence in their everyday lives at work and home.

5. For nurses, each component of the study points to their high level of connection to spirituality and the meeting of their spiritual needs. Perhaps spiritual concerns surface more readily and are more prevalent for nurses than other health professionals due to their constant physical and emotional proximity to their patients. In reviewing nurses' comments, they appeared to be more in tune with their own spirituality and more readily able to connect with and articulate how they meet the spiritual needs of their patients.

6. The reasons given by health professionals for not meeting their spiritual needs were lack of self-discipline, fatigue, stress, and relationship difficulties. It is possible that health care systems in flux are making increasing personal demands on health care personnel that are readily transported from work to home, particularly in this era of hospital down sizings.

CLOSING COMMENTS

In closing, it is reasonable to conclude that although spirituality has been inadequately addressed in formal education and training programs for health professionals, spirituality is very much a part of their working lives. Spirituality is, however, a truly complex and personal phenomenon that serves as a source of comfort and contemplation for some and outright confusion for others. This study has heightened the awareness and importance of spirituality in patient care and the personal lives of most respondents. As one person suggested, "This study made me much more aware of my spirituality, how I apply it, and what I need to do to nourish it." For the authors, it has provided clarity concerning methodology and has highlighted the need for further empirical examination of the significance of spirituality for both health care providers and health care consumers. Along with further investigation of the issues explored in this study, future research in this area should probe if:

1. persons with a stronger sense of spirituality are drawn to the provision of health care;
2. caregivers with a strong sense of spirituality provide better patient care;
3. spirituality should be included in curriculum and professional development of health care providers; and
4. health care providers with higher levels of spirituality practice better self-care.

In returning to Dunn's requirements for a complete state of well-being involving wellness of the mind, body, and the environment, including family, community life, and a compatible work interest, we must conclude that spirituality is very much part of Dunn's requirements. In the context of this study, we believe that many health care professionals would endorse the definition of spirituality by Reverend Jerry Nash. He suggests that:

> Spirituality is a way of being and acting so that we can breathe, grow, and be connected to ourselves, to others, to God (or in our words to a Supreme Other), to the cosmos in a salugenic (health producing) manner so that we can live meaningfully, age gracefully, and approach death purposefully with a sense of joy and completion [25].

To this we would add "and to offer the opportunity for all of this to be an integral part of the lives of those we serve."

REFERENCES

1. H. Dunn, *High Level Wellness*, R. W. Beatty, Arlington, 1961.
2. World Health Organization, *Constitution*, New York, 1946.
3. D. Ardell, *High Level Wellness*, Rodale Press, Emmasus, Pennsylvania, 1977.
4. J. Sefton, L. Wankel, H. Quinney, J. Webber, J. Marshall, and T. Horne, *Working Towards Well-Being in Alberta,* National Recreation and Wellness Conference, Coburg, Australia, 1992.
5. B. M. Mount and L. McHarg, *Montreal Children's Hospital Palliative Care Assessment Committee Report*, Montreal Children's Hospital, Montreal, Canada, 1987.
6. L. L. DeVeber, The Influence of Spirituality on Dying Children's Perceptions of Death, in *Beyond the Innocence of Childhood: Helping Children and Adolescents Cope with Life-Threatening Illness and Dying, Volume 2*, D. W. Adams and E. J. Deveau (eds.), Baywood, Amityville, New York, 1995.

7. C. L. Perry and R. Jesson, The Concept of Health Promotion and the Prevention of Adolescent Drug Use, *Health Education Quarterly, 12:*2, pp. 169-184, 1985.
8. C. A. Corr, J. D. Morgan, and H. Wass (eds.), *International Work Group on Death, Dying and Bereavement: Statements on Death, Dying and Bereavement,* International Work Group on Death, Dying and Bereavement, London, Canada, 1993.
9. J. D. Morgan, The Existential Quest for Meaning, in *Death and Spirituality,* K. Doka and J. D. Morgan (eds.), Baywood, Amityville, New York, 1993.
10. J. D. Morgan, The Knowledge of Death as a Stimulus to Creativity, in *Grief and the Healing Arts: Creativity as Therapy,* S. Bertman (ed.), Baywood, Amityville, New York, 1998.
11. R. Twycross, *How Whole is Our Care?* Address to the Seventh International Congress on Terminal Care, Montreal, Canada, 1988.
12. M. K. Stiles, The Shining Stranger—Nurse-Family Spiritual Relationship, *Cancer Nursing, 13:*4, pp. 235-245, 1990.
13. D. W. Adams, *Spirituality: How We Care for Ourselves and Our Patients,* workshop presented at the International Conference on Death, Dying and Bereavement, King's College, London, Canada, 1996.
14. J. A. Shelley (ed.), *The Spiritual Needs of Children,* Intervarsity Press, Downers Grove, Illinois, 1982.
15. M. F. Highfield, The Spiritual Health of Oncology Patients—Nurses and Patient Perspectives, *Cancer Nursing, 15:*1, pp. 1-8, 1992.
16. S. Eaton, Spiritual Care: The Software of Life, *Journal of Palliative Care, 4:*1&2, pp. 91-93, 1988.
17. F. S. Wald, *In Search of the Spiritual Component of Care of the Terminally Ill,* Yale University Press, New Haven, 1986.
18. F. S. Wald, Spiritual or Pastoral Care: Two Models, *Journal of Palliative Care, 4:*1&2, pp. 94-97, 1988.
19. J. Kaufman, Spiritual Perspectives on Suffering the Pain of Death, in *Death and Spirituality,* K. Doka and J. D. Morgan (eds.), Baywood, Amityville, New York, 1993.
20. H. Nouwen, *The Wounded Healer: Ministry in Contemporary Society,* Doubleday, New York, 1972.
21. I. Progroff, *The Cloud of Unknowing: A New Translation of a Classic Guide to Spiritual Experience Revealing the Dynamics of the Inner Life From a Particular Historical and Religious Point of View / Introductory Commentary and Translation by Ira Progroff,* Julian Press, New York, 1957.
22. M. D. Amenta, Pediatric Hospice Care, in *What Helps,* B. Martin (ed.), Children's Hospital of Los Angeles, Los Angeles, 1989.
23. G. McDermott, *Twelve Reliable Signs of True Spirituality,* Intervarsity Press, New York, 1995.
24. C. Korstanje, Sounding the Alarm: Church is Drifting toward New Age, Theologian Warns, *The Spectator,* Hamilton, Canada, Saturday, May 11, 1996, p. C8.
25. J. Nash, Personal correspondence to D. W. Adams, 1996.

SECTION 2:

Health Care and Spirituality:
Belief System Perspectives

Introduction

Reverend Richard B. Gilbert

"We should not presume, however, that spiritual contacts have the same character or meaning from one culture to another. Even if one's beliefs bear a resemblance to those of people one is trying to help, there may be crucial differences." Diversity is a gift, and current standards in health care as monitored by the Joint Commission for Accreditation of Health Care Organizations (JCAHO) *Standards* require us to affirm diversity and reject "different."

It is still easier to see "different," especially in spiritual and religious matters. It takes time to stay with a person in his or her own story. Spiritual questions, religious rituals, tough theological questions woven into ethical decision making, the anguish of suffering . . . all of this demands time, and it is time that is becoming scarce as we find ourselves falling deeper into the medical model for viewing everyone and everything. It is also time consuming because their questions become our questions, their longings snare our doubts and yearnings, and we want to retreat to a safe place "where we can just do our work," as a physician commented during Grand Rounds.

This chapter introduces a few faith traditions as examples of the larger discussion of diversity. Space did not permit including other faith traditions. We would remind you that one of the tasks of the chaplain is to represent the medical institution to the religious community. For the many traditions, new and old, that come into the care of your work place, it is the chaplain who can connect you to their beliefs, practices, and religious leaders. Even within familiar traditions, it is still necessary and helpful to invite the patient to share his or her own story and the meaning the patient gives to life events, losses, and the rituals claimed or shunned in the midst of a spiritual wilderness.

Dr. John D. Morgan, professor emeritus, King's College, and the director of the King's College Bereavement Conference, offers us a helpful look or grid at what we would call general or non-descript spirituality. It is a discussion of the many patients who simply do not (and should not) fit into more familiar patterns and structures. His theme is "Dying and Grieving are Journeys of the Spirit." His chapter serves as the first bookend bringing this section together as we walk through the universality of spirituality.

To balance Morgan's important discussion of the universal nature of spirituality and its participation in the grief journey, we offer the chapter by Professor Edgar Senne on spiritual care in the midst of the plurality of religions. We talk about a world of many religions, but still find many in health care working from the assumption that everyone is Christian, or at least believes in the God who Christians define. In other ways we are working with the system we call Western medicine, a delivery tradition that often assumes its approaches and biases from the Judeo-Christian tradition. Senne gives us the framework to first discuss plurality before we then can begin to discuss and appreciate the many world religions.

The Reverend Fr. Joseph Driscoll, author, poet, chaplain, and executive director of The National Association of Catholic Chaplains, brings us into the story of many Roman Catholic patients who seek their connection sacramentally, and the role of the chaplain (and others) in responding to those stories and expectations.

Rabbi Jeffery Silberman, chaplain and C.P.E. supervisor, has done very well with the challenge of bringing a very diverse community, the Jewish faith, into a clearer picture for us as we explore responding to the needs of the Jewish patient and family.

CHAPTER 5

Dying and Grieving are Journeys
of the Spirit

John D. Morgan

Dr. John Fortunato, a clinical psychologist who was in private practice in Chicago for many years, was, until recently, a member of an Episcopalian Benedictine community. Recently he has returned to the Roman Catholicism of his youth and has entered a contemplative monastery. The first chapter of his book *AIDS: The Spiritual Dilemma* [1] is entitled, "From the Bottom of the Heap." In it, Dr. Fortunato tells a story from his own life that bears repeating here:

> Mary was a proper Scottish lady in her late sixties who had married young. She had not had a happy life. Her marriage had failed; a hard thing for a proper Scottish lady to take. One of her sons was psychotic, in and out of institutions. Her career at the U.S. State Department had been an uphill struggle, mostly because Mary's sense of justice would not allow her to remain silent in the face of then-rampant inequity being doled out to her, and her Black and female co-workers.
>
> She always seemed to me a courageous but despairing person. A woman of great dignity . . . and sadness. A woman who blamed herself for everything that went badly in her life. A woman who carried around an enormous guilt.
>
> I suppose it was Mary's innate sense of justice that would not allow her to dismiss Wayne and me as her peers had done. Every Sunday morning, at the passing of the peace, as the rest of her age group made big circles around me, she would come directly up, firmly grasp my hand with both of hers, smile warmly, and say, "Good morning, my dear."

About a year later, Mary disappeared from St. Stephen's. It was such a frenetic place that I failed to notice her absence for a while. But when I finally inquired about her, I was told confidentially that Mary had lung cancer and was dying. Her way of coping with this final failure (as she apparently saw it) was to leave St. Stephen's and Washington and to remove herself to a rural Virginia town where she planned on dying alone. The parishioner who told me this added that I was not supposed to know it and that I must not try to contact her.

Well, I tried to honor her request, but I couldn't. I just couldn't. She had meant so much to me. So eventually, I sleuthed out her address and wrote. I told her how much I valued her having stood by Wayne and me the year before when we were going through hard times. I told her how much I wanted to reciprocate now that hard times had befallen her. I offered to come visit, run errands, read to her, whatever.

Four months passed. No response. I assume I had indeed gaffed by writing. I tried to forget about it. Then one day Mary's letter arrived. She wrote that she had been in the hospital and had really been unable to write. She told me how beautiful the letter seemed to her. She told me that Bill Wendt had been helping her grieve her impending death. And finally, she wrote that she would be moving back to Washington and would like nothing better than for us to have some time together to sit and talk, as she wrote, "Of shoes and ships and sealing wax, of cabbages and kings."

She returned to Washington about a month later, but before we could manage even one get-together, Mary MacLean Selcik died. I was bereft, left with a strong sense of incompletion both with her, and about her in terms of how unsettled she had seemed to the end. The night after she died, Bill Wendt, who had been at her deathbed, and I were officiating at the Eucharist. As we were taking off our vestments in the sacristy after the service, I mused to Bill that it seemed Mary had never made it to a peaceful place, that she seemed to have *died* with her courageous despair; dignified, but sad and guilt-ridden to the end.

"No," Bill said, matter-of-factly. "No, she made it. And it all had to do with the letter you sent her." I couldn't imagine what he meant; I had long since forgotten the letter. "The night before she died," Bill went on, "with her family around her, Mary pulled that letter from the drawer of her nightstand. She passed it around the room and made every single one of her family from the oldest to the youngest read it. And then she announced calmly and surely and peacefully, "That young man has given me a most wonderful gift. By his love, he has shown me that many kinds of people can be Christian . . ." And she added through her tears, ". . . even me. Even me" [1, pp. 28-31].

Fortunato continues:

Regardless of what Holy Orders I may ever be permitted to take, I will always view that day as my commissioning, my ordination. Because I came to know in that event that the most powerful place from which to renew the face of the earth is the bottom of the heap [1, p. 31].

In the last thirty years the care of the dying and bereaved has been improved. But at least equally importantly, the dying and bereaved have been our teachers and improve us as well. I begin each of my courses with a slide that says that the study of death is life-enhancing. I am convinced of the truth of this. We accept the limits of our financial resources, the limits of our short-term time or energy, but our culture continues to allow us to think that we can always pull out of our pocket another five years of life, another ten years of a relationship. As Robert Kastenbaum has noted, "It is possible for future scholars and practitioners to complete their formal education with only the wispiest of thanatological encounters" [2, p. 79].

The dying and grieving teach us that human life is a sexually transmitted terminal condition. A music therapist named Deanna Edwards wrote an award winning song called *Teach Me to Die*. In it she says, "If you teach me of dying I will teach you to live" [3]. The dying and grieving, those who are the bottom of the heap in our culture because they are not economically productive or consumed by a passion for the latest jeans or movie, teach us what is important in life. If we took death seriously, would we forget that when we say "good-bye" to a loved one, it might very well be that last good-bye? If we took the lessons of the dying and grieving seriously how many of us would forget to say "I love you" or "I am sorry"? Because we foster the illusion of immortality, we do not live fully in this moment. We continue to play silly games.

We have learned much from philosophical and theological traditions about the topic of spirituality. However, I think far more important is the lesson that we learn from the disadvantaged of the world: the dying, the grieving, and those who are dismissed by one or another prejudice in society; from those who are at the bottom of the heap. They too teach us about spirituality.

However, we might define the person, a theme which is found treated extensively in the book *Images of the Human: The Philosophy of the Human Person in a Religious Context* [4], each of us builds walls around the self so that the real person does not often shine through. We have to build these walls. One would have a hard time in society, in the church, in a university, in a department, in a classroom, if we allowed others to see our vulnerability, to see us as we think that we truly are. When we are privileged to work with the dying and the bereaved, a few bricks of those walls are taken out, on both sides. We allow others to enter behind those walls to see the self within, with all of the warts. It is a terrifying, awe-inspiring experience. It is one of the few times in my life when I believe that I am really being listened to, and certainly one of the few times when I truly listen in an I-Thou manner [5].

WHAT IS SPIRITUALITY?

It is my intention to discuss both from theory and from practical consideration. The theory is based on a philosophical consideration of the problem of knowing. The practical is based on the literature of caring for the dying and the bereaved.

A Theoretical View

A few years ago I was invited by a colleague to address his class about death and spirituality. I began the class with the remark that being confused about spirituality is, in a sense, the way it ought to be. The question of spirituality flows from the most basic questions we as humans ask: "What do I know?," "What must I do?," "For what can I hope?," "Who am I?"

> The *spiritual* is a dimension of our humanness. Most dimensions of our humanness are not uniquely human . . . [We share them with other creatures.] Spirituality is experienced at the meeting point, or as some would say, the merging point, between our self and that which we usually feel is not our self [6, pp. 52-53, *passim*].

Spirituality is the organization of consciousness [7, p. 540]; not some supernaturally oriented package of ideas. It is a focus on what we very natural beings, in this very natural world, can become [7, p. 540].

Spirituality is not some esoteric human phenomenon. The great faith traditions, and many of the philosophical ones, agree that the human person is in some sense spiritual, holds a unique place in creation. For Becker, "Spirituality is . . . an expression of the will to live, the burning desire of the creature to count, to make a difference on the planet because he has lived, has emerged on it, has worked, suffered and died" [9, p. 3]. Each choice that we make, whether it is as simple as deciding between a 29 cent throwaway pen or a $200 precise writing instrument, entails value commitments. These value commitments are the results of the spiritual nature of the person.

I believe that Plato and others had a basic insight about spirituality in their discussion of the problem of universals [10]. In the process of apprehension, the human mind is aware of the sense data received but in addition has the ability to transcend the immediate sense to arrive at a universal, a "oneness with respect to many" [11, p. 597]. Each human person is a material being which gets its existence one moment at a time. Yet, in spite of the immediacy of all experience, persons can think, that is, be aware of the common characteristics of things found in experience. Thinking, awareness of the common characteristics of things, is an example of the spiritual nature of the human mind.

The question, "do you like red wine?" is easily understood both by those who like the product and by those who do not. By analogy, it is even understandable to those who have never tasted wine. One should note that the question is not, "Do you like the red wine that is on your tongue at this moment." The question is "Do you like red wine?," that is, any red wine at all. When we stop to think about it, we realize that we have never tasted "any red wine at all" but we have only tasted "this red wine on my tongue now." In spite of the fact that all of our experiences of red wine have been in a particular place and time, and of a particular drop of red wine, I still understand the question "Do you like (any) red wine at all?" This ability to go beyond the immediacy of this moment and this place is spirituality.

Aquinas and others teach us about the self-reflective character of the human mind [12, p. 283]. The human thinking power can define what a thinking power is, reflecting on itself. This is an example of spirituality.

Spirituality is manifested in language, a symbolic referential system. We see spirituality in humor, the awareness of incongruity. Spirituality is manifested in ethics, a perception of the kind of person one envisions him/herself to be. Spirituality shows itself in creativity. Whether one is baking a pie, cleaning a room, or writing a poem, one creates what was not there before, what existed only in an intuition of possibilities. Spirituality shows itself in the religious, the awareness of a whole larger than oneself and a movement toward union with that whole.

A Practical View

However we as thinkers might debate the nature of spirituality, there is another approach to definition, and that is the practical meaning of the idea. Many who are privileged to work with the dying and bereaved believe that spirituality shows itself in the completion of life tasks.[1] The following lists some of the tasks that both the dying and grieving engage in while anticipating death.

---

[1] The term "task" is handy, but probably not very accurate. The term task seems to imply a specific beginning and end. The tasks of the dying and grieving do not fit into such a neat systematization [13].

- Develop a progressively deepening awareness of the seriousness of the illness and its implications through the dawning realization that certain hopes about recovery or stabilization are not being actualized.
- Gradually absorbing and coming to terms with the reality of the impending loss of time.
- Mourning past, present and future losses attendant to the terminal illness and death and the unrelated losses that have been revived in this loss situation.
- Experiencing and coping with the separation anxiety and fear elicited by the threat of permanent loss.
- Gradually decathecting from the image of the dying person in the post-death future and from the hopes, dreams, wishes, expectations, and plans that accompanied it.
- Starting to slowly incorporate changes in one's identity, roles, experiences, beliefs, assumptions, and expectations that reflect the current reality and will begin to prepare the griever for the reality that will exist after the death in a world without the loved one.
- Reviewing the past and attending carefully to the present in order to crystallize memories to keep after the death.
- Bargaining with God or fate for a reprieve, for more time, or for a different illness experience.
- Recollecting previous losses, grief, periods of vulnerability and other related experiences that have been revived by this loss.
- Contemplating one's own death.
- Considering what the future will be like without the loved one and experiencing associated reactions to it.
- Anticipating and planning for future losses and changes, both before and after the death [14, pp. 30-31, *passim*].

The above list gives us some of the dynamics that occur during the dying process. Daniel Callahan gives us, as it were, the criterion for an appropriate death when he says that death becomes acceptable ". . . when it comes at the point in a life when (1) further efforts to deter dying are likely to deform the process of living, or (2) when there is a good fit between the biological inevitability of death in general and the particular timing and circumstances of that death in the life of an individual" [15, p. 180].

In the literature today, the best known list of tasks is that in which J. William Worden speaks of the process of grief. Worden states that the griever has four major tasks. These are 1) to accept the reality of the loss; 2) to work through the pain of grief; 3) to adjust to an environment in which the deceased is missing; and 4) to emotionally relocate the deceased and move on with life [16, pp. 10-16, *passim*].

One moves through the tasks or journey of grief and the tasks or journey of dying, reflected in many of the suggested tasks above, by finding meaning. While death and bereavement are facts, dying and grieving are processes in which we engage. Like all processes, we engage in them in the manner in which we have been taught, the death system of our culture [17, p. 11]. "Time does not heal all wounds." Persons move from one phase in these processes to the other by doing grief work, that is:

> . . . a cognitive process of confronting a loss, of going over the events before and at the time of death, of focusing on memories . . . it requires an active, ongoing, effortful attempt to come to terms with loss [18, pp. 19-20].

We move on when we have found meaning in our own lives and in the meaning in the lives of the people who die, a search for meaning that goes on, as Catherine Sanders says, "relentlessly until some conclusion has been reached" [19, p. 95]. However we might define spirituality from a theoretical standpoint, practically it is found in this quest for meaning.

I believe that the following will be helpful in the analysis of spirituality. Barely skimming the surface of the history of thought, we see many definitions of what it is to be a person. These definitions range from "spiritual substance" [20] to "will to power" [21], and includes such awareness as the person as a moral creator [22], the person as a problem solver [23], the person as a network of relationships [24], the person as worker [25], the person as freedom [26], the person as sexual [27], the person as part of the Absolute [28], the person as redeemed [28], the person as destined to do the will of God [28].

Each of these views are intrinsically understandable. Each can be intelligently defended. Each make a certain kind of sense. We find ourselves agreeing with many of these positions, in whole or in part. Yet, the diversity of viewpoints teaches us the greatest lesson of spirituality: **the person is a self-creator, a being who decides one way or another what kind of being s/he will be**. Our spirituality gives each of us the particular integration of these identifying characteristics. We thus arrive at a more formal definition of spirituality.

> Spirituality refers to the ability of the human person to choose the relative importance of the physical, social, emotional, religious, and intellectual stimuli that influence him or her and thereby engage in a continuing process of meaning making.

Another way of discovering spirituality is to examine the difference between pain and suffering. The International Association for the Study of Pain states that pain is " . . . an unpleasant sensory or emotional experience associated with actual or potential tissue damage, or described in terms of such damage" [29, p. 5]. It may be acute, that is, a limited duration with a specific meaning; or it may be chronic, that is, unlimited duration and with no specific meaning, or a specific meaning that is already held. It is relatively easy to tolerate the pain of sunburn, a minor headache, a stubbed toe, an insult, a failure to receive what one perceives as his/her due. In chronic pain, physical or psychological, the pain no longer operates as a signal that something is wrong. The person feeling the unrelieved pain of a growing tumor already knows that something is wrong.

Suffering, however, has the connotation of "perceived threat to the integrity of the self, both physical and psychological" [29, p. 6]. That is, in suffering one has the sense of "losing it," of no longer being in control of one's own life, of helplessness and hopelessness. As Callahan states, there are two levels of suffering. The first deals with uncertainty, fear, dread. The second deals with "the meaning of life itself" [15, p. 100]. Suffering occurs when there is the sense that the level of pain has become so intolerable, that I can no longer be the person that I want to be. Aside from the very important differences in pain thresholds, a major contributing factor to how much pain one can tolerate without disintegration into suffering, is the perception of the world, the philosophy, the sense of meaning, that one holds: one's spirituality. A Buddhist who accepts the first Noble Truth [28, p. 148] that life is pain, will relate to pain differently, and presumably will suffer less than a materialist consumer who defines him/herself only in terms of possessions. One's philosophy operates as a buffer against suffering. Again, Callahan, "We are all fated to suffer and die. We are not fated to make one interpretation only of this necessity, or one response, or to have just one possibility of shaping the contours of our suffering" [15, p. 136].

All conscious human activity is a form of spirituality for reasons stated above; however, what is commonly spoken of as spirituality in discussions today is what might be called "self-aware spirituality," that is an awareness of oneself as a unique center of knowledge and valuation. Spirituality is a two-edged sword. It is our agony and our ecstasy. Because of it we are aware of our radical otherness, what Ortega y Gasset called our radical solitude [30, p. 126]. As we mature spiritually we become more aware that we are not *just* a product of nature or of nurture. We become aware that we are self-creations. This self-creation demands terrible responsibility and the loneliness that comes with responsibility.

Yet, at the same time, in our self-aware spirituality our ego boundaries become permeable. We are aware of the connection of ourselves with other persons, with the environment, with our understanding of God. We become aware of a higher order of the universe, a meaning in the universe, in which we participate but which we do not control. We become aware of the sacredness of every moment. We become very conscious of the limits of time, and of our *vocation*. Each of us is a spiritual being who knows that s/he is in the universe; with a need to make sense out of our lives; and we know that this is the one chance that we have to be the person that we could be.

Since the person is a meaning seeking being, spiritual pain is produced when one has the sense that his/her life is meaningless. No one can tell another where to find meaning. We can only support one another in the process of meaning creation. We offer each other social support, that is, asking another "How are you?," and staying long enough to get the answer [31].

Unlocking the Door to Spirituality

The International Work Group on Death, Dying and Bereavement have listed the following assumptions about the spiritual care of the dying and grieving:

1. Each person has a spiritual dimension;
2. The spiritual orientation influences mental, emotional and physical dimensions;
3. Dying and grieving can be times of spiritual growth.
4. Spiritual beliefs and practices are exhibited in widely different ways;
5. Spiritual needs can arise at any time or place;
6. A broad range of spiritual opportunities should be available for the dying and the bereaved;
7. Joy and humor are essential parts of human spirituality [32, pp. 34-41, *passim*].

Traditional faith systems have been very helpful in opening the doors to spirituality for the dying and the grieving by helping control fears and anxiety; by emphasizing those events in history that make life seem more understandable and give more people a sense of changelessness in the midst of change; by helping turn their best thoughts and feelings into constructive action; by transforming the tragic events of life through the direction of hope and the power of love; by leading to deeper sensitivity of the spirit, higher aspirations of service, and a firmer conviction that the cosmic purpose is best understood as creative goodness. Therefore, although grief is painful and disappointing, it does not lead to despair. Faith provides relief of guilt and sorrow; a longer view by a tie of present sufferings to time-honored sources of spiritual strength; and courage in the present and direction for the future [33, pp. 316-317, *passim*]. These aspects are not limited only to those within a major faith system.

Spiritual awareness can also be opened in ways other than questioning. Art therapy, music therapy, bibliotherapy, guided meditation, journaling, telling the story of one's life, examining photographs and other memorabilia are effective tools in opening persons to self-conscious spirituality [34].

CONCLUSION

In this chaper, I have shown that spirituality is fundamental to the human person. Spirituality shows itself primarily as a continual quest for meaning. The dying and bereaved teach us that the processes in which they move occur because of the meanings that they have found in their own lives and the lives of their loved ones. Thus dying and grieving as spiritual journeys is perhaps best summed up in the phrase of Herman Feifel, "To die—this is the human condition; to live decently and well— this is man's privilege" [35, p. 12].

REFERENCES

1. J. E. Fortunato, *AIDS: The Spiritual Dimension,* Harper and Row, San Francisco, 1987.
2. R. Kastenbaum, Reconstructing Death in Postmodern Society, *Omega, 27*:1, pp. 75-89, 1993.
3. D. Edwards, *Teach Me to Die,* from the album *Music Brings My Heart Back Home,* Rock Canyon Music, publisher, Provo, Utah, 1987.
4. H. Brown, D. L. Hudecki, L. A. Kennedy, and J. J. Snyder, *Images of the Human: The Philosophy of the Human Person in a Religious Context,* Loyola, Chicago, 1995.
5. M. Buber, *I and Thou,* W. Kaufman (trans.), Scribners, New York, 1970.
6. D. Klass, Spirituality, Protestantism, and Death, in *Death and Spirituality,* K. J. Doka and J. D. Morgan (eds.), Baywood, Amityville, New York, pp. 51-74, 1993.
7. P. Hefner, The Spiritual Task of Religion in Culture: An Evolutionary Perspective, *Zygon: Journal of Religion and Science, 33*:4, pp. 535-544, 1998.
8. E. Becker, *Denial of Death,* Free Press, New York, 1973.
9. E. Becker, *Escape from Evil,* Collier Macmillan, New York, 1975.
10. Plate, Phaedo, in *The Dialogues of Plato,* R. B. Jowett (trans. and ed.), Random House, New York, 1937.
11. W. L. Reese, *Dictionary of Philosophy and Religion: Eastern and Western Thought,* Humanities, Atlantic Highlands, New Jersey, 1980.
12. T. Aquinas, *Summa Theologiae,* I, q. 75, A. 1, in *Introduction to Saint Thomas Aquinas,* A. C. Pegis (ed.), The Modern Library, New York, 1948.

13. T. Attig, *How We Grieve: Relearning the World,* Oxford, New York, 1996.
14. T. A. Rando, A Comprehensive Analysis of Anticipatory Grief: Perspectives, Processes, Promises and Problems, in *Loss and Anticipatory Grief,* T. A. Rando (ed.), Lexington Books, Lexington, 1986.
15. D. Callahan, *The Troubled Dream of Life: Living with Mortality,* Simon and Schuster, New York, 1993.
16. J. W. Worden, *Grief Counseling and Grief Therapy: A Handbook for the Mental Health Practitioner* (2nd Edition), Springer, New York, 1991.
17. J. D. Morgan, Living Our Dying and Our Grieving, in *Readings in Thanatology,* J. D. Morgan (ed.), Baywood, Amityville, New York, 1997.
18. M. Stroebe, Coping with Bereavement: A Review of the Grief Work Hypothesis, *Omega,* 26:1, pp. 19-42, 1992-93.
19. C. Sanders, *Grief: The Mourning After,* Wiley, New York, 1989.
20. T. Aquinas, *Summa Theologiae,* I, p. 75, A. 2, in *Introduction to Saint Thomas Aquinas,* A. C. Pegis (ed.), The Modern Library, New York, 1948.
21. J. J. Synder, Fredrich Nietzsche: The Human Person as Will to Power, in *Images of the Human: The Philosophy of the Human Person in a Religious Context,* H. Brown, D. L. Hudecki, L. A. Kennedy, and J. J. Snyder (eds.), Loyola, Chicago, pp. 331-366, 1995.
22. I. Kant, *Foundations of the Metaphysics of Morals,* B. E. Liddell (trans.), Indiana University Press, Bloomington, 1970.
23. W. James, The Sentiment of Rationality, in *Essays in Pragmatism,* A. Castell (ed.), Hafner, New York, 1948.
24. G. Marcel, *Being and Having: An Existentialist Diary,* P. Smith, Gloucester, Massachusetts, 1976.
25. M. T. Ryan, Karl Marx: The Human Person as Worker, in *Images of the Human: The Philosophy of the Human Person in a Religious Context,* H. Brown, D. L. Hudecki, L. A. Kennedy, and J. J. Snyder (eds.), Loyola, Chicago, pp. 251-294, 1995.
26. J.-P. Sartre, Existentialism, in *Existentialism and Human Emotions,* J.-P. Sartre (ed.), Citadel, Secaucus, New Jersey, pp. 9-51, 1957.
27. D. W. Hudson, Sigmund Freud: The Human Person as Sexual, in *Images of the Human: The Philosophy of the Human Person in a Religious Context,* H. Brown, D. L. Hudecki, L. A. Kennedy, and J. J. Snyder (eds.), Loyola, Chicago, pp. 367-396, 1995.
28. H. Smith, *The Religions of Man,* Harper and Row, New York, 1986.
29. C. R. Chapman and J. Gavrin, Suffering and Its Relationship to Pain, *Journal of Palliative Care,* 9:2, pp. 5-13, 1993.
30. J. Ortega y Gasset, In Search of Goethe from Within, in *The Dehumanization of Art and Other Writings on Art and Culture,* J. Ortega y Gasset (ed.), Doubleday, Garden City, New York, pp. 121-160, 1956.
31. F. D. Ritchie, *Learning from the Experts,* lecture given at the 1995 King's College Conference on Death and Bereavement, 1995.
32. I. Corless, F. Wald, N. Autton, S. Bailey, M. Cocburn, R. Cosh, B. de Veber, I. de Veber, D. Head, D. C. H. Ley, J. Mauritzen, P. O'Connor, and T. Saito, Assumptions and Principles of Spiritual Care, in *International Work Group on Death, Dying and Bereavement: Statements on Death, Dying and*

Bereavement, C. A. Corr, J. D. Morgan, and H. Wass (eds.), King's (Ont.), London, Ontario, 1990.

33. T. A. Rando, *Grief, Dying and Death: Clinical Interventions for Caregivers,* Research, Champaign, Illinois, 1984.

34. D. Graydon, Casey House Hospice: Caring for Persons Living with HIV/AIDS, in *Ethical Issues in the Care of the Dying and the Bereaved Aged,* J. D. Morgan (ed.), Baywood, Amityville, New York, pp. 325-334, 1996.

35. H. Feifel, The Meaning of Death in American Society, in *Death Education: Preparation for Living,* B. R. Green and D. P. Irish (eds.), Schenkman, Cambridge, Massachusetts, pp. 3-12, 1971.

CHAPTER 6

Spiritual Care in the New Pluralistic Context*

Edgar P. Senne

I come to these comments from many years of engagement with the academic subject matter called History of Religions. For the last several years, I have been retired from teaching and less directly involved with the details of this subject. However, the implications of this study of the religions of humankind continue to be a kind of preoccupation with me, and all my continuing studies in one way or another relate to it. The History of Religions is a broad area of study, ranging in time from the beginnings of the human archaeological record, through prehistory and historical times to our present human experience. It is a study that tries to make sense of the infinite diversity of human religious experience. Diversity of spirituality is the very essence of such studies.

What is there in human experience that calls forth this religious response? It appears that, throughout time, humans have had a profound response to something at the very core of life. To say it another way, religion is not usually something people dream up while sitting under a tree chewing or smoking toxic substances. It is a response to what they perceive to be an encounter with the deepest and truest reality, the Ultimate Reality that lies at the depth of our most critical human moments.

Not surprisingly, these critical moments have included the proc-esses by which people take their food. Food represents the flow of life and

---

*An oral presentation at St. Anthony Memorial Health Centers, Michigan City, Indiana, October 1999.

the gift of life, and behind that gift is perceived to be the Mysterious Giver. Similarly, this Great Mystery is experienced in the life-giving waters and in the powerful light of the sun. It is experienced in the procreative processes and in our encounter with the mystery of death. In, with, and under these very ordinary earthly experiences, humans have always experienced the presence of the Ultimate Mystery of life.

It is in these experiences and at points like these that people have given names to that reality, naming it as a spirit or god; here they have clothed that Presence with personal qualities. This is how the gods and goddesses were born. Here is the origin of the icons and idols, and the myths and rituals that testify to the deepest truths of life and death. For better or for worse, this religious response has given meaning to human life. It has led to an infinite variety of myths, rituals, ethical codes, belief-systems, faith communities, and forms of spirituality. Indeed, this is the fountain from which flows all of the diversity in human spirituality, a diversity which is becoming ever more a familiar part of our experience.

THE NEW CONTEXT OF OUR TIMES

Thirty-seven years ago, when I was first thrown into this academic arena called "Comparative Religions," Hindus were in India, Muslims were in Middle-eastern countries and Indonesia, Buddhists were in Southeast and East Asia, and hardly anyone in my community had ever heard of Sikhs. As to Native Americans, it was assumed that they had forgotten all about their so-called "pagan" ways and were either dead or converted. It was, after all, God's plan that America would realize its "Manifest Destiny" by extinguishing these cultures, was it not? Such were the most common assumptions of nearly forty years ago. Here in North America, we had only to concern ourselves with Catholics, Protestants, and Jews, and we thought that was challenge enough.

All this meant that our studies about religions other than our own were studies about people in foreign countries. When college undergraduates asked why they should study these foreign religions, the answer most commonly was something like the following.

> As the global economy unfolds, you never know where your careers might take you. You may find yourself teaching or doing business in Japan or Saudi Arabia, or you may be soldiering who knows where. When you find yourself there, in the midst of another culture, it might be helpful to know something about what makes those folks tick and perhaps have some *a priori* respect and appreciation for them and their traditions.

The situation we have described has changed most radically in my own short lifetime. A few years ago a new textbook crossed my desk; it was titled, *World Religions in America* [1]. It is edited by an already well-recognized scholar, Jacob Neusner, and contains a series of chapters about different faith traditions, each written by a prominent scholar representing that tradition from the inside. *World Religions in America*—that's the new scene, not only in the large cities of the east and west coasts, but right here in the smaller towns of Northwest Indiana. My urologist is an Asian Indian, and his worldview has been formed by the spirituality of the Indian traditions. My internist is from Japan, and her spirit reflects the ethos of that land. My accountant is from Iran, and is a very observant Shi'ite Muslim. The family living two doors south of me, is an observant Jewish family. This is the new situation, and we have begun to speak of it as religious diversity, or diversity in spirituality.

I also want to identify a second group of people, ever more present in the new context, people who are deeply caring folks and on the very edge of the religious establishment or even outside it. I am referring to people who are thoughtful about theological and social-ethical issues and who care about matters of personal spirituality. Bishop John Spong refers to this group as Christians in Exile. Still others have walked away from any religious identity and done so with conviction. These folks believe they can no longer hold the traditional beliefs and trappings of the Christian tradition and are sometimes called members of the "Christian Alumni Association," a fast-growing segment of the American population. Having come to know a good many of these folks in recent years, I often find them thoughtfully and self-consciously secular, but they are secularists who are deeply committed to the project of serving fellow humans and protecting the life of the planet in every way they can. They are eager to work with and give their support to shelters for abused women and children, free health clinics, building and rehabilitating housing for those who need a boost, and any other effort that will move folks a little closer to a decent life. They are the humanitarians who are sometimes derisively called "secular humanists." I thank God for them, often finding them to be more reliable allies in humanitarian projects than many others who are comfortably situated in the religious establishment. These folks may or may not have what we usually think of as a form of spirituality, but they have a presence, which needs to be appreciated and respected.

Let's consider a few statistics about our present diversity. In North America, according to a current Internet source,[1] 85 percent of those

<hr />

[1] http:www.adherents.com

surveyed count themselves as Christians (60% Protestant and 25% Roman Catholic); 8.7 percent consider themselves non-religious; 2 percent are Jewish; 1.4 percent are Muslims; just under 1 percent are Buddhist; and .5 percent claim some form of Hinduism. Less than half of 1 percent list themselves as having a connection with groups such as Baha'is, Sikhs, New-Agers, and a long list of others.

Those percentages may, at first, seem small, even insignificant, but they represent a fast growing population. It means that at least 15 to 20 percent of the people around us are other than Christian in their self-understanding. Synagogues have been very visible among us in many communities. But now we are beginning to see more and more mosques (or Islamic Centers), Hindu temples of various kinds, Buddhist "churches" and temples, and still other religious gathering places. Unless we bury our heads deeply in the "stuff" that covers our desks, we must come to terms with the presence of our neighbors of other faiths and worldviews. What is more, if we are people in public and parish ministries, it is our calling to help the people we serve to deal with this new phenomenon in ever more thoughtful and caring ways.

REFLECTIONS ON THE NEW CONTEXT

For the persons who represent faith traditions other than Christian, the new context must still seem like "the same old, same old." If you fit into that category, you know what it is like to be a minority voice in this society. You have had no illusions about how the Christian majority has viewed your faith tradition, and how little interest there is in understanding it. It must often feel as though that majority "Christian" presence is in your face and on your backs. If what we are calling "the new diversity" is to hold any promise for religious minorities, perhaps it lies in the hope that there will be a place of greater respect and equality at the table, where representatives of the faith traditions gather to share their common concerns for the mending of a broken world.

In this new context of greater diversity, Christianity will be called upon to give up its privileged place. We are heirs of the 1500-year tradition of Constantinianism, heirs of a religious, political, and social situation that once was "Christendom." Under this arrangement, Church and society were virtually the same; the power and glory of the one was the power and glory of the other. Even in the United States, where we work so hard to keep church and state separate, religion and the dominant social-political ethos have been so mutually supportive as to make the situation very little different from that which dominated

Europe for so many centuries. Christians in this country have certainly been accustomed to privilege and dominance, and it is only in recent decades that there are signs of that being diminished. In election campaigns, candidates can still manipulate this situation to their advantage, and they almost always do.

That era, we are told, is rapidly coming to an end. It began to be dismantled in Western Europe several decades ago when the effects of the so-called Enlightenment began to be a part of the mentality of the general populace. Religious indifference, implicit and explicit secularism, and the presence of those faith traditions that had their origins in distant lands—all this marks the beginning of the new era, the "post-Constantinian" era or, as many would call it, the "post-Christian" era. The Christian establishment is losing its exclusive and triumphant position. It must share the stage with serious folks of other faith traditions and none.

Religious and social analysts have been telling us this for some time now. In my own study, it has been the Canadian theologian, Douglas John Hall, who has most helped me to see the nature of our own new situation. Hall has written a three-volume theological work during this decade, the first volume in 1991 and the third in 1996. The individual titles in this trilogy are, *Thinking the Faith, Professing the Faith, and Confessing the Faith,* and they share the significant subtitle, *Christian Theology in a North American Context* [2]. In this extended work, Hall goes to great length to establish the fact that the two northern countries of the Americas are fast coming into what for them is a very new situation. This new situation, according to Hall, calls for a complete rethinking of the Christian theological tradition, as well as a search for new ways to live out Christian discipleship.

Another author, Darrell J. Fasching, offers his reading of the new era in his little book, *The Coming of the Millennium: Good News for the Whole Human Race* [3]. This is not your ordinary book about the coming of the new millennium. Fasching argues that the very essence of the biblical message, both of the Old Testament and the New, is rightly summed up in God's work of welcoming strangers and God's call to his covenant people to join in welcoming the stranger. Fasching goes on to point out that Christians have spent most of the past two millennia proclaiming an exclusive Gospel, one which was Good News for the few and the harshest rejection for the rest. This, he insists, is a long-time distortion of Jesus' message, quite the opposite of the call to welcome the stranger.

Fasching then articulates an interpretation of the Christian message, which offers Good News for the whole human race, a salvation that is a pure gift of God's grace, unconditioned even by the human response. It is the message of the God who welcomes all, loves all, and saves all [3, p. 4]. It is not my purpose in this chapter to explicate, defend, or refute Fasching's universalistic thesis. It is a compelling case that he makes, one made with erudition and sophistication and not to be quickly dismissed.

But Fasching points to a central theme, which can be useful in thinking about the new era in which we live. It is a theme that runs through the whole Hebrew and Christian scriptures, the theme of God welcoming the stranger. The Hebrews themselves were once strangers and wanderers, and God welcomed them. "I will be your God, and you will be my people." As God had welcomed them, they were then called upon to welcome the stranger wherever they would meet him or her.

Fasching offers a fascinating interpretation of the story of the tower of Babel [Gen. 11], seeing in this story an important lesson—the concept of the stranger. The people described in this story felt themselves invincible as long as they were all alike, as long as they spoke the same language and valued the same things. Their uniformity and cohesiveness would enable them to build a tower to the very gates of heaven, and they would, thereby, make themselves a great name. But God saw that what they held sacred was not actually God's presence, but their own social unit, their own tribe, nation, or city; that was the highest good, the sacred.

So, God confounded the people of Babel, took away the idolatry of their uniformity and made them strangers to each other. They would be scattered to the four corners of the earth, and they would now speak different languages, develop different cultures, value things differently; they would be strangers to each other. That would be very uncomfortable, because they would prefer to have everyone be just alike. Difference would unsettle them and make them fearful. Soon there would be distrust, hatred, and bloodshed. Nevertheless, Fasching points out, it is God who created this diversity. God knew that where we are all alike, our love is really for ourselves and our kind; but where we are different, our love must reach out across the boundaries to the stranger. When this happens, we are participating in God's own welcoming activity. Thus, diversity enters the picture, not as a curse but as a gift and a blessing [3, pp. 27-37].

Who really is the "stranger?" Whoever is not like us, that one is the stranger. In one sense, that means every person is a stranger to us, if not totally and always, then partially and oftentimes; our spouses, our children, and even we ourselves are sometimes the stranger. How much more the one who speaks a different language, whose physical features are notably different from ours, whose cultural manners and national background are different from ours, and whose spiritual outlook is so different from our own. In all these differences, we meet the stranger.

And who is the greatest Stranger of all? Is it not God who is the ultimate stranger? Indeed, "God's thoughts are not our thoughts, and God's ways are not our ways" [Is. 55:8]. No matter how much we think we know of God, it remains infinitesimal. God is the wholly other, the one who is utterly different from us. How shall we know that One? The biblical tradition teaches that we meet God when we welcome the stranger.

This theme of welcoming the stranger plays a major role in the Hebrew scriptures. Jacob once wrestled all night with the stranger, and (lo and behold) in doing so, he wrestled with God [Gen. 32]. The result was an enormous blessing and a promise that created the community of Israel. In an earlier example [Gen. 18], we read, "The Lord appeared to Abraham as he sat by the oaks of Mamre." And how did the Lord appear? He appeared in the form of three strangers. Abraham offered his generous hospitality to the strangers, and, in doing so, he welcomed the Lord. The story goes on to tell how Abraham cared enough about the strangers of Sodom to plead and bargain with God on their behalf. Unfortunately, when he and the three strangers reached Sodom, the men of Sodom failed to welcome and respect those strangers. Instead, they wanted them to be objects for their own control and use. It is in this abuse, this failure to welcome the stranger, that Fasching locates the real sin of Sodom. It is a sin far greater than any sexual practices to which they may have given themselves, says Fasching, for in rejecting the strangers, they were rejecting God [3, p. 48].

Those who call themselves Christian keep meeting God in the stranger named Jesus. This is most powerfully set before us in the parable of the last judgment [Matt. 25]. There we are taught that God regularly appears in the form of the stranger. When the people stand before the Judge, they hear a surprising announcement. He says, "I was hungry and you fed me, I was thirsty and you gave me drink, I was a stranger and you welcomed me, I was naked and you gave me clothing, I was sick and you took care of me, I was in prison and you visited me." Those who are standing there under judgment are thoroughly puzzled by the verdict. They remembered doing some of these things for strangers, but they surely had not seen the Lord's face in the face of the stranger. Whether knowingly or unknowingly, when we welcome the stranger, we welcome God. It is probably unnecessary to elaborate on the reverse side of this lesson. Quite simply, when we turn away from the stranger, we are turning away from God.

"Diversity in Spirituality"; who is a greater stranger than those whose faith traditions are so different from our own? Who is more different from us than those who seem to us to worship a different God? Christians have, for many centuries, met those strangers with the invitation to believe and be saved or else await eternal damnation, God's total rejection. Less often has the stranger of another faith been met with respect, a desire for understanding and appreciation. We have wanted them to renounce their difference, so that their thoughts would be like our thoughts and their ways would be like our ways; then, we thought, God could welcome them as God has welcomed us. I do not say that it is only Christians who have taken this approach to the stranger of other faiths; people of some other traditions have done so as well. Surely, it is time to rethink this approach to the stranger.

We turn now to a consideration of several of the ways in which we might approach the stranger of other faith traditions. Many contemporary scholars who concern themselves with the encounter of the religions in our time have identified three approaches. They speak of the Exclusivist approach, the Inclusivist approach, and the Pluralist approach. Allow me to briefly identify each of these approaches, summarizing the analysis of Diana Eck in her 1993 volume *Encountering God: A Spiritual Journey from Bozeman to Banaras* [4]. I shall offer the summary in her own words.

> **The Exclusivist** says, "Our own community, our tradition, our understanding of reality, our encounter with god, is the one and only truth, excluding all others."
>
> **The Inclusivist** says, "There are, indeed, many communities, traditions, and truths, but our own way of seeing things is the culmination of the others, superior to the others, or at least wide enough to include the others under our universal canopy and in our own terms."
>
> **The Pluralist** says, "Truth is not the exclusive or inclusive possession of any one tradition or community. Therefore, the diversity of communities, traditions, understandings of the truth, and visions of God is not an obstacle for us to overcome, but an opportunity for our energetic engagement and dialogue with one another. It does not mean giving up our commitments; rather, it means opening up those commitments to the give-and-take of mutual discovery, understanding, and, indeed, transformation" [4, p. 168].

Surely, most of us will recognize the Exclusivist approach. I grew up going to Mission Festivals, and here I kept hearing about the millions who were headed for hell every day, because they did not have the right faith. This Exclusivist approach has been the primary strategy of missionary movements through the ages. It was the charter for the conquest of the Americas, the entire continent of Africa, the Indian subcontinent and many other lands in the nineteenth century. This approach to the stranger is based on the conviction that all who do not explicitly confess Christ as Lord will be eternally lost. The Exclusivist has no doubt that God cannot now and will not in eternity welcome that stranger. If given a chance to defend that position, the Exclusivist will predictably recite a line from one of Peter's sermons in *The Acts of the Apostles*; it says, "There is salvation in no one else, for there is no other name under heaven, given among mortals, whereby we can be saved. " In response to this way of using Scripture passages as proof-texts, Krister Stendahl has remarked that phrases such as this one "grow legs and walk right out of their context" [4, p. 171].

Diana Eck argues, quite convincingly, that this approach to the stranger has significant social, ethical, and political implications [4, pp. 170-178]. We could walk through the history of Christian conquest and we would see how this view of the stranger has been used to justify massacres and the total eradication of cultures. What we think about God's regard for the stranger will justify how we regard and treat them.

Some years ago, I found myself face-to-face with the Inclusivist approach. I was sitting with a group of my students in a Vedanta Center in Hyde Park, Illinois. The Guru was explaining the higher wisdom of Vedanta, one of the more philosophical expressions of Hinduism. He said, "There is surely much truth in all religions, but the highest of them all, the peak of the mountain is the Vedanta. It is the summation of all other religions. All are included in Vedanta; none is beyond it." Hearing these words, I felt like I had, as they say, "been had," swallowed up by a tradition so much richer and broader than Christianity. But, somehow, I did not feel okay about the way in which my faith tradition was being absorbed into Vedanta. This approach to other faith traditions we call Inclusivism, and Christians have done this same thing to others. The Roman Catholic statement from Vatican II, "The Relation of the Church to Non-Christian Religions" is an example of cautious inclusivism [4, pp. 181-185]. Catholic theologian Karl Rahner went a step further by creating the category of "anonymous Christians." When Rahner uses this phrase he "means faithful people of non-Christian religions who do not 'name the name' of Christ, but who are nonetheless saved by [Christ's] power and grace, even though they do not know it" [4, p. 183].

When you have only heard the voices of Exclusivism, the Inclusivist approach sounds gentle and generous. But, if you are the one being "included," it feels very condescending. I didn't like being an anonymous Vedantist, and I think it might not feel particularly good to the devout Hindu, Muslim, Buddhist, or Jew to be called an anonymous Christian.

The third approach is that of the Pluralist. Pluralism "is an inter-pretation of the plurality of religions and spiritualities, with which we are surrounded in this new era. It is a way of evaluating and responding to that religious and cultural diversity." Pluralism, says Eck, goes beyond the fact of diversity; it is an active engagement with it. Pluralism is more than tolerance, important as that is; it is the search for mutual understanding through engagement. It is not simple relativism; it assumes that participants come to the table with their faith commitments intact, with something to share. It is not syncretism, not a smorgasbord of spiritualities, a place for picking and choosing and piecing together one's own "feel-good" spirituality. It is based upon respect for differences, not a blurring of difference. Finally, Pluralism requires interreligious dialogue, which means active and openhearted listening in search of understanding and accompanied by a willingness to be changed by what one learns [4, pp. 191-199].

Let us now conclude these few remarks about the new situation being met by those in spiritual ministries. A responsible exercise of our callings, according to our perspective, requires that we educate ourselves about the faith traditions that surround us. This is something that is relatively easy to do, at least in a beginning way. It requires that we seek a respectful and appreciative approach to the faith of the neighbor, the one who is, in so many ways, a real stranger to us. Everything hinges on how we deal with our encounter of that stranger, knowing, as we do, that it is the face of God that meets us in the face of that stranger. On a personal level, let me say that it has been my experience, with myself and my students, that the more deeply we come to understand another faith tradition, the more we are driven to a new apprehension of our own faith tradition. A serious and openhearted search into other religions leads not to conversion away from but a deepening into one's own faith tradition.

REFERENCES

1. J. Neusner (ed.), *World Religions in America: An Introduction,* Westminster/ John Knox Press, Louisville, 1994.
2. D. J. Hall, *Thinking the Faith, Professing the Faith, Confessing the Faith: Christian Theology in a North American Context,* Fortress Press, Minneapolis, 1991, 1993, 1996.
3. D. J. Fasching, *The Coming of the Millennium: Good News for the Whole Human Race,* Trinity Press International, Valley Forge, Pennsylvania, 1996.
4. D. L. Eck, *Encountering God: A Spiritual Journey from Bozeman to Banaras,* Beacon Press, Boston, 1993.

CHAPTER 7
The Roman Catholic Patient

Reverend Fr. Joseph Driscoll

The tiptoe quiet of the early morning hospital corridor echoes the approaching procession of feet. In the darkened ward, a sister holds a single candle lighting the way for the vested priest behind her. He holds the gold ciborium, containing the consecrated hosts of Holy Communion. In Sister's other hand is a small bell, which she rings as the procession turns into the ward or room in an attempt to arouse the Catholic patient from his or her sleep. Sometimes there is a need for a further shake to awaken the sleeping patient, who opens her or his eyes to a descending Communion wafer and the Latin acclamation of faith: *Corpus Christi,* the Body of Christ.

Later in the day, the priest may return for some conversation or to afford the opportunity for a person to go to confession, and, in either case, always closing with a blessing utilizing the sign of Christ's suffering, death, and resurrection: the Cross. A look at the table beside the patient's bed may reveal more of the faith practices of their Catholic beliefs: A missal or book of prayers, a holy card with a picture and prayer to a favorite saint, or perhaps a bottle of holy water sitting on the night stand.

Hanging from the neck of the patient, any kind of blessed medal on a chain may be visible: the Blessed Mother, St. Michael, or the popular "miraculous medal." Sometimes the patient will be wearing a cloth "scapular" which bears the print of the Sacred Heart of Jesus, or Our Lady of Perpetual Help, or some other holy picture depicting a particular devotion. Encircling the patient's folded hand are the rosary beads which are wooden, plastic, or glass, the color of black or brown, or perhaps made of silver, crystal, or sometimes even gold.

This above scene is a painted miniature picture, circa 1963, of the belief system and faith practices of the Roman Catholic patient in a Catholic hospital. For many older Catholic patients, these sights, sounds, smells, tastes, and touch are familiar manifestations of their living faith. In order to understand the spiritual needs of the sick or dying Roman Catholic patient and their families, one needs to appreciate the belief system that underlies the faith practice seen above. As we shall see later on, though the particular rituals did change after 1965, all of the essential ingredients of this hospital scene are still at the heart of this belief system. For in essence, Roman Catholicism is a body religion expressed in body ritual.

ROMAN CATHOLIC BELIEF SYSTEM

God in Christ

St. Paul, in his *First Letter to the Corinthians,* speaks eloquently to the reality of the mystery of our God, who is both concealed and revealed, simultaneously. We are trying to see our God, but as St. Paul observes: "At present we see indistinctly, as in a mirror" [1]. We seek the face of God, and like this image familiar to the second century Greek world, we rub the metal more and more in our life journey, trying to get the clearest image we can of this God from the material world that is given to us.

In essence, to call Roman Catholicism a body religion is to affirm the incarnational theology that sits at the center of our belief system. This God, so mysterious and beyond all comprehension, is at the same time our God who "so loved the world that he gave his only Son, so that everyone who believes in him might not perish but might have eternal life" [2]. This incarnation of God was in Christ, the Word who became flesh and made his dwelling among us [3].

Jesus then is the *mysterion* (Greek) or *mysterium* or *sacramentum* (Latin) of God, meaning the mystery or, more to the point, the visible sign of this hidden mystery of God [4]. The mirror, coming back to St. Paul's image, is rubbed as we see more clearly revealed the fullness of God in his Son, Jesus.

God's love is manifest in Jesus, who came into this world and who lived and walked among the people of Palestine. His love was redemptive as he came to touch people where they hurt and to restore them to health and wholeness. His powerful healing presence prompted the people to declare in an acclamation of faith: "God has visited his people" [5].

Jesus' ministry was one of healing. One fifth of all the gospel texts (Matthew, Mark, Luke, and John) are stories of healing. There are forty-seven separate stories (not duplications) wherein Jesus encountered a woman or man with a physical or mental illness, and in that faith encounter, brought about a healing [6]. His reputation grew and so did people's faith in this God of their ancestors whose promise of restoration was now at a time of fulfillment.

Jesus touched people at their deepest core. Healing was not merely physical, but mental and spiritual as well [7]. Deeply rooted in his Jewish tradition, Jesus knew that illness was not isolated and individual, but rather connected and social in the matrix of family and community. The evil and sin that surround these relationships were often the point of discussion when teachers and prophets discussed the mystery of sin and illness [8].

This linking of sin and sickness was reflected clearly in Jesus' healing ministry. He not only effected the physical or mental cure but, looking deeply into a person, touched not only the skin but the soul wherein there resided what was often the dis-ease of the person coming to him. The pronouncement of a cure almost always was accompanied by a pronouncement that a person's sins were forgiven as well [9].

The ultimate act of healing was in Jesus' own suffering and death. Not a single isolated act of a tragic violence, but rather a unifying act of a redemptive love. The earliest witness to faith in Jesus was a witness to faith in the suffering, death, and resurrection of Jesus, the Christ. All sin, and with it the effects manifest in sickness, suffering, pain and ultimately, death, are healed in this supreme act of selfless love on Calvary. The Cross, for the Christian, would forever be the sign of healing and restoration to life and wholeness.

This incarnation of God's healing love in Christ would be further enfleshed in the body of his followers. Core to the Roman Catholic's belief system is this truth, namely, that Christ's presence continues in his Church.

God in Christ in the Church

Before Jesus left this world to return to his Father, he made clear his identification with those who were ill or dis-eased in any way. "I was sick and you visited me." Any disciple of his who came upon the sick was coming upon Jesus himself. His compassion for those who were ill occasioned him to list them among "the least" of the brothers and sisters into whose care he was entrusting the body of what would become his Church [10].

The community of disciples who followed Jesus early on took his name. It was at Antioch that these followers first became known as "Christians" [11]. So, too, the community of disciples took on the ministry of Jesus and like himself, sought to bring good news to the sick and the poor. The presence of God made flesh in Jesus is now made flesh in the Christian community. Jesus missions his disciples repeatedly to go out casting out demons, laying hands on the sick and anointing them with oil [12].

The history of the Church bears witness over these 2,000 years to individuals and communities who continued the healing mission of Christ through every conceivable outreach to the homeless, orphaned, sick, elderly, and dying. Since the renewal of the Second Vatican Council (1963-65), religious communities everywhere, particularly in our own United States, have been encouraged to return to the history of their foundation as religious communities and to rediscover the charism that inaugurated the mission that impelled their leaders.

The first religious sisters in the United States were twelve French Ursulines who landed in New Orleans in 1727 to nurse the sick, and since that time literally tens of thousands of religious, primarily women, have expanded that ministry on horseback and buggy, dotting cities and towns from East to West across these United States. Theirs is as bold and adventuresome a journey as the Lewis and Clark expedition, only of a much longer duration [13].

God's love in Christ in the Church is "the animating principle of health care" [14]. For the Catholic patient this love of God embodied in Christ continues in the Church, and especially in the Sacraments.

God in Christ in the Church through the Sacraments

For the Catholic patient, the God we cannot see clearly is touched, tasted, smelled, listened to, and seen, if even indistinctly, in the actions of God in Christ in the Church. These actions are experienced in a unique way through the seven rites known as sacraments. We are touched by hands laid on our heads or smeared with oil on our bodies. We taste the bread of life and drink from the cup of Christ's suffering. We smell the fragrance of the perfumed oil and listen to the words of absolution. We see all of the above: bread, wine, oil, hands, the signing of the Cross—and more—in the rituals that assist a person in her or his journey in search and in return to God [15].

These seven sacraments—Baptism, Confirmation, Eucharist (Initiation), Penance and Anointing of the Sick (Healing), and Holy Orders and Marriage (Commitment)—are special signs of grace handed down by Christ through his Church [16]. They are "powers that come forth from the Body of Christ, which is ever-living and life-giving. They are actions of the Holy Spirit at work in his Body, the Church" [17].

The Catholic patient's faith and prayer life have been drawn toward the life of grace received in the sacraments. These are not simply signs or symbols, in the sense that they merely represent God or an aspect of God's healing power. The very celebration of the sacrament is a moment of grace wherein God is truly present in the action.

Jesus himself embodied his healing presence and performed his healing actions in and through the material world around him. He used spittle, laying on of hands, mud, and washing [18]. He took bread and lifted a cup of blessing. So too his Church in her long tradition continues the incarnation of Christ in a body religion with its embodied rituals.

For the Catholic patient, the intimate connection of God-Christ-Church-Sacraments lies at the heart of his or her belief system. Each connection makes clearer the reflection of the God of us all who is ultimate mystery. To separate one from the other is usually not possible for the Catholic believer. This connection is the body of Christ given in love by God, who seeks to reach out and heal this sick and suffering world.

With an understanding of this belief system, we can now move into the significance of the faith practices of the Roman Catholic in the spiritual care that is needed in sickness and, ultimately, dying.

ROMAN CATHOLIC FAITH PRACTICES

Pastoral Care of the Sick

The Cross

The earliest, simplest, and most profound of all Catholic faith practices is the embodiment of God's deepest love in the sign of the Cross. When an infant is presented to the Christian family in baptism, she or he is immediately signed on the forehead with the sign of the Cross when greeted at the entrance of the Church. Throughout her or his life, this same child, and later adult, will place his or her hand in holy water at the Church door and make the same sign of the Cross when entering Church for Sunday Eucharist.

When beginning and ending prayers, or receiving absolution after confession, or after taking holy communion, when sealed on the forehead with oil at confirmation, in a nuptial blessing or a ceremony of ordination, and finally when ill and desirous of the power coming from anointing—the Cross is signed on the Christian believer. This practice signifies for the believer the centrality of the paschal mystery: the life, death, and resurrection of Christ.

The Community

Certainly in illness we experience some of the most dire challenges to the human spirit. We are confronted with our "powerlessness," "limitations," and "finitude" [19]. We need the experience of our God embodied and held in the desperation of our embrace. Pastoral care, therefore, involves the holding environment of the Church and the rituals that express this care and healing of the community. All of the actions of the Cross are done in the environment of a "liturgical and communal celebration" [20]. Even if the community cannot be physically present, as in the case of a pastoral visitation in a household, the rituals of the Church always emphasize the whole Church at prayer with and for the person receiving Christ in a particular or sacramental moment.

Often in the case of a patient, when a minister brings the Eucharist or a priest comes to preside at the anointing, the family members or staff are invited to participate and be that healing community when in the home or the hospital room. In the case of anointing, the priest will sometimes invite those present to lay hands on the sick person after he does in the place designated in the ritual.

The United States Bishops' latest directives for Catholic health care underline the ministerial role played by health care professionals who participate in "a special vocation to share in carrying forth God's life-giving and healing work" [21]. Nurses, physicians, social workers, pharmacists, therapists, environmental personnel—all have an opportunity to see themselves as sharing in God's healing work. Facilitating this care of the spirit is the lead spiritual care professional, the *certified* chaplain.

The Chaplain or Spiritual Care Provider

Illness, especially sudden or unexpected, sends a shock wave through the person, disrupting the ordinary and regular routine of one's life. The physical and emotional shock reverberates in the soul, the deepest part of the human spirit, wherein a myriad of feelings can shake a person into "anguish, self absorption, sometimes even despair and revolt against God" [22].

The chaplain or other professional spiritual caregiver helps steady the faltering person through crisis intervention, skilled listening, empathetic responding, or, when needed, ethical consultation and overall facilitation of the communication of emotional and spiritual care for the patient and their family. The chaplain attends to the spiritual needs of the patient and, when appropriate, helps guide the person to her or his ultimate source of healing and meaning through it all.

In ministry to a Catholic patient, an important aspect of spiritual care is sacramental care. The celebration of the sacraments should take place within the context of this holding environment of listening and responding to the faith journey emerging in the pastoral conversation. Sometimes this does not occur because the large numbers of Catholics and fewer ordained priests (necessary for the administration of the Sacrament of Anointing) can unfortunately lead to a mechanistic approach to the celebration of the sacraments.

The United States Bishops made clear the difficulty when the celebration of a sacrament lacks the time and preparation which create a more open environment for the person. "Faith grows when it is well expressed in celebration. Good celebration fosters and nourishes faith. Poor celebrations weaken and destroy faith" [23].

Another difficulty can arise when a patient does not feel worthy to receive the sacraments because of the alienation from the Church, or a sense of unworthiness, or some unresolved religious issue from the past. In these instances, which usually are shared in the course of pastoral conversation, the chaplain is an important facilitator of the healing process. Many times the patient will express a need to go to confession and through this sacrament will feel an important resolve and reconciliation in his or her journey toward health and wholeness.

The Sacraments of Healing

Whenever one speaks of the seven sacraments of the Catholic Church, the Eucharist is at the center—not surprising since the Eucharist is the re-enactment of the sacrifice on Calvary wherein Christ gave his life for us. The Eucharist is both a sacrament of initiation into the Christian community and it is also a sacrament of healing. In the latter instance, it is often conjoined with Penance (confession) and the Anointing of the Sick in what are sometimes called the Sacraments of Post-Baptismal Healing.

Whenever a sacrament is celebrated, the gathered assembly is invited to that moment by the reading of the revealed Word of God. In the case of the person who is ill, this word "awakens the faith of the sick person and of the community to ask the Lord for the strength of his Spirit" [24]. For example, when holy communion is given, the Eucharistic minister will most often precede with a scripture and prayers from the ritual. Even in the days of early morning communions, the priest and sister were coming from the Eucharistic celebration where the Word had been shared in the assembly.

When a priest comes to administer the Sacrament of the Anointing of the Sick, he will often inquire whether the person would like to go to confession first. This need is often evident when a person has been alienated or has not practiced their faith for some reason.

The origin of the Sacrament of the Anointing is in the passage from *The Letter of James* 5:13-16.

> If anyone among you is suffering hardship, [that one] must pray.
> If a person is in good spirits, [that one] should sing a hymn of praise.
> Is there anyone sick among you? He [or she] should ask for the
> Presbyters of the Church. They in turn are to pray over him [or her],
> Anointing him [or her] with oil in the Name of the Lord. This prayer
> Uttered in faith will reclaim the one who is ill, and the Lord will
> Restore [that one] to health. If [that one] has committed any sins,
> Forgiveness will be [theirs]. Hence, declare your sins to one
> Another, and pray for one another, that you may find healing.

In this passage, there are three elements which constitute the Church's ritual of anointing. First, there is the laying on of hands (praying over the person), which is an ancient ritual for calling down the Spirit upon a person. It is likewise a healing gesture as touch itself most often brings comfort and a vital connection to the healing community.

Second, the person is anointed with oil which is blessed by the Bishop during the Easter Vigil on Holy Saturday. An ancient tradition is evidenced in the importance of the blessing wherein the oil presented was given divine power [25]. The current practice is to make the sign of the Cross on the forehead and on the open palms of the person. The following prayer is said during the actual anointing:

> (while anointing the forehead) Through this holy anointing, may the
> Lord in his love and mercy help you with the grace of the Holy Spirit.
> (while anointing the hands) May the Lord who frees you from sin
> save you and raise you up.

Finally, there is a Prayer after the Anointing, chosen from various options that correspond to the patient and his or her particular circumstances (before surgery, in extreme illness, in advanced age, etc.).

This three-fold action is the celebration of the Sacrament itself. However, it is usually preceded by the Liturgy of the Word and oftentimes with the reception of Communion. If celebrated in the context of a communal rite, there is often music and a gathering afterward for food and sharing.

The effects of the Sacrament are the taking away of sin, the strengthening of the sick person, and, in some instances, restoration of bodily and mental health.

At a point in the history of the Sacrament of the Anointing, the guideline for reception moved from serious illness to "danger of death." For this reason, patients often were alarmed if a priest came into the room. This meant that their death was thought to be imminent. The anointing was postponed until the last moment and was known as "extreme unction," or more popularly, "last rites."

With the renewal of the liturgical rites following the Second Vatican Council, the Anointing of the Sick was returned to its original context as a sacrament of healing and not a sacrament leading to death. In the renewed ritual, there was a clear separation between pastoral care of the sick and pastoral care of the dying.

Pastoral Care of the Dying

For the Christian believer, death trumpets not the final victory. The whole paschal mystery of Christ is a journey through death to life in a movement toward our "final destiny" [26]. We hold on to the life we know, but when we move from the process of healing into the process of dying, we do so held not by our own strength, but by our faith. The Church in the renewed ritual separates "Pastoral Care for the Sick" from "Pastoral Care for the Dying." In care for the sick, the rite calls for visitation, communion, and anointing. In care for the dying, the rite is broken down into viaticum, commendation of the dying, and prayers for the dead [27].

As indicated earlier, the Eucharist is at the center of the Church's liturgical rites. It is also "the last sacrament of the earthly journey" [28], and so when ministered to the dying person, this sacrament is called viaticum. Viaticum literally means "with you, on the way," in this context, food for the journey [29].

This sacrament does not need a priest for its celebration, though in fact people will often want to call the priest out of an earlier practice of calling for him at the end for the "last rites." The Eucharist can be ministered either in the bread or by the precious blood, if someone is too weak or unable to swallow solid food. If the dying is prolonged, a person may have the Eucharist each day through the end.

The Rites also have prayers to commend the dying which can be offered with the person and their family, especially after a person has slipped out of consciousness. And finally, the ritual has prayers that may be offered around the body after the person has died.

A patient may also request to be anointed when she or he is dying. This sacrament can give he or she the healing and strength that she or he may need for the final journey. It is, however, proper that the section "Pastoral Care for the Dying" be the ordinary ritual, unless a person requests differently or the need is ascertained in the course of caring for the person.

Other Faith Practices

In addition to the seven sacraments, there are other rituals and practices that embody and support the faith lives of Catholic believers. These sacred signs with spiritually beneficial effects are called sacramental [30]. Unlike the sacraments which are the continuing presence of Christ himself in the "new law" [31], these devotional signs come in different ages out of the piety of different cultures as ways of sustaining and enlivening faith. These include blessings (i.e., of a house), objects (i.e., medals, statues, ashes, incense) or other materials made holy with meaning.

The *Constitution on the Sacred Liturgy* from the Church speaks respectfully of the place of sacraments and sacramentals in the worship life of the believer: "the liturgy of the sacraments and sacramentals sanctifies almost every event in their lives; they are given access to the stream of divine grace which flows from the paschal mystery of the passion, death, and resurrection of Christ, the fount from which all sacraments and sacramentals draw their power. There is hardly any proper use of material things which cannot thus be directed toward the sanctification of men [and women] and the praise of God" [32].

These graces are embodied in the faith practices of Roman Catholics and are resources for them to draw upon in their times of crisis, especially illness and suffering.

CONCLUSION

The scene in the hospital corridor today is quite different from the early dawn procession of the sister and the priest of thirty years ago. Whereas 100 percent of the Catholic chaplains were ordained priests in 1965, only a small minority of professional chaplains today are ordained priests, as evidenced by their membership in The National Association of Catholic Chaplains, where only 19 percent are priests [33]. Though the evident decline in numbers of priests is a factor, a more fundamental shift happened at Vatican II as all the baptized faithful in the Church were called to share in the ministry of Christ with their own gifts as a member of the People of God. Today, the Catholic chaplain entering the patient's hospital room is more apt to be a sister, deacon, or layperson. Many Catholic laywomen are beginning a second career as a chaplain after raising a family, and in some cases, after obtaining an advanced degree from a seminary.

Lone sacramental priests in hospitals have been replaced with pastoral care departments where women and men, ordained, lay and religious, Catholic, Protestant, Jewish, and Muslim all work together.

The priest of thirty years ago who had no special training in ministry to the sick has given way to the professionally trained and board-certified chaplain; more than 70 percent of the Catholic chaplains in the United States who hold membership in The National Association of Catholic Chaplains are certified to provide spiritual care [33]. Among other changes in the health care environment, the spiritual care of persons has become more integrated into the total health care of a person in and now outside the institutional setting. Insights and skills gleaned from new understandings from the behavioral sciences have affected the way in which sacraments are celebrated with those who are sick or dying.

Though the faith practices have undergone changes during the last thirty years, the underlying belief system still remains. We still seek our God. The clearest image we have is in the person of Jesus Christ, especially as manifest in his passion, death, and resurrection. For the Catholic, Christ is experienced clearer still in his Church and in a unique manner in his presence in the Sacraments.

A Catholic patient today may hear the knock on the door of his or her room and see a layperson come in, greet them, and sit down for a visit. Communion may now be a part of a pastoral conversation, some Scripture reading, an invitation to express in prayer the heart of what the person has just shared. If family members are present, or staff as well, they will likely be invited to share in the prayer and sacrament.

The celebration of the Anointing of the Sick is often done in a communal parish setting at the Eucharist several times a year. With one-day surgery more often the norm, some parishes are inviting those who are going in for surgery the following week to gather after the Sunday Eucharist to be anointed with other members of the parish family.

Oftentimes, family members and a person's physician or nurse will be invited to lay hands on their loved one after the priest so that there is a fuller expression of the richness of this celebration of the sacrament. People will sing, pray together, or sit quietly as the ritual embodies the presence of God in this moment.

We see God "indistinctly, as in a mirror," says St. Paul. The Roman Catholic tradition, however, through her embodied ritual, strives to be faithful to a God who so loved us that he became flesh among us. Through the sacraments, we are able to more clearly see, taste, hear, smell, and touch this wonderful God of healing and life.

ENDNOTES

1. 1 Corinthians 13:12
2. John 3:16

3. John 1:14a
4. *Catechism of the Catholic Church,* no. 774.
5. Luke 7:16
6. Champlin, *Special Signs of Grace,* p. 82
7. NCCB, *Ethical and Religious Directives,* General Introduction, p. 3
8. *Catechism,* no. 1502
9. *Directives,* ibid.
10. Matthew 25
11. Acts 11:26
12. *Catechism,* nos. 1506-09
13. For this and other stories of the women religious who carried the healing mission of Jesus across this country, I refer the reader to Suzy Farren, *A Call to Serve: The Women Who Built Catholic Healthcare in America,* 1996, The Catholic Health Association of The United States.
14. *Directives,* Ibid.
15. *Catechism,* no. 1501
16. *Special Signs of Grace,* p. 21
17. *Catechism,* no. 1116
18. *Catechism,* no. 1504
19. *Catechism,* no. 1500
20. *Catechism,* no. 1517
21. *Directives,* General Introduction, p. 5
22. *Catechism,* no. 1517
23. "Music In Catholic Worship", no. 6 in *The Liturgy Documents: A Parish Resource,* p. 191.
24. *Catechism,* no. 1518
25. For a succinct account of the history of the Sacrament of the Anointing, see Joseph Champlin, *Special Signs of Grace,* p. 84ff.
26. *Directives,* p. 9
27. Champlin, p. 86
28. *Catechism,* no. 1210
29. Champlin, p. 92
30. Champlin, Ibid., p. 123
31. *Catechism,* no. 1210
32. "Constitution on the Sacred Liturgy," no. 61, in *The Liturgy Documents: A Parish Resource.*
33. Statistics from the National Association of Catholic Chaplains, February 1997.

Recommended Reading

Catechism of the Catholic Church, English Translation for the U.S.A.—United States Catholic Conference, Libreria Editrice Vaticana, Pauline St. Paul Books and Media, 1994.

Champlin, J. M. *Special Signs of Grace: The Sacraments and Sacramentals,* The Liturgical Press, Collegeville, 1986.

Ethical and Religious Directives for Catholic Health Care Services. National Conference of Catholic Bishops, Committee on Doctrine, United States Catholic Conference, Washington, D.C., 1995.

Faren, S. *A Call to Care: The Women Who Built Catholic Healthcare in America,* The Catholic Health Association of the United States, St. Louis, 1996.

Huck, G. (ed.). The Liturgy Documents: A Parish Resource. Liturgy Training Program, Archdiocese of Chicago, Chicago, 1980.

CHAPTER 8

The Jewish Patient

Rabbi Dr. Jeffery Silberman

In the Jewish community one finds many levels of religious observance and practice. While some Jews might draw a direct connection between their illness and their faith, many Jews experience illness as an event separate from the rest of life. They presume that medical science, not spirituality, would best respond to their needs.

Yet, the use of the term spirituality has come to be commonplace in all of American culture. Only a few years ago this word was shunned in all respectable settings as being too new age or just plain strange. Spirituality's renewed general cultural validity has posed a dilemma regarding its application and role in mainstream Judaism. Among rabbis and Jewish chaplains we struggle to define Jewish spirituality in the life of our community and for Jewish patients.

In providing Jewish spiritual care to patients, rabbis and Jewish chaplains recognize the power that Jewish prayer, ritual, and teachings have to assist in the search for meaning and value. These rabbis and chaplains are not mystics or faith healers who claim miraculous spontaneous healing. Jewish spiritual care providers, unlike therapists or psychiatrists, do not look for pathologies. They are teachers and people of faith who help Jews strive toward spiritual wholeness, personal meaning, and a deeper connection to God and the Jewish community through the wisdom and care of the Jewish tradition.

Jewish spirituality offers a recognition that all life is sacred and that it is linked together in profound, if not fully knowable, ways. Spirituality in a modern context does not mean anything fringe or cultist. Spirituality pertains to the soul of a person. Many Jews, according the demographic studies, have no formal religious affiliation yet think of themselves as being Jewish and spiritual. While it may be argued that being religiously Jewish requires community, these unaffiliated Jews, as well as those who hold formal membership in synagogues, are seeking something which responds to their need for personal meaning and value. For example, when one faces a terminal diagnosis such as metastatic cancer, that individual may redefine his/her life during the time remaining with a set of new priorities. The quest for something spiritual to guide that redefinition may be answered by Jewish religious tradition or by individually tailored models which derive from that tradition. This distinction will be developed later in this chapter.

SPIRITUAL NEEDS AND RESPONSES AT THE TIME OF ILLNESS

Jewish spiritual care and healing address both the mind and the heart. All of us want to know and understand what is happening to us when we face illness. We also seek comfort and solace when we feel pain, loneliness or fear. In turning to the sources of Jewish tradition we want to know what our tradition teaches, how it may guide our ritual observances at life's important transitions, such as illness or death. One traditional way this may happen is in an encounter with religious texts. From the *Talmud* (the primary body of Jewish legal opinions) to the *Shulhan Aruch* (the codification of Jewish Law) to the prayer book, rabbis and Jewish chaplains strive to make Jewish wisdom about healing and the spirit available to Jewish patients. Through study and reflection, we can come to understand the Jewish teachings about *Nefesh* (the soul), *Sh'chenah* (the in-dwelling presence of God), and *Refu'ah* (healing).

When confronting illness we also want to feel the support and care which religion offers. Jewish religious community is a primary vehicle for such care, traditionally through *Bikur Cholim* (the communal responsibility of visiting the sick). Yet, for those without access to the Jewish community, a trained and compassionate rabbinical counselor may assist the Jew in making that connection in the midst of a crisis. Through Jewish song and prayer, through listening and consoling from a tangible Jewish presence, we may feel linked to a greater sense of Jewish community.

When any one of us falls ill, many questions arise around life, its meaning and death. The wisdom of the Jewish tradition is a central resource for Jewish spiritual care. Our goal is to bring that wisdom and the spirit of Jewish care to those in need. Two short aphorisms give a taste of what the tradition proffers. "Three things drain a person's health: worry, travel and sin" [1]. "Three things restore a person's good spirits: beautiful sounds, sights and smells" [2]. Jewish spiritual care and healing complements medical care and treatment as it values one's soul, as well as one's body.

The American Jewish community does not enjoy the cohesiveness that once was a hallmark of Jewish communities. We are separated by our own internal religious diversity, as well as by external factors and geographical boundaries. The American Jewish community is the most highly educated and well informed community in our history. Thus, many cultural factors and philosophic movements influence Jewish religious life. These influences manifest in the diversity of lifestyles and beliefs of American Jews. For example, Jewish feminist thought, Jewish mysticism, and secular humanism affect some in the Jewish community. These ideologies and other movements impact our appreciation and practice of Jewish spirituality, especially in times of vulnerability such as illness and hospitalization. Consequently, there is no single model of Jewish practice or belief in the general Jewish community, much less so among Jews facing or living with illness.

Furthermore, the current medical environment dictates that many aspects of patient care are radically different from just a few years ago. Being a patient has been radically altered from past experience. The length of stay, the severity of conditions, the recovery period and the staffing in hospitals are all different. The patient may be in and out in one or two days. This means the patient's adjustment to the illness and time of access to them by the chaplain is all too brief. No longer can the chaplain or rabbi anticipate several days in which to respond to a request for a visit. There is limited interaction with the physician, the nurse, and all of the myriad of staff that a patient typically encounters. In short, the opportunity for human contact, much less for addressing spiritual concerns, is diminished in the current health care setting.

JEWISH RELIGIOUS PREMISES

Understanding the dimensions of Judaism and Jewish life in America help one appreciate the variegated nature of spirituality for Jewish patients. There are four main formal streams in Jewish religion [3]. There are also smaller factions which reflect particular emphases and concerns [4]. While these different streams and factions of Jewish religious life are broader than just Jewish patients, they inform the dynamics encountered with Jewish patients. Other fundamental influences, such as the role of community and history, imprint upon the Jewish patients and how they interpret their hospital experience. In what follows I will discuss some of these influences and aspects of diversity in Jewish life and how they present in the Jewish patient.

Community

The first of these, the role of community, illustrates this significance most clearly. In traditional Jewish life it is a fundamental assumption that the individual cannot fully actualize Jewish religiosity apart from the community. The Jewish community historically has been the foundation of Jewish identification, as well as Jewish observance. In contrast to Christianity, the Jews were not so much expected to articulate theological beliefs in concert with an established creed, as they were expected to participate in the religious life of the entire community. This entailed an active role in the life of the synagogue, the religious educational system, the community social service network, and so on. Jews lived in close proximity to one another, whether by preference or under political edict, and functioned in many respects like an extended family in their behavior.

A second aspect of Jewish community which illustrates a central value of connections and caring is *Bikur Cholim* (the communal responsibility of visiting the sick). Through the shared concern and support for community members who were suffering, the Jew was connected to all Jews. It was a religious duty that brought people closer together and this behavior defined a part of their spirituality. In our own day, the responsibility for *Bikur Cholim* is not vital for many American Jews. No longer connected to one another in the same ways, Jews, as many other religious communities, are unaware of the daily fate of their co-religionists. It is common that someone may become ill, enter and leave the hospital before anyone, especially their religious community, finds out. The commitment of time to such a "voluntary activity" as *Bikur Cholim* holds little priority. Communal commitment to connection and caring draws few Jews to active participation in the task of visiting the sick.

A modern variation of this theme of communal responsibility can be discerned in the attitude which many American Jews have toward the state of Israel. This is a third aspect of community dynamics in American Jewish life. While this has changed somewhat in the current political atmosphere, for nearly the last forty years a segment of the Jewish community defined its identity with Judaism through ties to Israel. The close feeling and commitment to Israel which accompanied this interest appeared very much like the sense of extended family that Jews of earlier centuries felt within and to their self-contained religious communities.

For many Jews, the search for spirituality or religious renewal can be traced to a desire to recapture feelings of community or connection. The Hebrew word *Shlemut* (wholeness) captures this notion as representative of coming together as a whole or, in terms of illness, restoring the unity of heart, mind, and body. Etymologically this term is related to the Hebrew word shalom, which means peace. This summarizes some of the power of its symbolic meaning for Jews living with illness. The opportunity to see another Jew or rabbi when ill may be the most effective way in which to respond to a Jewish patient who is in need of this connection to community.

History

The Jew in general and the Jewish patient in particular is cognizant of the fact that history has assigned a unique place for Jews. This dimension of Jewish life affects Jewish self-perception. Even the Jew who lacks a formal Jewish education carries a sense of the constrictions which many nations in the past have imposed upon the Jewish people. This is part of the Jewish collective unconscious, inseparable from the Jew whether or not one has experienced prejudice first hand. The Jew therefore sees him/herself as other, as different. This self-perception of difference may intensify under circumstances of vulnerability. The Jewish patient's response to being alone and isolated in the hospital room may reflect irrational fears and unfounded concerns of bias which isolation and vulnerability generate in all persons.

Another dynamic rooted in history which will affect interaction with Jewish patients in a vulnerable situation is how they regard overtly religious Christians. While there may not be rational connection, many Jewish patients in a largely Christian setting will be wary of anti-Semitism in the behavior of staff toward them. The approach of a Christian chaplain or clergy may be perceived as an attempt to convert the Jew. Recent experience demonstrates that this type of missionizing unfortunately is not merely a thing of the past. Sensitivity to this dynamic is essential in understanding the Jewish patient in the hospital context.

In a similar way, the Jewish patient may express the notion that he or she has no religious needs whatsoever. The Jewish mind is drawn to the logical and rational. Both Karl Marx and Sigmund Freud, who were born Jewish and are generally identified as Jews, asserted that religion was insubstantial and unnecessary for intellectual development. Judaism, as understood by Marx and Freud, could easily be rejected by other Jews. Another origin of this attitude, more sympathetic to religion, was the writings of early twentieth century rabbi and Jewish philosopher Mordecai Kaplan. Kaplan offered a definition of Judaism as "an evolving religious civilization." While his intention was never to divorce religion from the rest of Jewish life, that is how some have interpreted his message. Thus, many Jews see themselves as culturally Jewish but not religious in any way. Intellectually, they have separated the Jewish civilization from any kind of personal faith. They claim no belief system, while at the same time not denying their Jewish identity. Obviously, these Jews would not readily admit to having spiritual needs, yet they still carry a consciousness of Jewish history.

JEWISH THEOLOGY AND OBSERVANCE

Jewish religious belief, as noted, is far from monolithic. Philosophers and theologians have long sought to define the essence of what Judaism is. This project has almost always yielded a highly subjective perspective of what is at the core of Judaism. For example, it is hard to imagine a Judaism without Torah (the 5 books of Moses). Yet, there are an infinite variety of interpretations as to what is meant by Torah in Judaism [5]. It is therefore reasonable that each individual Jew would hold a unique understanding of what Judaism means to him or her. The implications of this idiosyncratic belief make it difficult to know what might be meaningful or effective in addressing a Jewish patient's spirituality.

Jewish religious practice and belief can be assessed to a limited degree when one identifies with a particular stream in Jewish life. Thus, the Reform Jew is likely to be not very strict in adherence to dietary laws or regarding the kinds of labor prohibited on the Sabbath. The person who identifies with Conservative Judaism may be much more concerned about the types of food eaten, yet may not have an objection to eating from plates that are not strictly kosher. The Reconstructionist Jew, under most circumstances, would be hard to differentiate from a Conservative Jew in practice since historically they are related. The Orthodox Jew would typically have a range of personal religious practices which for men could include wearing a yarmulke (male head coverings) to not touching a woman other than his wife. And for women could include covering the hair with *Sheitel* (wig) to observing all of the laws of *Niddah* (ritual purity). Yet, despite these labels and the tendencies they indicate, there is a complexity of Jewish belief which defies any simple categorization.

There is an old story which demonstrates further the complexity of Jewish theology and belief, as well as religious observance.

> There was a small town Epikorus (one who has rejected Jewish religious beliefs in pursuit of philosophic truth) who heard of a great Epikorus who lived at a distance and he decided to seek out this master. The small town Epikorus traveled long hours and days to

reach the home of the great Epikorus. When he arrived he asked to see the master and was told, much to his surprise, that the great Epikorus was at the synagogue. The small town Epikorus assumed the master was there ridiculing the teachings, but upon his arrival, he was told that the great Epikorus was leading prayer. The small town Epikorus waited until the service was over and approached his mentor with a question. "What were you doing leading prayer? How could you, who is known as the great Epikorus, who scoff at the teachings of the rabbis, participate in prayer?"

The great Epikorus replied. "I am an Epikorus, not a heathen."

The essential message of the story is that whatever one's religious or non-religious identity, the Jew may hold a place in the community and observe its normative practices. Unfortunately, this is not a simple matter for the Jewish patient.

Jewish religious practice of the patient is informed by many factors. The Judaism of one's youth may be far removed from an individual's current lifestyle and yet, when ill, there may be a return to old ways. Esoteric notions and concepts, such as from the *Kabbalah* (Jewish mystical literature), may become more important when one is ill than the standard behavior of thrice daily prayer. While Jewish religious belief and practice is without absolutes, at the same time any given practice, such as *Kashrut* (Jewish dietary laws), may become essential to an individual Jew when confronted with illness.

RELIGIOUS ISSUES FOR JEWISH PATIENTS

At the time of illness, the religious or spiritual issues for Jews do not differ fundamentally from that of any other person in a situation of vulnerability or crisis. All people look for meaning, support, and comfort, as well as a source of guidance and instruction. Therefore, I first suggest some generalizations about issues for hospital patients. I will then add to the discussion some specific religious issues for Jewish patients.

Ritual is often more important during a time of illness than otherwise in the life of the person. The particulars of what the person finds meaningful may vary greatly from one person to another. A Jewish patient may request to recite the *Kaddish* prayer for dead relatives or friends. Or the Jewish patients may insist upon receiving only kosher food, even when this is not ordinarily part of their religious observance. Such requests often reflect the extent to which the person is feeling alone, disconnected, or frightened by their present circumstances. Yet, it is important that these requests be honored whenever possible, in that they can also indicate a sincere religious need.

For some, faith is deepened and a "religious conversion" takes place when they are hospitalized and facing serious illness or death. When one is faced with illness, emotional defenses and responses are intensified. The intensity of response applies to religion as well. Changes may manifest as increased interest in religious observance or rituals. Some may draw closer to God or to their faith tradition. Others may adopt a more stringent form of religious practice. Previous religious observance or beliefs are not necessarily indicators of how one may react to the experience of illness. Profound changes may occur when a person faces a crisis or terminal prognosis. For example, a Jewish patient may require a *Chumash* (Bible with basic Jewish commentaries) or a *Siddur* (daily prayer book) or some other Jewish religious text in order to adopt a more religious attitude while hospitalized.

One may observe a greater attachment to religion or a strong, previously unarticulated, rejection of religion. The Jewish patient may reveal anger at or rejection of God or religion. Under such circumstances, this rejection of faith may be a way of expressing the pain of feeling abandoned or hurt. The chaplain needs to listen carefully to this person, offering empathy and care, even in the face of anger. The ability to express one's true feelings at God or God's representative may yield an opportunity for eventual reconciliation.

A person's relationship to God becomes significant at times of illness. The patient looks for opportunities to connect and strengthen the feeling that God is present and cares. The Jewish patient, like others, often recalls past actions which may now be identified as short-comings or sins. These can be associated with the causes of the current illness and, therefore, the person seeks, directly or indirectly, forgiveness from God. Rabbis and other chaplains need to apply a framework of religious understanding to the behavior of people who are sick and recognize their needs, both reasonable and unreasonable, at this vulnerable time.

Illness frequently evokes a sense of one's need for forgiveness. In the Jewish tradition, the idea of forgiveness is almost exclusively associated with the holy day Yom Kippur (Day of Atonement). Forgiveness is sought at that time through prayer and fasting. The focus of the liturgy is relationship to God, yet the rabbis teach that forgiveness should begin with family and friends. Confronted with serious illness, the Jewish patient may turn his or her attention toward obtaining forgiveness. This may or may not be a conscious effort, yet the sensitive rabbi or Jewish chaplain can recognize the presence of these issues. One prayer designated for final confession near the time of death is called the *Viddui* (confession). This prayer which may be recited by the rabbi, as well as by the patient, provides a traditional vehicle to reconnect with God by affirming one's misdeeds and God's oneness. It can begin the process of reconciliation, as one sheds the guilt which frequently accompanies the need for forgiveness.

For a Jewish patient to reconcile with God is not an especially conscious process. In truth, it is somewhat foreign for Jews to speak in such terms. But the essential meaning of reconciliation is not substantially different for Jews. It speaks to an alienation from God or a feeling of abandonment by God. It is not always obvious in the feelings of anger or isolation that the issue is one's relationship to God. The Jewish patient may assume that there is no relationship at all with God.

The process of bringing one back to God may well begin with the reconciliation with family. Talking about what separates people from one another is a good way to move toward that goal. Being able to listen to what other family or friends are saying is the hardest part of reaching a coming together. The rabbis teach in a book of Jewish wisdom literature the following:

> If you have done your fellows a slight wrong, let it be a serious matter in your eyes; but if you have done your fellow much good, let it be a trifle in your eyes. And if your fellow has done you a slight favor, let it be a great thing in your eyes; if your fellow has done you a great evil, let it be a little thing in your eyes [6].

Using models from the Bible which speak to human estrangement from God may open the door to further exploration of this dynamic.

We can further identify some of the typical dynamics associated with the experience of illness. Commonly, we use psychological language to describe some patient behaviors, yet often these same dynamics directly impact upon the religious and spiritual dimensions of illness as well. A person may experience fear of dying or of death. There may be psychological manifestations of the loss which people experience in hospitals. A person may hold their feelings inside, unable or unwilling to talk about them. The patient may exhibit a lack of trust. These situations may give rise to a request by the Jewish patient to see a rabbi, even if the person has not previously been affiliated with a synagogue. A trained Jewish spiritual caregiver would be the best resource at this time. However, in the event that one is not available, most community rabbis will serve to respond to such calls.

In summary, the issues of Jewish patients are similar to those of other religious people facing illness and death. The particulars of Jewish life may significantly effect the ways in which these issues appear. For the chaplain dealing with Jewish patients and seeking to support their spiritual quest at such a time, the task is complex. I would encourage

Christian chaplains to seek out the advice and consultation of a trained Jewish chaplain to assist them with Jewish patients.

PRACTICAL ASPECTS OF JEWISH SPIRITUALITY

For many American Jews the framework of formal Judaism is unfamiliar. They may have concluded their own religious education at twelve or thirteen years of age with the celebration of a Bar or Bat Mitzvah (literally, son or daughter of the commandment) [7]. Regular religious observances and religious practices, much less formal theological concepts, elicit little personal meaning. Yet, there are some Jewish religious resources which communicate universally that may aide Jewish patients in reclaiming aspects of the Jewish tradition in their search for spirituality.

Prayer

The most accessible resource of Judaism at the time of illness may be prayer. While the traditional language of prayer in synagogues is Hebrew, any of the traditional prayers may be translated and said in translation according to rabbinical authorities when one does not know Hebrew.

In order to acknowledge the different streams in American Jewish life we must note that prayer in traditional Judaism is primarily fixed in its formulation. Orthodox Judaism denotes the where, when and how of the liturgical day for Jews. For example, the prayer known as *Me Shebayrach* (May the One who blessed . . .) [8] is said at the reading of the Torah (Hebrew Scriptures) in the synagogue. Yet, it is common for liberal rabbis to recite this prayer at the bedside of a Jewish patient. Familiarity with traditional prayers, while preferable from a communal perspective, is not required of the individual Jew. More and more, Jews have begun to learn the language of spontaneous prayer. This is so important that many Jewish teachings illustrate permission to pray in one's own terms. A Hasidic story demonstrates this point.

> A boy from a small rural village where there were few Jews and no synagogue, one day accompanied his father to the city to do some marketing. While there, they went into a synagogue. The boy had never been in a synagogue before and he was impressed and moved by the sight of the congregation at prayer. He, too, wanted to pray. But he did not know how. His father taught him only to say the letters of the Hebrew alphabet, but no more than that. So a thought occurred to him. He began to recite the alphabet over and over again. And then he said, "Oh Lord. You know what it is that I want to say. You put the letters together so that they make the right words."

That too was a Jewish prayer [9]. For the traditional Jew, there are prayers which are suited to every occasion in life. If one adopts a traditional model of observance, then one can use a fixed formula throughout the course of life to acknowledge God in all that one experiences. On a daily schedule, there are prayers to be said morning, noon, and evening. There are prayers before one eats and after. There are prayers upon rising in the morning and when one washes. Quite clearly, it was the intention of the rabbis who formulated the cycle of prayers in Jewish life that one connect all dimensions of life with the spirit.

An example from daily prayer which may be helpful to the Jewish patient are the section of morning prayers known as *Birchot ha-Shachar* (morning blessings). In these prayers, we thank God for many things which we normally take for granted, including for the miracle of being alive. In the prayer *Asher Yatzar* (blessing of creation of human beings), the marvels of the human body are mentioned. Even for one who is ill, there are still things for which one can be thankful. To connect spiritually with the Jewish tradition, these prayers can be an effective vehicle.

However, it has been noted that few Jews normally adhere to this extensive pattern of prayer. At best, we speak these prayers in conjunction with those times when we are more aware of God's presence. Thus, at meals, on the Sabbath, and during holidays, Jews are more likely to give thanks, offer praise, or ask for something or confess. Nonetheless, there is a profound comfort in knowing that such formulas do exist and that one can return to them when there is a need.

Shabbat—Sacred Time

In seeking to increase one's spirituality at the time of illness, Jewish prayer and ritual are open doors to a better sense of Jewish identity and connection. The same may be said of the ritual observance of *Shabbat* (the Jewish Sabbath). For one who is ill and in the hospital, life is generally interrupted. Normal habits and patterns of living are disturbed. Of course, it is also true that when one is not feeling too well, one is usually not ready to undertake a new set of religious requirements or obligations. Yet, while the traditional observance of *Shabbat* demands a great deal, access can be quite simple. There is another Hasidic story which illustrates this point.

> Looking out the window on a weekday morning, the Hasidic teacher, Nachman of Bratzlav, noticed his disciple, Chaim, rushing along the street. Reb Nachman opened the window and invited Chaim to come inside. Chaim entered the home and Nachman said to him, "Chaim, have you seen the sky this morning?" "No, Rebbe," answered Chaim.

"Have you seen the street this morning?" "Yes, Rebbe." "Tell me, please, Chaim, what did you see in the street?" "I saw people, carts, and merchandise. I saw merchants and peasants all coming and going, selling and buying."

"Chaim," said Nachman, "in 50 years, in 100 years, on that very street there will be a market. Other vehicles will then bring merchants and merchandise to the street. But I won't be here then and neither will you. So I ask you, Chaim, what's the good of your rushing if you don't even have time to look up at the sky?" [10].

This story captures the spirit in Jewish life of the Shabbat. This suggests how Jews can regain a sense of the sacred time in their experience, whether in the hospital or at home.

The Jewish holidays offer another vehicle for reclaiming the spiritual from traditional Jewish practice. Obviously, the time of illness in the hospital separates one from home and family. All of the normal routines are changed. Yet, the ability to share in some way the traditions of the Jewish holidays can be very important to the Jewish patient. The symbols, such as the *Hanukiah* (8-branched candelabra) or the *Pesach Seder* (ritual meal celebrated for the Passover holiday), can effect great spiritual comfort for the Jewish patient. They permit the Jewish patient to distinguish Jewish sacred time from normal time and life. Following the lunar-based Jewish calendar, a Jew can mark the times of holy days, *Rosh Hodesh* (the beginning of the Jewish month), and the beginning time of the *Shabbat,* on Friday evening.

Mitzvot—Religious Intention

When I was in high school, I had the opportunity to travel to the Hasidic Jewish community outside of Detroit for a weekend. I was part of a youth group from a Reform Jewish synagogue. We arrived at the synagogue a short while before the beginning of *Shabbat* and the rabbi asked that, beginning now, we wear yarmulkes (Yiddish for male head coverings). He then suggested that adopting a Jewish way of life did not mean, as we assumed, following all of the 613 *mitzvoth* (commandments) that were in the Torah. Rather, he said, that it means taking on one mitzvah at a time and making it one's own. That may be the focus and intention of developing a spirituality for Jewish patients.

In an Orthodox Jewish life style, religious practice is observed in every dimension of one's life. These religious observances and behavior are derived from the body of *Halacha* (Jewish religious law). Liberal Judaism grants autonomy to the individual to choose those aspects of tradition that are meaningful in their own lives. For the Jewish patient, there are implicit limitations dictated, for example, by the person's medical condition which he or she must follow according to rabbinical authorities. Thus, the concept *Pikuach Nefesh* (literally, danger to the soul) requires that a Jew whose life would be threatened may not observe the fast for the *Yom Kippur* holy day. The religious observances offered to the Jewish patient as a way of connecting to his or her spirituality must be tempered by reason and practicality.

Liberal Jewish religion in particular has struggled with the ways in which to relate to traditional practice. This dynamic is not dissimilar than what is experienced by the Jewish patient. As noted, it is often a practical impossibility for the Jewish patient to adopt all of the patterns of traditional Jewish observance. Therefore, it is important to place the goal in the context of what is possible. To increase or better access one's Jewish spirituality when ill, a Jew needs to decide what is realistic and what is do-able. A key concept to convey to Jewish patients is *Kavanah* (intentionality). In using this concept we understand that one's motivation and commitment are of primary importance, even more than what one may actually be able to do. Another Hasidic story illustrates this theme.

> A villager who prayed at the House of Prayer of the *Baal Shem Tov* on the High Holidays had a son who could not learn to read even one letter. Because the boy could not pray from a prayer book, his father never took him to services during the holidays. But when the boy turned thirteen, his father decided to take him to the House of Prayer for the Day of Atonement.
>
> Now, this young boy had a pipe on which he used to play as he sat in the fields watching over his sheep. He took this pipe with him to services and the father didn't notice. Hour after hour, the boy sat in the House of Prayer and said nothing. When the Afternoon service began, he asked his father if he might play on the pipe. His father angrily forbade it and took the pipe from the boy. Finally, the Concluding Service began. Suddenly, the boy snatched away the pipe from his father's hand and blew into it with all his might. The congregation was startled and confused by the sound. But the *Baal Shem Tov* went on with the service. At the end of the day the rabbi declared that the little boy's pipe music had carried all of the congregations' prayers up to heaven [11].

The intention of his heart was more powerful than the prayers of a great rabbi and the entire congregation. This is the message which the Jewish patient can hear when limited in what he or she may observe of tradition.

God

A relationship with God in the history of Jewish theology is premised upon the idea of *brit* (covenant). This covenant was established in

Jewish tradition first with Noah, then Abraham, and finally, with Moses and the Israelites. Modern Jewish thinkers, notably Rabbi Eugene Borowitz, have pressed for retaining this idea as the central element in a personal Jewish theology. Two qualities of God are the basis for the covenant with Israel, God's *Mishpat* (justice) and *Rachamim* (mercy). These two ideas can at the same time cause great fear (that God would punish with illness) and great comfort (that God is compassionate and gracious) in the Jewish patient.

Clearly it would be presumptuous to explore all of the ramifications of Jewish belief in God in this chapter. Yet, it can be noted that there are many levels at which one may find a connection to God in the face of illness. Using the framework of Martin Buber, we can focus on the personal qualities of God. Thus, there are the representations and representatives of God which we find in the synagogue community and rabbi. Like Tevya the Milkman in Fiddler on the Roof, one's relationship with God may have a quality of friendship or companionship. Many Jews familiar with Eastern religions like Buddhism have discovered meditation practices derived from Judaism and found God in the silence of their own heart.

We need not go far to learn that the path to God is open to all who seek God's presence and care. From the book of Micah, we read:

> He has told you, O man, what is good,
> And what the Lord requires of you:
> Only to do justice
> And to love goodness,
> And to walk humbly with you God [12].

The Jewish patient may find a relationship to God in the texts of the Jewish tradition, in the connection with a rabbi or Jewish chaplain, or in the *Ruach* (spirit or breath) that resides within.

ENDNOTES

1. Babylonian Talmud, tractate Gittin, page 70a.
2. Babylonian Talmud , tractate Berachot, page 57b.
3. The four are Reform, Conservative, Orthodox, and Reconstructionist. Each reflects a different level of observance of Jewish traditional practice, as well as different theological and philosophical positions. The interested reader is encouraged to see Joseph L. Blau's *Modern Varieties of Judaism*, New York: Columbia University Press, 1966.
4. Small movements in Jewish life include Humanistic Judaism, New Age Judaism or Jewish Renewal, and Jewish Vegetarianism.
5. See the essay by Louis Jacobs "Judaism" in *Jewish Values*, Keter Publishing House, Jerusalem, 1974.

6. Fathers According to Rabbi Natan, Chapter 41.
7. This ceremony marks the formal passage of a Jewish child into adulthood.
8. The Me Shebayrach prayer is a blessing which asks for healing of body and spirit. It carries a primary significance in the Jewish community for one who is ill.
9. From H. H. Donin, *To Pray as a Jew,* Basic Books, New York, p. 17, 1980.
10. From M. D. Shapiro, *Gates of Shabbat,* CCAR, New York, pp. 1-2, 1991.
11. F. Klagsbrun, *Voices of Wisdom,* Pantheon Books, New York, p. 439, 1980.
12. Micah 6:8

SECTION 3:

Health Care and Spirituality: Ethnic and Gender Perspectives

Introduction

Reverend Richard Gilbert

The debate over "political correctness" rages on in most corners of society. While it is important to be "correct" in language, it is equally important that we be "correct" in our understanding of practices, beliefs, needs, values, and expectations that emerge from different groups and *as they choose to give them meaning*.

In this section we have contributions of "groups" or communities of people that reflect issues of ethnicity or gender. Dr. Gerry Cox, a researcher and teacher who also speaks from first hand experience in his work, writes about the spiritual pathways of Native Americans (First Generation Americans) as they experience life events and health concerns.

The Reverend Robert Miller, who has done extensive research, writing, and work in the trenches on issues of men and life and men and faith, offers needed insights about men, how men respond to health crisis, disease, and trauma, and how men choose or choose not to give meaning to life events.

Chaplain Karrie Oertli, a hospital chaplain and C.P.E. Supervisor, delves into the spiritual and experiential journey of the woman. She brings meaning and respect to what it means to be a woman and delineates the feminist concerns, needs, and issues surrounding health care and life events.

This division concludes with a very rare and honest look at a population of patients who can bear not only the medical concerns that assault them, but also the misinformation and misapprehension by the caregivers. Chaplain Sue Jelinek addresses the concerns of the Gay-Lesbian-Bisexual-Transgendered patient, carefully pointing out ways that our misinformation and biases add judgment and can influence how we do or do not provide care.

CHAPTER 9

The Native American Patient

Gerry Cox

Emile Durkheim defines religion as, "the belief in Spiritual beings" [1, p. 44]. To have spirituality is to have renewal of the soul and spirit [2, p. 74]. Native Americans historically believed in spirits and in the afterlife. In all religions, death management practices emerge to deal with loss.

The practices in Native-American religions parallel those in other religions. Native Americans like Christians view death with fear and yet as a spiritual release. For the Native American, death is a separation of the body and the soul [3, p. 45). Concepts of spirituality effect both attitudes toward dying and death and the death-management practices. All spirituality is about roots. To be spiritual, one must live a rooted life, a life rooted in tradition and history [4, p. 1].

Traditional Native-American culture has many features in common with traditional Christian practices. While religion is a word that has no equivalent in the languages spoken by Native Americans, they are intensely spiritual peoples whose spirituality is exhibited in their art and everyday living [5, p. 200]. Like Christians, Native Americans do not view death as something to be ignored, but rather as a natural part of life. Death is not to become an obsession nor to be feared [6, p. 58].

ELEMENTS OF RELIGION

There are fourteen elements of religion and death management practices. First, the conception of the sacred. A visitor to a religious place, person, or event would typically be struck by the fact that the situation is viewed by the people involved as holy rather than profane. It is characterized by a sense of awe or mystery. The Native American is religious in kind. Native Americans have a sense of the sacred that permeates even the most casual and personal attitudes of the individual. The Native American understands herself or himself and the world as part of a religious view [7, p. 23]. While the individual is essentially spiritual, the Native American will turn to a priest or a shaman or other qualified person to deal with the sacred. They have the knowledge of how to deal with the sacred.

Among Native Americans, those who deal with the holy were singled out from childhood for special religious training. They would be taught the sacred ways of the people [8, p. 3]. As the shaman might have a vision quest, Jesus had his vision quest in the wilderness [9, p. 111]. The traditions of Judaism and Christianity parallel those of the Native Americans. The story of Samuel from the Hebrew Bible and the Seminaries for Youths in Christianity historically are examples of such traditions.

Second, Durkheim suggests that all religions contain magic as a basic element as well [1, p. 58]. Magic in religion can be typified by the basketball player who prays before making a free throw, by the child who prays for a bicycle, and by the parent who prays for a magical cure for a child who has no scientific hope. Certainly the use of magic among Native Americans can be typified by the Sun Dance ceremony of the Cheyenne and the rites of the Lone Tipi [10]. Magic is similar to religion in that it serves some of the same functions.

Both magic and religion deal with the supernatural, both use specialized personnel to deal with the supernatural, both are based upon faith, and both explain why events occur. To the Navajo, all sickness and disease, whether mental or physical, is believed due to supernatural causes such as an attack by a witch or one of the Holy People, or by breaking one of the rules of life [11, p. 99]. Certainly many Christians believe that their misfortunes are due to the devil or their own breaking of the rules. Spiritual wholeness is given by religious identification and by sound moral teaching that results from such teaching [3, p. 220].

Attitudes are also an element of religion. Magic is different from religion in that it is specific in its goals. One orders that another fall in love, die, get sick, or whatever. In religion, the goals are more transcendental such as long life, unity with God, salvation, and freedom from sins. In magic, one has different attitudes as well.

In religion, the attitudes are typically reverence, awe, respect, but could be ecstasy or terror as well. In magic, one commands that events occur rather than pleads or begs. Magic is more utilitarian and technical than is religion [1, p. 405]. For the Christian, Baptism seems to be able to magically guarantee one's entry into Heaven. Communion magically gives the grace needed to live the Holy Life. For the Native American, an attitude might be reverence for Earth Mother as an expression of the work of the Great Spirit in creating the environment in which the human beings live.

A fourth element of religion is ritual. Ritual serves the function of making sacred objects, ways of doing things, and supports belief. Rituals provide the routine that supports stability and predictability in religion. Rituals could be a way of making a piece of pottery, weaving a rug, carving a sculpture, a sand painting, or casting a piece of metal. Before the whites came, Native Americans had beliefs and rituals that fit their way of life and spiritual needs [12, p. 254]. The Navajo viewed themselves as tied to the sacred earth, and the materials that they used to weave had traditionally come from the earth: the wool from sheep, the dyes from wild plants and berries, the looms from the trees [13].

Religious rituals give order to one's life. This allows religion to deal with the strains of everyday living. The Blessing Way ritual of the Navajo is a clear example of a ritual in Native American religion. As a key ritual in the Navajo religion, the Blessing Way was a ceremonial that was concerned with peace, harmony, and good things [14, p. 2]. Like the Catholic sacraments, the Blessing Way is used for births, weddings, and other life events, but the Blessing Way is also used for good hope, to acquire property, protection against accidents, and to invoke a blessing on all aspects of domestic and social life including childbirth, weddings, adolescent rites to install tribal officers, to bless a new house, and other blessings needed for daily life [14, p. 3]. Lifeway rituals may be used to cure injuries caused by accidents or illnesses while the Mountainway Chant would be used to cure gastrointestinal and other illnesses [14, p. 3].

Probably, most Christians would expect that being religious and spiritual would lead them to have good hope, to acquire property, to have protection against accidents, and to invoke a blessing on all aspects of their domestic and social life. The Navajo believed that the misfortunes of sickness and premature death are the result of not following the rules and that ceremonials could restore order in the individual by performing exact rituals that would require supernatural forces to withdraw their punishment or sickness from the individual [11, p. 98].

The Changing Woman is the favored people among the Holy People of the Navajo. She had much to do with the creation of the Earth Surface people [15]. Like Christ to the Christian, She is one with God. She, too, has an eternal presence [15]. For the Pueblos, contact with the supernatural is the aim of all ceremonies. Spiritual healing can occur with the aid of the supernatural [16, p. 123].

For the Apache, ceremonies were performed as cures, to set things right, or to ward off evil. The majority of ceremonies were carried out by the shaman [11, p. 135]. The many rituals of the Catholic Church have their parallel in the Blessing Way and other Navajo ceremonies. Native American spirituality provides those who are ill dying, and their survivors, a framework to cope with crises and trauma of life.

Fifth, all religions also have belief as an essential element. A major function of belief is to support religious rituals. Durkheim argues that, in principle, religion is supported by beliefs, and yet beliefs are often modeled after rites to account for them [1, p. 121]. As demonstrated by the book *Sky Lore of the American Indian* [17], the Native Americans had beliefs similar to Judaism and Christianity concerning creation, the solar system, and the acts of nature. Oral traditions yield stories such as these for the ancient Jew as well as the early Christian. The beliefs of one religion are typically viewed as legends or myths to those who are not believers.

The origins of religious beliefs are a sixth element of all religions. Revealed truths typically come from deities or from their prophets. God is described as speaking to Abraham and to Moses in the Old Testament and the Hebrew Bible. God spoke to Mohammed and told him what to write in the Koran. God also came to the Navajo and gave them the Blessing Way. After the original word is given to the people, the members of the religion and their leaders develop what the word means. Those who carried on the oral traditions of the Jewish word did not all follow the same text. The Yahwist, the Elohist, the Priestly, and the Deuteronomist sources all have slightly different versions of the word of God and the events of the people of God [18]. The early Christian versions of the word of God vary depending upon whether one reads Matthew, Mark, Luke, John, or the words of Paul. Similarly, the word of God as exhibited in the Navajo Blessing Way has more than one version [14]. The Monster Slayer who came to save the Navajo people is similar to the coming of Jesus for the Christian [19, p. 52].

The traditions of the Navajo combine belief, and ritual as a part of social justice. The Navajo Church focus is upon curing as was the focus of Jesus upon curing [19, p. 52]. Spiritual healing is not only a part of Native-American religions, but it has occurred among the founders of religions, saints, and disciples as well [20, p. 124]. In an oral tradition that covers much time, stories have a way of changing as development and revision is always possible.

Durkheim would also view animism as an essential element of religion. He sees two kinds of phenomena occurring. One is nature in the form of the great cosmic forces such as the wind, rivers, stars, or the sky or in the objects of nature such as plants, animals, and rocks have spiritual being. The other type of animism is that of souls occupying a spirit world [1, p. 65]. In the first type, spirits are seen as becoming the wind, stars, sky, and other natural phenomena with the power to control their natural forces and to impact the lives of the people. These spirits were seen as responsible for what happens in the universe [1, p. 333]. Mother Nature, the Sun God, the Moon God, and the God of the River Nile are all examples of such animism. The Blessing Way emphasis upon Gopher Man, Gopher Woman, Green Frog People, and the Maiden Who Became a Bear demonstrate the other concept of the first type. The Navajo legend of the Maiden who became a Bear is a part of the Healing Ceremony [16]. The concept of spirits of the people occupying the bodies of animals is a part of many tribes of North American Native Americans. These animals spirits have their guardian spirits as well. The transition to guardians for people is quite simple. If animals have guardians and people can occupy the bodies of animals, then people have guardians as well [21]. Spirits help people, befriend them, guide them, and for those who are blessed by the spirits, they become shaman [22, p. 15].

Christians would talk about guardian spirits called guardian angels. For the Native American this can be one's guardian spirit [23, p. 17]. The second type of spirit of animism is seen in ghosts or spirits of another world who come to visit the people. In Christianity, the Devil comes to tempt Jesus. The Blessing Way of the Navajo tells of the Horned Monster, the Eye Killers, the Big Centipedes, the Overwhelming Vagina, the Rock Monster Eagle, the Big Ye'i, and other world spirits that come to attack the people [14]. The occult may have the same threat of danger for Christians. Evil spirits come to take the souls of the living. The Black Mass and other occult activities are designed to attack Christianity and Christians as the monsters are to attack the Navajo.

The eighth element of religion is veneration and worship of spirits [1, p. 309]. While it is probably true than humans have worshiped just about everything on earth that could be worshiped, it is usually not the object that is worshiped at all, but rather the spirit or being that inhabits the object or which is represented by the object. For the Hopi, Kachinas were not deities, but rather were the spiritual essence of various life entities that could help the people [24, p. 23]. Like the Christians, the Navajo worshiped a God. Most North American Native American tribes worshiped a supreme deity [3, p. 12]. For the Navajo, the supernatural is conceived as ever present and ever threatening; thus, ritual is integrated and interwoven with all phases of daily life and believed as essential with all phases of daily life to maintain harmony with the universe [25].

Ninth, all religions also have myths. Myths can be defined as "articulation of the mysterious in story and symbol" [3]. Durkheim viewed myths as having an essential role in religion and suggested that if myth were withdrawn from religion that it would be necessary to withdraw the rite also because myth determines the character of the religion [1, p. 100]. Christian myths concerning Jonah, Noah, Abraham, the flood, and the parting of the Red Sea to allow the Passover are quasi-historical. The Native-American parallels of the Orpheus tradition of the Ghost Dance [26], the myth of the Navajo as the first humans ascending from the underworld, the origin myth of the Sun Dance of the Cheyenne [10], and the Blessingway myths of Changing Woman [14] are also quasi-historical. Such myths are typically long ago so that it is difficult to empirically test their validity. Myths also are a part of the belief structure of the religion. Myths probably function to validate or justify beliefs and rituals. It is doubtful that it is necessary that myths actually be true to be believed and supported in religion. The function of myth is to support belief and ritual. It is not the basis for belief.

Tenth, all religions have a set of things which serves to designate the particular religious group that Durkheim called its totem [1, p. 121]. For Catholic, the totem would include the Rosary, the Sacraments, the Church, religious medals, and clerical garb. For the Navajo, the totem would include the purification ritual of the Indian sweat bath, the sand painting, the weaving of the rug, and the making of baskets. Such totems are social totems. Social totems give the members of the religion a sense of identity and a social solidarity that would not be possible without the totem. The members do the rituals and practices of the totem together and get a sense of belonging by doing so. A totem could also be mystical presence in birds, animals, or natural objects. Such a totem could be called a mystical totem. Tribes that depended upon the buffalo or other animals for survival would develop rituals and beliefs concerning the animal to give them power over the animal to allow its capture. The vision quest of the Southern Plains tribes was to obtain a guardian spirit that would take the form of an animal, bird, or inanimate object [27]. Durkheim describes such activities among the Australian tribes and among some Native American groups [1, p. 236].

An eleventh element of religion would be the notion of ancestor worship. Like Christianity, Native-American groups have a belief in an afterlife [19, p. 45]. The notion of complete extension of the personality at death is difficult to accept. When a person has a close relationship for an extended time with another person, the death of that person leaves a void. The dead can remain part of the life of the living. It is not unusual to have someone describe the visit of a deceased loved one in a dream or semi awake state. It is even more common to have the living describe a feeling of the presence of the deceased in one's life. Their influence continues to be a part of the life of the living. Christians may communicate with the deceased through prayer or meditation. The Navajo may communicate with the deceased through animals. Death does not end life. It is a part of life. Death permeates life.

Death is not just something which happens in the future. It is a part of the daily lives of people. Facing the future of death makes life more livable. It makes life have a sense of urgency. It makes death a goal rather than a threat to one's being. Everyone dies. All who one knows will die. When a loved one dies first, the living must go on with life without the dead. The living often continue to make the dead part of their life. Those in the afterlife may remain in an intimate relationship with the living [19, p. 45].

An additional element of religion is that all religions incorporate some form of artistic expression. This can be expressed through art, music, dance, dramas, and literature. From the Greeks through the Renaissance in the West, music has been considered part of the process of healing the body and the soul. The concepts of holistic care emerged from antiquity, lost their popularity over the centuries, and emerged again as a method of healing [28, p. 111]. Shaman have used sound and music for centuries to deal with spirits and to effect cures [29, p. 34]. Even in the "white" culture, music therapy is based upon a medical model of healing that is measurable and predictable [30].

The Chippewa, Navajo, Cherokee, Pagago, Seminole, Sioux, Cheyenne, and most other tribes used music to heal the sick [31, pp. 27-36]. Shaman have drums, and common medicine practitioners have rattles [23, p. 163]. Creative expression has been found to be a valuable link to the healing process for children and promotes mental and physical health [32, p. 138]. Not only is music helpful for curing, but drama and music are also helpful for those who grieve [33, p. 136]. Poetry, photographs, and art are also effective elements in healing [34, p. 167; 35, p. 255; 36, p. 3; 37, p. 173]. All Native-American religions and all Christian groups incorporate some elements of artistic expression.

A thirteenth element of religion is an attitude toward death. Attitudes toward life and death are learned. Religion is one source of learning. Native-American and Christian attitudes toward death are somewhat similar. The major difference is that Christians would believe that Jesus Christ is necessary for salvation. However, the concept of a Christ who returned from the dead is abhorrent to the Navajo [19, p. 45]. The concept of human mortality is present in both. Both have the concept of soul and afterlife. Both the Christian and the Navajo put great emphasis upon prayer.

The ritualistic prayers and chants of the Navajo have their parallel in the Catholic prayers and chants. However, a difference is that Christianity focuses upon belief and faith while Navajos focus upon ritual activity [19, p. 46]. A major difference is that the sacred words of the

Christian are written in a sacred book while the sacred words of the Navajo are passed down in an oral tradition.

In both the traditions of Judaism and Christianity, oral traditions were a major part of their history, as with the Navajo. In recent years, the sacred words of the Navajo have been written [14, 30]. Death is a major subject in the oral tradition of the Native American [34] as is life to the Christian.

The last element of religion is the explanation for evil. Death is perhaps the greatest evil that religion explains. In Christianity God allows human freedom which explains evil; other religions have their anti-gods to explain evil [1, p. 468]. While there are many evils in life, death is one of the evils that all peoples must face. Death is not simply an event which ends life, but death is a part of life. It is not simply a future event, but death is an ever present event. The limits of time that one can live force people to make the most of their lives while they have them. Death becomes a teacher for life.

Like all groups, Native-American tribes often lived a precarious existence. War, famine, or disease could easily end their lives. While all tribes did not talk of a separate place for the good and those who were evil in an afterlife as do Christians, at least most tribes believed in an afterlife [19, p. 45]. Like the Christian, the Native American is able to face death with less fear and apprehension because of a belief in an afterlife.

NATIVE AMERICAN VALUES

The values of Native Americans are a part of their spirituality. Native Americans had different values regarding the accumulation of wealth. Most were taught that one should not be too rich for fear of witchcraft [40, pp. 17-19]. Native Americans had no concept of private property. Native Americans did not produce goods for sale and for profit [5, p. 200]. The concept of amassing goods as a goal was also not a part of the culture. Yet they were still taught that one should work hard and not be lazy [40, p. 12]. The later introduction of "white" education even further eroded the cultural system.

While much of the culture has been lost, many Native Americans are rediscovering their "roots." Several patterns have emerged. Native Americans are generally more aware of how they are related to others in their kinship system than are most white people. For Native Americans, one's clan or lineage is a part of his or her life. It is important and has duties and obligations that go with such membership. One may be called upon to be a story teller, dancer, drummer, or whatever. Most

Native-American communities provide their children with more time and experiences with grandparents and other older relatives which leads to less of a generation gap. While white society tends to devalue elderly people, Native Americans still value the elderly. Native Americans are more likely to care for their elderly at home. While those who are more "white" may use nursing homes, the general pattern is for the elderly to be cared for at home with relatives. This means that children and others have the opportunity to have first-hand knowledge of the dying process.

Native Americans have a network of sharing and assistance that is organized along kinship lines. This tends to include money, child care, housing, rides, help with work, and whatever is needed. Generosity and sharing are strong cultural values. The "give-away" ceremonies are still practiced among many groups. Rather than saving and acquiring, Native Americans shared and gave away property. The giving and sharing was a part of their spiritual life [5, p. 219].

The practice of public ceremonies along kinship lines is still strong. Unlike white families which no longer have reunions or other family gatherings on a frequent or regular basis, Native Americans continue to have family-oriented ceremonies. Even dying has a ceremony. Ceremonies were a part of all activities from eating to weddings. Spiritual life is inseparable from economic, political, and social life [5, p. 200].

The Federal government has impacted the Native Americans. Some policies were directly and deliberately designed to weaken or breakup the Native-American family. Placing children with white families or in boarding schools took away the traditional role for Native-American families. The paternalism of the government has to a large extent replaced the family. Like many white welfare families, Native-American families were not allowed to make their own decisions or to direct their own lives. White patriarchal assumptions about proper families also disrupted Native-American families that were matriarchal or egalitarian. Problems of alcohol, unemployment, poverty, and so forth have further weakened the Native-American family. White racism has further weakened the family. White capitalism may further weaken the family. The huge dollars that are becoming available to Native Americans through casinos, bingo, selling resources, or other "white" ways threaten the way of life of Native Americans.

Yet, some Native-American communities are attempting to preserve their culture and to maintain their traditional ways. Like the white families, there are many strong, joyful families that are maintaining the traditional culture and having successful family life. Those who have managed to continue to integrate their spiritual life with their everyday life have generally been able to maintain their traditional ways. While many cultural traditions may exist only in books, many more have been preserved. While the traditional family is endangered, it still survives.

Native Americans have a different culture. The lifestyle of the various tribes differs greatly, but some cultural patterns do emerge. First, the white culture is future-oriented. The Native-American culture tends to focus upon the present. Rather than living a life of anticipation and seeking of the future, Native Americans tend to focus upon the present timelessness. Anglos also live by the clock. Time is greatly important to the white culture. Calendars and time are not important in the native cultures. To amass goods and property and to have savings is the white way. For Native Americans, goods are to be shared and savings used. There is no value to amassing property. Habituation to hard work as a way of life is a white cultural practice. For Native Americans, and particularly for men, drudgery over a period of years to earn a living was not a part of the culture. The white culture is also greatly attached to science and its ways. A physician may be baffled by the Navajo who wants to leave the hospital to have a "sing." Science is not a part of the way of life of the Native American.

MEDICAL CARE AND DYING

The medical care of Native Americans has been fragmented and confused. As many have been forced to reservations or restricted areas maintained by the Federal government, many traditional methods have been lost over time. White medicine has also been introduced over time. Many Native Americans also live in cities and are the primary users of "white" medicine. While each of the approximately 300 tribes has their own beliefs and practices regarding health and illness, generally, most would believe that health is the result of living in harmony with nature and having the ability to survive under extremely difficult circumstances. Humans have an intimate, personal relationship with nature.

The earth is alive and has a desire to be healthy as well. Like humans, the earth is occasionally ill and at other times healthy. It, too, can be out of balance. The earth is the friend of the human. It gives food, shelter, clothing, and medicine to humans. The earth belongs to life, life belongs to the land, and the land belongs to itself.

Humans must reciprocate and be the friend of the earth. One who is in harmony with the earth will be in balance and will be healthy. Health is in the control of the individual. Everything in nature and in life has a purpose. The land feeds and clothes humans. Every illness or pain has a purpose. One must pay the price for what one does. Every human has the power to control one's self. This spirit power is the source of illness and pain. One must pay the price for one's acts whether in the past or in the future. Science may view the cause of disease as from some bacteria or other empirically controlled cause, the Native American views illness as not being the result of bacteria or germs or whatever, but rather it is the price that one must pay. The specific views of selected tribes will be discussed later.

TRIBAL HEALING

The traditional healer of the Native American was the shaman. The traditional culture Native Americans have generally maintained their belief in the healing ways of the shaman. The shaman is to be knowledgeable in the ways of the earth, humans, and nature. To be a recipient of the medicine power, one must live one's life in balance.

There are four directions, four seasons, four ages of humans, and four kingdoms of life. One must renew the commitment to this balance every day [41, p. 62]. The shaman is to determine the cause of the illness or pain and then must develop the proper treatment of the illness or pain. The special ceremonies may take from a few minutes to several days. Shaman are taught by other shaman. It takes years to learn the craft. One is never finished with the learning. Unlike the white physician, the shaman looks to more than the physical causes of an illness. The shaman tries to determine the spiritual causes of the illness as well. A dream or a vision may be the medium for healing by helping the shaman find the cause of the illness [42, p. 247]. Holistic medicine may be an attempt to recognize the multiple causes of illnesses. Just as each life has a purpose, the shaman's purpose is to find the cause of an illness and to cure it.

To heal, the shaman does not stop with the idea that a drug or other medicine can cure. To cure, the shaman administers physical medicine, but he or she also administers spiritual medicine. The treatment is a process that not only heals the physical illness, but also administers to the spiritual needs that must be addressed to bring the person back into harmony or balance [43, p. 224]. The medicine power enables the possessor of the spirit to have personal contact with the invisible world of the spirits [41, p. 63]. If one is meant to die, then there is nothing that the shaman can do. One cannot defy nature.

What can be done, will be done. More than that is unnecessary and may be an affront to nature. Death is not to be feared, but life is to be appreciated for oneself and for one's loved ones.

The Old Testament of the Native Americans

The Native-American spirituality can be described as the Old Testament of the Native Americans. The Native-American Bible is not yet written, but it may be as equally inspired as the Hebrew, the Christian, or the Muslim bibles. Theologians need to seriously study Native-American theology. Unfortunately, words like animism, shamanism, tribal religion, and so forth are not the scholarly words of theology. The Native-American Old Testament includes a creation story, covenants, history of its people, and relations with the creator. As Christians have given part of their legacy to the Jewish people, Christians could also give part of their legacy to Native-American peoples. The world views of Israel and of Native Americans have much in common. Each believed in a Creator who was God, that God was God for all peoples, that a covenant existed with God, that God provided the people with prophets and healers, that God provided law and a way of life for the people, that God provided a "promised land," that God spoke through dreams and visions, that God would deliver the people from suffering, and that God could become incarnate on earth. Native-American religion has a place in the religions of the world.

Attitudes Toward Dying and Death

While generalizations are dangerous, the variety of cultural expressions of dying and death do have some commonalties for the various tribes. Most tribes express a willingness to surrender to death at any time without fear. The Lakota Chief Crazy Horse was noted for his chant before going into battle that, "Today is a good day to die." Every day is to be lived as if it were one's last day. One must enjoy and live fully. Just as one cannot buy land, one cannot buy life. Death is waiting. One cannot escape. One does not seek death before its time, nor does one avoid death or try to delay its occurrence. No one is ever truly alone. The dead are not altogether powerless. There is no death, but rather simply a change of worlds [41, p. 25].

Apache

Apaches are not one tribe. Their ways are not the same for all groups. The Western Apache are noted for the lack of words. When one is suffering from an illness or pain, one may be "sung over." When one is the object of a ceremony, it is considered to be wrong to talk to the person. The only people who talk to the patient are the shaman and the relative who is in charge of food preparation. The patient only speaks openly when asked to pray [44, p. 228]. Curing ceremonies typically begin in the early evening and continue until nearly dawn the next day. While it is permissible to talk openly and freely with the patient prior to the ceremony, it is not permissible after the ceremony begins [44, p. 226].

The attitudes of the Apache toward the elderly are a paradox. The elderly are spoken of as poor even if they have property. The elderly do not have the best clothes, the best food, or even sleep in the most desirable places. They are recognized for having lived a long life and if they have a clear mind are a vital part of family affairs [45, pp. 514-515]. "Throwing away" of the elderly was practiced historically. This meant that when one was too old to walk or ride, he or she would be abandoned. They would leave them food and water and return in a few days to bury or to push the wickiup in on top of them [45, p. 515]. For the Chiracahua Apache, old age was a time of prestige.

One would wish for a long life and old age in prayers, chants, and ceremonials. The old kept active and when they were not able to be active, they usually died within a few days [46, p. 40]. Apache shared their surpluses with relatives. Today, older people who receive retirement checks often give them to younger relatives. Old age is a time of giving to younger relatives [47, p. 168]. The Eastern Apache, the Western Apache, and the Northern Apache all express fears of ghosts and will perform dances to obtain protection from ghosts [48, p. 193]. Other dances also are performed for a sick child, a sick woman, or a sick man [49, pp. 174-179]. For the Apache, the shaman can be a man or a woman, an adult or a child. The power is given to one by the spirit. One can use it or avoid it. It is a choice. What one experiences is only a little part of the world. One can use the power to go to the greater part of the world.

A few are given the power to reach the spirit part of things. Those people become the shaman or di-yin [50, p. 65]. The shaman who uses his or her power against the forces of the spirit world might lose and a patient might die. If a patient dies, it is not the fault or shame of the shaman who presided at the ceremony. It is because the powers of the spirits were too strong [50, p. 65]. The power of the shaman to the Apache is just as real as the power of hospitals and medicine to whites [50, p. 66].

Once one dies, the ghost becomes of great concern. One does not use the name of the dead. They may be too busy and to interrupt them may cause anger [51, p. 15]. To honor the dead and to avoid their wrath, the Apache would set aside part of their fields as the fields of the dead. They would not cultivate these fields for three years even if it meant starvation for the family [49, p. 178].

The dead can cause illnesses. Owls, ghosts, dreams, witchcraft, and affronts to supernatural powers cause illnesses. The shaman cures with herbs and medicines and the appeasing of the powers that caused the illness [51, p. 18]. Most Apache view the illnesses of the Spanish and white peoples as being too strong for the shaman

[51, p. 29]. If the shaman does not cure these diseases, it is not his or her fault.

The treatment of the Apache was a ceremonial matter. A person with an illness or his or her family invited the shaman to do a ceremonial. If the shaman or shamans accepted, a ritual was performed. If the person lived, the shaman had successfully dealt with the spirits and the disease. If the person died, it was the person's time to die or the spirits were simply too strong. If one lives, it was meant to be. Suffering is a natural part of life. One must confront destiny and death with a spirit of acceptance [3, pp. 119-121]. For the Apache, it was also acceptable for the person with the illness to refuse the treatment of the shaman and to die in peace [51, p. 61].

Navajo

For the Navajo, the hatqali, chanter, or shaman is a person who is familiar with the chants, songs, and requirements of the chants. An elderly shaman chooses one to learn the ways of the chanter. Often this will be to a son, brother, or other male relative. After years of study, one may also become a chanter.

It may take as long as eight years to learn the songs and methods of painting in the sand [52, p. 177]. Like the Apache, the chanter may refuse to answer every call for his services. The person with the illness or his or her messenger may request the services of the chanter several times before the chanter agrees. After the chanter learns the cause of the illness and the condition of the patient, the chanter may still refuse. Ordinarily, the chanter will accept. Typically, women do not perform as chanters, but some have done so. Many women know a great deal about medicine and are used by the shaman to obtain medicine. The Navajo consider disease to be the result of breaking a taboo or an attack of a witch. A diviner may be called to determine the cause of the illness. After the divination, the shaman may call a medicine man or woman to treat the person with medicine, and then the shaman will sing for the ill person. Sometimes, the same person performs all three tasks. A fee is charged for all of these services.

The practice of motion of the hand is a gift to the chanter. The hand movements of the diviner help to determine the cause of the illness. Like those searching for water, the diviner knows when the hand moves a certain way, that she or he has found the cause for the illness. Sand paintings may also be a part of the ceremony. Stargazing is another attached to sand painting rituals. When the painting and the stars combine, the diviner can determine the cause of the illness. Four colors are symbolic for the diviner. White or yellow mean that the patient will recover. Red means that the illness is serious. Black means that the patient will die. Diviners also use listening. What they hear tells them the cause of the illness. If someone is heard crying, the patient will die. The goal is to achieve harmony with nature.

Generally, the Navajo have hope in their religion. When they suffer misfortune or have illness, they believe that their ceremonies will help them through their crisis. As the person is dying, the individual will be removed from the hogan and taken to a nearby shelter or to an unused hogan. The person will be dressed in the best clothes and jewelry no matter how much suffering he or she may be experiencing. Several close family members and the healers will remain with the ill person. As death nears, only one or two may remain [53, p. 141].

Health is the natural human condition. Health is the balance or harmony with nature. When one loses the balance, one has weakness of health that appears in the form of injury or illness. This means potential death. It is a serious matter. The sick are to be treated with care and kindness. When the illness causes death, one must then avoid the dying and soon to be deceased person to avoid illness from the ghost. When Navajos work in hospitals, they typically avoid contact with dead bodies. If they do have contact with the dead, they may very well miss work to go through a cleansing ritual.

Lakota

The Lakota or Sioux had healers who were typically senior men or women who had a calling to be healers in dreams or visions that were beyond their control. One was obligated to begin healing work [54, p. 173]. While the Navajo healing sessions are individualized, the Lakota healing sessions are meticulously formalized. It may take years to accumulate the power and reputation to move from assistant and singer to healer [54, p. 174]. Like the Navajo, the Lakota have to request the assistance of the healer. He may refuse. Various healers are available, and it is necessary to obtain the correct healer [54, p. 174]. The healing rituals for the Lakota are logical. The rituals make sense. One is surrounded by friends. They do not wait in a waiting room. Strangers do not administer to the patient. The sense of wholeness and harmony will allow the patient to gain a better understanding of himself or herself and will lessen fears of the illness and offer an acceptance within the community [54, p. 176]. To the Lakota everything was filled with spirits and powers that controlled or otherwise affected the lives of the people. The mountains, the buffalo, the eagle, the wolf, and the fox all had mysterious forces and medicine [55]. Humans are no better or worse than other living things. All things have a spirit. Every animal is a special gift. Illness is a part of life. It is to be accepted.

MEDICINE

The use of medicine by Native Americans is a major part of their healing arts. Over 200 drugs that are now used in white medicine have their origins from Native Americans [43, p. 224]. Native-American healing arts have included sweat baths, rituals, and herb medicines. The basis of the healing lies in nature. Even the medicines are natural. Rituals are even used when picking the plants for the medicines. The distribution of the medicines also has its rituals. The health care of white culture also includes medicine, but it does not include ritual. When white medicine allows the shamans and healers to perform their rituals, the healing of Native Americans is enhanced. Quite often, Native Americans perceive the cause of their illness to be something other than what the physician has diagnosed.

The hospitals are unfamiliar, they are forced to wait for long periods, and they are among strangers who do not know them. Physicians and nurses are often demanding and impatient. This may cause the patient to become silent, to leave, or to develop great fear. White medicine is typically not explained to the patient. It is refused, not taken, or may be discarded when the hospital staff is no longer present. Medicine is a part of nature. White medicine appears to be unnatural in bottles or syringes.

Health care providers must recognize what they are communicating to Native Americans. Native Americans are used to being diagnosed by others without a lot of questions or personal history questions. Note taking is also bothersome to a culture with oral traditions. Out of respect one listens closely to another. One does not write while another is talking. However, most Native Americans are no longer full-blooded. The mix of the cultures is great enough that many of the traditions are no longer so powerful. If one is to be in balance or harmony with nature, one must die when it is one's time. A man will not behave without dignity and cry out for interventions that will only prolong the process. It is better to die today than to be shamed by living tomorrow.

WHAT CAN NATIVE AMERICANS TEACH US?

The lessons of the Native American are clear. A natural death is better than an artificial one involving futile interventions. The Navajo singer chants, makes sand paintings, moves her/his hand, and whatever to try to restore a person to health. As a specialist, a fee is charged as does a doctor, but she/he includes magic. Sun Dance in its various versions, too, tries to make a successful outcome by the use of magic.

White medicine does not use magic, but it can learn from those who do. The Native American does everything that he or she can to try to make a successful outcome. This involves both rational techniques as in white medicine and the use of emotional involvement. While it may end in disappointment and it may be more psychological than real, magic does allow the person to know that he or she did all that could be done. Native-American medicine heals the spirit as well as the body. When a person dies, the physician loses a patient. When the Native American dies, it was his or her time to die. It was not the fault of the shaman or the family. Historically, white physicians did not have the techniques and medicines that they now have. They, too, relied on supernatural interventions.

Over time, death became viewed as the enemy. For the Native American, death is natural and not an enemy. Suffering is a natural part of life. The emphasis upon winning has lead to guilt. Neither the physician nor the family lost. The patient did not lose either. The patient died.

THE ROLE OF RELIGIOUS SPIRITUALITY IN DEATH

In the daily life of the Native American, spirituality is an inevitable part of every facet of life. Spirituality and prayer are inseparable to the Native American. To separate spirituality and prayer would mean cultural death for the Native American. Every day is a holy event, unlike the Christian who may view one day of the week as a holy day. All that the Native American undertook began and ended with the influence of a spiritual kinship with nature. Spirituality invaded and benefited every part of the Native American's daily life. Like the Christian, the Native American looks to this spirituality to explain the successes and failures of daily life. The guiding spirit or force which rules nature can help him or her through daily life and its struggles.

While the Native American typically did not build churches like Christians, nor have a Bible or hymnals or whatever, the Native American seemed to be equally spiritual and religious in his or her daily life. Native Americans believe that every living thing, including animals, plant life, and the elements, are spiritual items. The Native American gave reverence to the all-powerful and ever present spirit. The dead, too, are a part of the spirit world. In their theology, the abode of the dead is a blessed place and the dead themselves are bringers of blessing. The funeral ceremony allayed not the fear of those who survived but, rather, allayed their grief [12].

While death beliefs varied from one tribe to another, some patterns do exist. Tribes that are sedentary like the Pueblo and the Navajo seem to exhibit more fear of the dead than tribes that are hunters and gatherers like the Sioux or the Apache. The Hooghan (anglicized to hogan) is the center of every blessing in life: happy births; the home of one's children; the center of weddings; the center where good health, increase in crops and livestock originate; where old age—the goal of life—will visit regularly. The hogan means a long life of happiness. Those reaching old age in the hogan have nothing to fear, including death. The Navajo prays the Blessingway for the blessing of death in old age. The hogan in which such a death has occurred is not destroyed. The family may witness such a death. The four days of mourning which are otherwise customary are not observed. Family life continues in the same hogan. It remains a home [14]. The Navajo would prefer to no longer use a hogan where someone had died if the Blessingway was not observed. They have a purification ritual for the items that the deceased left behind before giving them to survivors so that the dead cannot harm them.

Other groups, like the Papago, destroyed property that was not buried with the dead in order to keep the survivors safe from the dead [12]. The Navajo would bury the dead in their blanket and leave their jewelry on the body. Since Native-American groups did not embalm, they normally buried their dead as soon as possible after death whether in the ground or air burial. Funeral practices of Native Americans are based upon the attitudes toward death and the dead. Some mourn for a time such as the Navajo who mourn for four days after the burial. Others, like the Salish Sioux, hold a feast after the burial [56]. Christians, as well, do both after a death. While one may theologically celebrate the triumph of the soul over death, one still mourns his or her loss. Funeral rites are rites of passage. The rite is designed to allow the dead to pass into the domain of the dead.

For life to be meaningful, it must lead somewhere. Its destination is death. Death can therefore be life's ultimate fulfillment or life's ultimate failure. Few moments can rival the moment of death for bearing religious significance [39].

CONCLUSION

Regardless of tribe, Native Americans view death as the natural end of life. It needs to be natural. Let the dying die. All religions have many common elements. Fourteen are discussed. The spirituality of Native

Americans is similar to that of Christianity. Both Native American religions and Christianity have much in common. Both exhibit similar patterns of spirituality. The death management practices of both groups have parallels as well. Spirituality of the people is shown through their management of death.

> Oh, my brother, come back to me,
> Come back, my brother, I am lonely,
> My brother come back and we
> will give you a small present [12].

The confrontation with destiny and death is the confrontation with one's spirituality. As the legend has it, the sleeping Indian outlined by the Wind River Mountain will someday rise again [3].

REFERENCES

1. E. Durkheim, *The Elementary Forms of the Religious Life,* Free Press, New York, 1915.
2. W. Stolzman, *The Pipe and Christ: A Christian-Sioux Dialogue,* Tipi Press, Chamberlain, South Dakota, 1991.
3. C. F. Starkloff, *The People of the Center: American Indian Religion and Christianity,* Seabury Press, New York, 1974.
4. M. Fox (ed.), *Western Spirituality: Historical Roots, Ecumenical Routes,* Fider/Claretian, Notre Dame, 1979.
5. J. Mander, *In Absence of the Sacred: Failure of Technology and the Survival of the Indian Nations,* Sierra Club Books, San Francisco, 1991.
6. L. A. DeSpelder and A. L. Strickland, *The Last Dance: Encountering Death and Dying,* Mayfield, Palo Alto, California, 1996.
7. National Geographical Society, *The World of the American Indian,* The National Geographical Society, Washington, D.C., 1974.
8. J. Grimm, Reflections on Shamanism: The Tribal Healer and the Technological Trance, *Teilhard Studies, 6,* Fall 1981.
9. C. Myers, *Who Will Roll Away the Stone? Discipleship Queries for First World Christians,* Orbis, Maryknoll, New York, 1994.
10. E. A. Hoebel, *The Cheyenne: Indians of the Great Plains,* Holt, Rinehart and Winston, New York, 1960.
11. B. P. Dutton, *Indians of the American Southwest,* Prentice-Hall, Englewood Cliffs, New Jersey, 1975.
12. R. M. Underhill, *Redman's Religion: Beliefs and Practices of the Indians North of Mexico,* University of Chicago, Chicago, 1965.
13. J. B. Katz, *This Song Remembers: Self Portraits of Native Americans in the Arts,* Houghton Mifflin, Boston, 1980.
14. L. C. Wyman, *Sand Paintings of the Navajo Shooting Way and the Walcott Collection,* Smithsonian Institution Press, Washington, 1970.
15. S. Moon, *A Magic Dwells: A Poetic and Psychological Study of the Navajo Emergence Myth,* Wesleyan University Press, Middleton, Connecticut, 1970.

16. V. Laski, *Seeking Life,* American Folklore Society, Philadelphia, 1958.
17. M. Littmann, *The People,* Hansen Planetarium, Salt Lake City, Utah, 1976.
18. L. Boadt, *Reading the Old Testament: An Introduction,* Paulist Press, New York, 1984.
19. R. N. Rapport, *Changing Navaho Religious Values: A Study of Christian Missions to the Rimrock Navahos,* Peabody Museum of American Archaeology and Ethnology, Cambridge, Massachusetts, 1954.
20. J. D. Sweet, *Dances of the Tewa Pueblo Indians: Expressiosn of New Life,* School of American Research Press, Santa Fe, 1985.
21. A. Hultkrantz, *Belief and Worship in Native North America,* Syracuse University Press, Syracuse, New York, 1981.
22. M. Wood, *Spirits, Heroes and Hunters: From North American Indian Mythology,* Schoeken Books, New York, 1982.
23. A. Hultkrantz, *Shamanic Healing and Ritual Drama: Health and Medicine in Native North American Religious Traditions,* Crossroad, New York, 1992.
24. R. Kaiser, *The Voice of the Great Spirit: Prophecies of the Hopi Indians,* Shambhala, Boston, 1991.
25. R. F. Spencer and J. D. Jennings et al., *The Native Americans,* Harper and Row, New York, 1965.
26. A. Hultkrantz, *The North American Indian Orpheus Tradition,* The Ethnographical Museum of Sweden, Monograph Series, 2, Stockholm, 1957.
27. W. K. Powers, *Indians of the Southwest Plains,* Capricorn, New York, 1972.
28. B. Cole, *Music and Morals: A Theological Appraisal of the Moral and Psychological Effects of Music,* Alba House, New York, 1993.
29. J. Alvin, *Music Therapy,* Basic Books, New York, 1975.
30. L. Bunt, *Music Therapy: Art Beyond Words,* Routledge, New York, 1994.
31. D. M. Schullian and M. Schoen, *Music and Medicine,* Henry Schuman, New York, 1948.
32. S. Jennings, *The Handbook of Dramatherapy,* Routledge, New York, 1994.
33. P. F. Kellerman, *Focus on Psychodrama: The Therapeutic Aspects of Psychodrama,* Jessica Kinglsey, Philadelphia, 1992.
34. G. Combs and J. Freeman, *Symbol, Story, and Ceremony: Using Metaphor in Individual and Family Therapy,* W. W. Norton, New York, 1990.
35. J. Weiser, *Phototherapy Techniques: Exploring the Secrets of Personal Snapshots and Family Albums,* Jossey-Bass, San Francisco, 1993.
36. E. L. Phillips, *Love, Poetry, and Psychotherapy,* Irvington, New York, 1985.
37. M. R. Morrison, *Poetry as Therapy,* Human Science Press, New York, 1987.
38. S. D. Gill, *Sacred Words: A Study of Navajo Religion and Prayer,* Greenwood, Westport, Connecticut, 1981.
39. S. D. Gill, *Native American Religions: An Introduction,* Wadsworth, Belmont, California, 1982.
40. R. Hobson, *Navajo Acquisitive Values,* Peabody Museum of American Archaeology and Ethnology, Cambridge, Massachusetts, 1954.
41. B. Steiger, *Medicine Power: The American Indian's Revival of His Spiritual Heritage,* Doubleday, Garden City, New York, 1974.

42. L. Irwin, Cherokee Healing: Myth, Dreams, and Medicine, *American Indian Quarterly, XVI,* pp. 237-257, Spring 1992.

43. J. Highwater, *Indian America,* David McKay, New York, 1975.

44. K. H. Basso, To Give Up on Words: Silence in Western Apache Culture, *Southwestern Journal of Anthropology,* 26:3, Autumn 1970.

45. G. Goodwin, *The Social Organization of the Western Apache,* The University of Chicago Press, Chicago, 1942.

46. D. C. Cole, *The Chiricahua Apache: 1846-1876 From War to Reservation,* University of New Mexico, Albuquerque, 1988.

47. R. J. Perry, *Apache Reservation: Indigenous Peoples and the American State,* University of Texas, Austin, 1993.

48. R. J. Perry, *Western Apache Heritage: People of the Mountain Corridor,* University of Texas, Austin, 1991.

49. T. E. Mails, *The People Called Apache,* Prentice-Hall, Englewood Cliffs, New Jersey, 1974.

50. J. L. Haley, *Apaches: A History and Cultural Portrait,* Doubleday, Garden City, New York, 1981.

51. H. H. Stoeckel, *Survival of the Spirit,* University of Las Vegas, Reno, Nevada, 1993.

52. E. Shorris, *The Death of the Great Spirit: An Elegy for the American Indian,* New American Library, New York, 1971.

53. G. A. Reichard, *Social Life of the Navajo Indians,* Columbia University Press, New York, 1928.

54. R. J. De Mallie and D. R. Parks (eds.), *Sioux Indian Religion: Tradition and Innovation,* University of Oklahoma, Norman, 1987.

55. B. Copps, *The Indians,* Time-Life Books, New York, 1973.

56. R. W. Habenstein, *Funeral Customs the World Over,* Bulfin Printers, Milwaukee, 1983.

CHAPTER 10

The Male Patient

Reverend Robert Miller

The challenges and changes that sickness and health problems confront one with are not easy for either sex—but the typical male patient may possibly present unique challenges for a health care provider or pastoral caregiver.

Some feel that the broad cultural differences between men make stereotypical descriptions extremely difficult. Certainly men of different races and ethnic backgrounds do vary in openness, ability to communicate openly and freely, their trust of (and responsiveness to) medical personnel, etc. However, leaving specific ethnic issues aside, there are enough similarities between men of all cultures and races to generalize some common issues in health care giving with male patients specifically.

Generally speaking, most men may not handle hospitalization or personal health problems very well. Frequently, a caregiver may sense in a man a certain emotional flatness, perhaps even a dispassionate "detachment" about his condition. There may be a certain inability to communicate about the "deeper issues" involved with a serious medical condition, even a lack of openness or honesty. There may certainly be anxiety, impatience, frustration, or fear on a man's part—although it may be well hidden. Caregivers may encounter resistance, anger, or even outright rejection or denial in dealing with medical realities or situations. Family dynamics may seem to interfere with effective medical or pastoral care. Often a woman (wife or mother, for example) has become the health care initiator for male health problems and may end up speaking for "her man" throughout the process (sometimes thus impeding the adaptation process).

From a specifically masculine framework there are several reasons why all of this may be so (because the above reactions may certainly be seen in all patients to some degree). These perspectives will be elaborated upon in the succeeding pages. But to begin, several foundational "male issues" need to be understood:

1. The world of personal vulnerability and weakness, and the often sudden awareness of one's mortality that sickness can engender, is a foreign world for many men. The majority of males are uncomfortable with feelings in general and the feelings that these issues bring up specifically. The "inner world" may be an unfamiliar place to them. They may feel very threatened by what is happening, and this may reflect onto health care providers or caregivers.

2. Men are threatened by a sudden lack of "control" over their own bodies and lives. It challenges many of the cultural and familial patterns men have grown up with and live under every day. They may perceive themselves as no longer able to be the protectors or caretakers of their families, nor able to find self-worth in their job or work (at least temporarily). These are important issues for men specifically.

3. The process of dealing with sickness or health problems is not an "efficient" process, and many men place great value on right-brain, problem-solving approaches to life's problems. Health issues and life-crises in general (uncontrollable by their nature) directly threaten a man's often very "efficient" neat little world.

4. Most men grow up strongly influenced by cultural and ethnic mores, as well as developmental "conditioning" to wear certain "masks" or "personas." They have heard and learned from their earliest days that "real men" avoid emotional "weakness" (*Men are not supposed to cry*"), and are always "in control" of themselves and their life. Denial is a major coping mechanism for men who most often simply don't know *how* to relate to the things happening to them because of the dearth of role models in both culture and family.

ONE MAN'S HEALTH CRISIS

Dennis Byrd was a six-foot-five, 270 pound defensive tackle in 1989, the year when he was drafted by the New York Jets football team. He had an outstanding rookie year, ending with seven sacks, one short of the Jets' rookie record, and was named to one All-Rookie Team. He was in his third year of professional football, rapidly gaining a reputation for himself, when the Kansas City Chiefs came to Giants Stadium on November 29, 1992. The second half had just begun when, in attempting to sack Chief's quarterback David Kreig, he crashed into a 280-pound teammate, breaking his neck and causing almost total paralysis.

Over the next six months, he would grapple not only with hospitals, specialists, doctors, therapy sessions, and wheelchairs, but also with his image of himself and his purpose in life. Despite his strong and unshakable faith in God, Dennis grappled with the shocking fact that his entire world had suddenly and tragically changed forever. In the powerful book he later wrote called *Rise and Walk,* he expressed poignantly what his own unexpected struggles were like.

> Tortuous feelings and emotions were flooding through me for a long time. Questions without answers beat through my brain. It's hard to explain how much my physicality meant to me, how much it means to any professional athlete. I had a beautiful wife, a beautiful daughter . . . those things were really important to me as a man, but so was my body. I was fast, I was strong, among the best in the world at the game I loved. My body said "Hey, look. I'm a professional football player. I do *this.*" Now I wondered how I could validate myself to her (his wife Ange) without being a football hero. I wondered how she'd feel about me if the football player was gone . . . [1, pp. 154-155].

SICKNESS IS NOT "EFFICIENT"

For a man like Dennis Byrd (and many others), the sudden confrontation with one's mortality and human vulnerability can be a true shock. Like Byrd and thousands of other men before, sickness and health problems are *rarely* "dealt with" as efficiently, painlessly, or "cleanly" as men would like. Many men unfortunately treat their bodies and inner spirits as they do their automobiles. When there is a problem with the engine or brakes, for example, a man brings it to a mechanic who he fully expects will professionally replace or tune up whatever is amiss. All is quick, clean, efficient, and (except for the bill!) relatively painless.

However, men seem to expect that *all* of life's problems and pains should be dealt with as efficiently and painlessly as this. It is all too easy for men to ignore their inner world, their lurking insecurities and fears, or else consciously trample them under by strength of will in the belief that all feelings and emotions are "useless appendages" in the business of everyday life. (After all, according to the traditional mores of our culture, *"men are not supposed to cry!"*) Thus, feelings of loss or personal weakness, along with those of compassion, sensitivity, and others, are relegated to the "out-basket" of life because they refuse to disappear into place as efficiently and neatly as many men would like!

For most men, this world of personal weakness, loss, and grief is an alien country with a completely foreign language. They do not know the "foreign language" of emotions, feelings, and inner honesty about themselves. This is something that our culture and their heritage has taught them is "better left to women," something totally irrelevant to the "male world" of action, control, independence, and autonomy. A man literally has to be *re-taught* to 1) acknowledge the *reality* of what is going on, 2) recognize and identify what is happening emotionally and psychologically, and then 3) how to express, release, adapt, and cope with these inner realities.

Thus, at the core it is men's *image of their selves as men* that may be the most serious hindrance to emotional, physical, and spiritual health. It is here that health care providers and caregivers may find an entry to bring pastoral care, encouragement, and perhaps effect a change of attitude. Caregivers can help men begin to realize that they are not mechanical machines operating out of some scientifically predetermined, behavioristic causality. Males are not emotion-less, superhero-strong, independent "islands" operating in a vacuum. They can be fearful, weak at times, struggling with life-crises, but at the same time be strong, self-aware, honest, and faith-filled. This is the inner beauty of the "deep masculine." Men need to realize that they are an integral combination of physical body, inner spirit and soul, personality, and emotion. Men's hidden inner world, their feelings, are ignored and overlooked only at great peril to their integral psychological balance.

GENDER DIFFERENCES IN
APPROACHING LIFE-CRISES—ONE COUPLE'S STORY

> The serious problems of life, however, are never fully solved. The meaning and design of a problem seem not to lie in its solution, but in our working at it incessantly [2].

Steve and Sue are a happily married couple with three children. They have worked hard at their relationship. But, after more than twelve years of being together, Steve freely admits that they often wonder how they ever got together in the first place.

"My wife and I are as different as night and day," Steve says. "We often joke about just how radical the differences are between us. We end up concluding that only God, in his warped sense of humor, could have brought us together and nurtured our relationship over the last 12 years of marriage.

"We cope with the big hurts in life very differently as well. Yet somehow we accept each other's differences and continue to nudge each other towards wholeness, which is what it's all about anyway. The following chart depicts at a glance the two ends of the coping spectrum that we have typically encountered in our relationship:

SUE	STEVE
Freely expresses her feelings	Just feels numb inside
Turns to friends for support	Tries to go it alone
Allows tears to flow freely	Keeps things inside
Seeks help from all available sources	Feels stigmatized to seek help
Seeks information, reads books	Wants to get it over with
Doesn't rush the process	

Steve continues with a few comments on these differences between he and his wife. "The above dynamic reflects our own experience from 12 years of marriage, and it might reflect your own as well. I really don't relish the fact that I sound like such a typical male! I think that I should somehow be more enlightened than that. I hate to admit it, but I admire my wife for her innate coping skills. I try to be in touch with what our society calls the more "feminine" qualities. Suffice it to say, though, that they just don't come very naturally.

"When it comes to the question of why men and women handle situations uniquely, so much comes down to the 'dirty' word 'socialization.' Men and women are so different, and in so many ways! I am fascinated by the difference between the sexes . . . the bestseller list always contains a blockbuster title or two that attempts to sort things out. . . ."

Men and women are different. This basic truth seems self-evident to all, but, in today's gender-sensitive world, it is a truth which continues to be analyzed. Sexual and biological differences are fairly obvious examples, but the realm of psychological and behavioral differences seem to be more in dispute. Couples like Steve and Sue are not unique. Men and women take very different approaches to handling everyday life issues, and the crises that health problems bring on are no exceptions to this. (Anyone who has ever been in a close friendship with a member of the opposite sex has probably had the thought so well expressed by the popular book by John Gray entitled, *"Men are from Mars, Women are from Venus"!*) [3].

Certainly men and women do share many common psychological growth patterns. But each sex has their own unique ways of developing those basic behavioral, psychological, and personal traits that make us who we are. This is not the place nor time to enter into arguments surrounding gender-related personality traits, but suffice it to say that it is my belief that men do develop some uniquely masculine aspects of personality (as women do feminine traits).[1]

Neither these male aspects and behavioral tendencies nor the female aspects or tendencies[2] are "better" than the other. Both sexes complement each other physically, psychologically, and in many other ways, as divine "natural law" planned it to be. Jungian psychology likewise demonstrates that men have a feminine side to their personality (called *"anima"*), as women have a masculine side (*"animus"*) to theirs. So, what are described here are not unchanging dictums about men's and women's behavior in times of sickness, but more *inclinations and tendencies*. These inclinations may help health care providers and caregivers better understand male behavior patterns in times of sickness or crisis, and offer relevant clinical or pastoral care. They are certainly not proscriptive of *all* male (or female) actions or attitudes.

> The masculine aspect of personality may be variously described as logos, or outgoing reason, active creativity, controlled aggressiveness, psychological firmness, the capacity to strive for goals and overcome obstacles enroute [4, p. 33].

As inferred above, one basic tendency in masculine nature seems to center around men's need for *independence* and *autonomy*. Maintaining a certain independence and freedom in action and attitude is very important for many men. (This may well reflect the basic survival needs of our pre-historic male ancestors.) *Competitiveness* tends to thrive among men; indeed it is the way many men "feel out" status and rank with their peers. Likewise, men often feel tension between *maintaining a social image* (being in control) and the inner emotional turmoil that may boil up in crisis. Expressing that inner turmoil, of course, is not only socially "unacceptable" but would be a sign of weakness for many. Hence, a caregiver should understand why hospitalization (with all the fears, upheavals, and challenges it always brings) can be an extremely threatening process for some males.

All of this differs from women, who tend to be more highly *relational* than men. Women often have a *support network* that encourages and

---

[1] Richard Rohr identifies the characteristics of uniquely "masculine energy" very effectively in his tape series "A Man's Approach to God," tape 2. John Sanford also discusses this point in a number of his books.

[2] John Sanford (a Jungian psychotherapist and writer) describes the feminine aspect of personality as "Eros, or the capacity for relationships, understanding, awareness of others, creativity through receptiveness, an indirect way of attaining goals, patience, compassion, the valuation and nourishing of life." He then cautions "everyone contains possibilities for both masculine and feminine development, and no one can approach wholeness without development in both areas" [3].

promotes sharing on many levels—personal, emotional, etc. Likewise, women are far more likely to *express their emotions*, and display empathy, and compassion in response to the emotions of others.

Maryland grief counselor Tom Golden sums up some of these differences very accurately when he says "The keyword for women is *intimacy*, which is a measure of the degree that women are related to each other. Men have a keyword of *independence*. The object of their striving . . . is to maintain and enhance their independence and position" [5].

Along with these psychological differences, research is emerging which indicates that chemical and hormonal differences may affect the underlying nature of men and women. For example, William Frey, in *Crying: The Mystery of Tears,* theorizes that declining amounts of the hormone prolactin in men after adolescence make it more difficult for them to access tears in times of great emotion [6]. In their 1976 book *Grief in Cross-Cultural Perspectives,* Rosenblatt, Walsh, and Jackson examined the grieving of eighty-seven different cultures. They did not find one culture in which men expressed more tears than women, and found nine cultures in which men did not cry at all. This highlights another distinction between men and women, namely that men do not use tears as much as women when dealing with their grief [7]. A *Time* magazine article several years ago also reported research showing that differences in the size of a membrane connecting the two hemispheres of the brain might give women a greater connection between verbal capacity and feelings, leaving men less able to verbalize feeling states [8]. *Newsweek* recently covered the research being done on differences in how men's and women's brains actually function, using MRI and other brain mapping technologies [9].

All of this indicates the basic point that men and women can be quite different in how they approach essential life crises. There are substantial psychological, physical, and cultural reasons for this. Thus, it should not be a surprise that how men deal with sickness could also be quite different than women. The generic advice often heard for dealing with life-crises (let out your feelings, don't be afraid to cry, etc.) may not work as easily for a man as a woman. A man's struggle with health crises can be a unique journey through an often very foreign and strange land.

BEHAVIORAL PATTERNS IN MALE PATIENTS

There are a number of general features in the uniquely male way of handling life-crises which tend to set them apart from women. These are not exclusively male, nor definitive of all men, but are instinctive *tendencies and patterns* in men (factors that may certainly be present in women as well).

First, men are inclined toward *private expression of their "losses" or crises,* where few emotions are shown publicly, or even admitted personally. Feelings are held within oneself for a variety of reasons—because men are not relational but autonomous by nature, because men do not wish to "burden" anyone else by their "useless" feelings, and because men are simply not comfortable with (or even aware of, at times) the turmoil and pain inside of them.

The private expression of one's crises is not necessarily an unhealthy factor for a man. The essential issue is the *acknowledging and honoring of inner losses and griefs* however a man does it, *not* the necessary public or outward expression of those feelings. Again, male and female "crisis styles" are *complimentary* not *contradictory.* Grief therapist Thomas Golden believes that the key for men expressing grief (for example) is *knowing that they are respected* first [5, p. 10]. When a man knows that he has the respect of other men, that they will "honor" his autonomy and accept his "weakness," he will feel free to take the risk of admitting his insecurity and other fears.

Second, many men in crisis or sickness feel it is important for them to *maintain control and their "image."* Maintaining a tight control over his emotional world is a way a man attempts to maintain control of his life and everything that happens to him. Most men have learned while growing up that "Emotional vulnerability denotes weakness." So, when a man "breaks down," revealing his inner uncertainties, his independence can be threatened, and there is fear of losing one's image or status with other men in the competitive "game of life." Thus, when the challenges of health problems confront a man, he may instinctively tend to deal with this "problem" as he does with all others—by staying calm, in control, "on top of" things, showing no weakness.

One man exemplified this inclination to control when he told me "My wife is too emotional about things. I'm not comfortable with her when she does that . . . it's a foreign world for me. I've got to keep her going and stay strong, even though I'm hurting like crazy and don't know what to do." This man found his own coping processes "complicated" by his wife's strong emotions, since he felt he "had" to be the "strong one," thus maintaining his "image" at a time when his own inner turmoil was crying out for acknowledgment.

Last, there is in men a *tendency toward action and activity* at times of crisis, grief, or loss. Men value independence in thought and action, and are not always as good handling inner emotions. Thus, at times of crises, men tend to utilize what is already a strength for them, namely taking concrete action and "doing things" (described by John Sanford as "*outgoing reason, active creativity*" in his book *Kingdom Within* [4]). Because the difficult feelings experienced at times of sickness, death, or other crises *cannot* be handled cleanly and efficiently, and are often immensely frustrating for men (who can't really "do" anything about them), men seem to need something that *can* be actively and efficiently done.

> It's not easy to be a man. If I express my grief I lose because I violate the male stereotype of the strong man who shows no emotions. However, I know if I don't express the pain of grief, I will also lose because suppressing my feelings will bring me more problems. I'm in a no-win situation.
>
> Frank (a widower after 38 years of marriage)

Thus, control can be brought to an intrinsically out-of-control situation, and a man can feel like he is accomplishing something constructive and healthy.

Concrete and creative activity can become a tremendous source of healing for men in the coping processes of crises or sickness. In choosing appropriate actions ("creative actions"), a man can enter into his inner world's fears, begin to process the frustration and pain, and acknowledge its role in his life. Using a man's innate inclination toward activity can also become a way for men to honor their inner world issues in unique, "memorializing" ways. (One man, for example, chopped and stacked wood to help vent his grief energy; another man found that painting was the most therapeutic thing he could do in crises.) This concept of "creative activity" is such a vitally important one for men that it deserves much consideration and reflection for all caregivers dealing with men [10].

TOWARD A "PROCESS": HOW MEN HANDLE LIFE-CRISES

Just as there are stages of development and growth in men's lives (I outline three basic developmental stages of life that a man goes through [10, pp. 61-71], other writers have offered similar patterns [2, 11, 12]), there are also significant differences in men's reactions and responses to crises in their lives. We may discern a developmental "process" in men's attempts to "successfully" deal with crucial life-issues such as sickness. The healing that ultimate acceptance, awareness, and successful coping brings can emerge anywhere along these levels. However, the degree and depth of acceptance and coping, as well as individuation and personal growth, depends on successfully negotiating the furthest levels. As might be expected, the levels depend on a man's degree of honesty, self-awareness, willingness to change, and his spirituality.

Level 1

Denial and rejection: going on as if the loss or grief made no difference at all in a man's life. There is not only emotional numbness and denial, but also a lack of (or inability to take) any reflective time, inner work, or significant faith response.

A man remains the prototypical "John Wayne" or "Marlboro man"—emotionless, stoic, unaffected by the "weakness" of feelings, personal mortality, or loss issues.

Level 2

Mere coping: making the "minor" life adjustments needed to cope with life crises or losses and get along in now different circumstances. Life is difficult for a while, emotions seem overwhelming briefly; but a man "learns" to ignore these things, and makes subtle lifestyle changes to ease his pain. However, basic issues surrounding the crisis or loss, as well as any negative emotions, are not dealt with yet. Inner consciousness and self-awareness has still not progressed much past barely "breaking the surface" of self-reflection and emotional honesty.

Level 3

Healthy and "successful" dealing with the life-crisis itself: the negative, challenging emotions of crisis or loss are honestly expressed, and the personal turmoil of the demanded re-adjustment is slowly but effectively dealt with. Dr. Kübler-Ross' stages perhaps *are* followed "successfully," all the way to ultimate acceptance of the situation.

This level always takes a period of time to be fully realized. (As a personal example, when my own father died in 1967 it took me nearly 18 years to fully "put it to rest," and be at peace with him and his passing.) However, although self-consciousness may have begun, the deeper ramifications of realizing one's personal "mortality" may *still* not have penetrated or radically changed the "deep masculine." One further level is possible, where life-crises become *"necessary wounds"* moving a man into the deepest places of his being.

Level 4

Deep personal life issues touched and wrestled with: here a man "wrestles" with his own spirit, his God, and the "ultimate questions" of life. Perhaps there is a movement into a new "stage in life." A man's self-awareness becomes greatly increased through long-term faithful reflection, prayer, and "inner work." Often a new "balance" or a profound sense of integration or wholeness emerges deep in one's being.

This stage is generally reached and entered unconsciously, without an active "choice" or decision. It simply "happens" when a man is open to the call to "move deeper," and when he has a certain integrity of lifestyle, a strong spirituality, and deep self-awareness.

Not reaching this stage does not imply one has *not* fully become a man—levels of self-awareness, faith sensitivities differ widely between men. But, as Carl Jung says so well, "[Though] I cannot blame the person who takes to his heels [at facing these inner trials and struggles] . . . neither can I approve his finding merit in his weakness and cowardice . . . I find nothing praiseworthy about such capitulation" [13].

PRACTICAL SUGGESTIONS FOR CARE IN THE MALE PATIENT RELATIONSHIP

1. Respect and understand the "male situation." Many men have been raised with strong cultural and familial blocks to emotional openness, to what they perceive as "weakness." There will often be inner tension between "being in control" or being "strong," and the pain and hurt and frustration (perhaps unfamiliar feelings) felt within themselves.

2. Encourage men to be open and honest with themselves. Do not allow them to play long-term "games" of denial, particularly in situations of serious medical or personal consequence.

3. If appropriate and needed, help the male patient become aware of his inner world, to become familiar with the "landscape" of that perhaps very foreign world. Remember though that many men simply do not know how to express what is going on inside them. The world of emotions, tears, verbalizing inner "movements" is a foreign language to many. Help them with words or questions—"do you feel like you're angry about this . . . frustrated . . . worried," etc. Questions like "How did you react to this . . ." may be easier for men to answer than feeling-centered questions.

4. Give men "permission" to be "weak." A close friend of mine calls this a "grieving permit": permission to be or feel something other than what their expectations or images "demand." When men don't feel they have to be strong for someone else (or themselves), they may be more open to getting in touch with their own hurts.

5. It may be more comfortable for many men to approach their medical situation from a "problem-solving mode." This might include looking at a situation more analytically, attempting to logically clarify the "problem" (i.e., medical condition, possible issues involved, etc.), coming up with specific practicable options for him to undertake, and

defining or clarifying a "goal" or "endpoint" for the entire process. This approach is a methodology many men feel comfortable with and use often.

6. The "bigger context" of all a man is going through in dealing with sickness is the sudden confrontation with one's own human limitations. This is not an easy thing to see for any person. If needed or appropriate, caregivers can help encourage men to face their own "mortality." No man (despite what he may think) is completely the "master of his own destiny." Sickness forces him to confront that.

7. In dealing with issues surrounding a man's medical condition (or other personal issues), caregivers should not overlook the impact upon a man of losing his job, or having his ability to work seriously impaired due to a medical condition. In the masculine psyche, a man's job, profession, or some meaningful employment is a vital part of a healthy self-image. Most men need to return to work as soon as possible; and research has shown that men feel better if they are working.

8. For successful coping with life crises, a man's personal pains, "griefs," and crises must be acknowledged and honored somehow by talking, thinking, crying, writing, daring, confronting, or whatever. The key word here is *honored and acknowledged*. Encourage a man to take creative and concrete action to honor the losses or "griefs" he deals with. A little activity to "process," channel, or somehow deal with pent-up energy, frustration, or pain is valuable for men, as long as it is not incessant activity that avoids inner issues.

> Dennis was a 72-year-old man married to a younger woman who loved him dearly. They had two small children together, as well as his own older children from an earlier relationship. Dennis was a hard-working man who was forced to retire from his job in early 1995, but then unfortunately slowly began to also lose his eyesight.
>
> He was depressed for months, but was unable to open up about his struggles in these areas to anyone, even his wife or several close friends. Though raised Catholic, he practiced no faith. He was a rigidly "closed" man, isolated and independent, perhaps a paradigm of the "friendless American male." Dennis' griefs unfortunately were never dealt with or acknowledged. He committed suicide in their apartment 6 months after his retirement.

9. Anything a caregiver can do to encourage a man to take *creative action* about his present condition is extremely beneficial. As stated previously, men tend to be "action-oriented." Being able to DO SOMETHING engages that "active" part of a man's psyche. Examples here could include exercise, letter-writing, a repetitive action, creating memorials, solitude, and silence etc. [10, pp. 143-168].

10. Help provide or encourage relationships and sharing in whatever pattern or form is available or helpful for a man (whether with spouses, close male friends, clergypersons, or whomever). In times of crisis and pain, men need *friendships* where there is understanding, support, and encouragement and *relationships* in which they can share their fears or worries. If this is not done so much by well-chosen words (often difficult to find), then it can be manifested by the gift of "presence" at least. How men do this—with whom, in what ways, what words are chosen—is really not as important as the actual doing.

11. A man may need help in communicating issues or concerns with his own family members (especially children). Caregivers should always be sensitive to the dynamics not only of the male patient, but also as they affect and relate to those closest family members. Be sensitive to family tensions, to women who may be "speaking for" the man, and to such surrounding issues as support systems, communication styles, and possible life-changes.

12. Refer men to a support group, if this is relevant to the situation. Hearing other men whom he has gained respect for, sharing about the same type of problems or situations, can be extremely helpful. Some researchers have found that men work best in closed groups with separate subjects planned for each session.

13. Ultimately, all men and women need to learn the "hard lesson" that is one of the greatest secrets of wisdom and inner peace—only suffering and pain can truly bring one to consciousness. Most people simply do not naturally move into deeper realms of consciousness, self-awareness or inner peace without having "walked through the fire" first. Sickness (and the subsequent confrontation with one's "mortality") can be a "necessary wound" for a man, opening the doorway to a deeper place of inner consciousness and wisdom.

14. More and more medical studies and research are proving an age-old truth known by spiritual people—a healthy pursuit of spirituality improves a person's health, not just mentally but physically. One psychiatrist and author called the relationship between religion and health "The Neglected Factor," and contends that churchgoers of all income levels (and people who pray regularly) are healthier, live longer, recover more quickly, and even have better sex and happier marriages than people who do not go to church.

There is a strong lesson here for health care providers and caregivers. Remind the male patient that there is a Power greater than him in this world, and that prayer and worship can be an empowering force to recover more quickly, find personal satisfaction, and develop a positive attitude toward life. (This is not even counting the benefits in the next life!)

15. Always lead men to spirituality and God gently, without forcing them. In whatever fashion a man may conceive his "higher Power," be open and prepared to lead him to that "divine place" where only God can touch one's deepest hurts.

CONCLUSION

There may be many medical needs and personal issues which arise when dealing with a male patient. But perhaps those entrusted with the care of male patients can best assist them by gently helping them to peel away timeworn, encrusted layers of male inculturation, and to peer behind the resolute masks of false bravado and "strength." What lies beneath the surface of a man, that which sickness and medical problems so unwillingly extract—fear, concern, loss of control, weakness—need not necessarily be enemies. They can be "friends" pointing to deeper wisdom.

Ultimately, caregivers' best "work" may be helping facilitate in men the willingness to adapt their self-images, to learn the "dark" and different language and wisdom of the inner world. The health care process for men is thus not just about coping successfully with the immediate medical problems or exigencies. It can also be the first step of a journey into the most precious commodity a man has in this world—himself. It may be an uncomfortable and unfamiliar journey, but one that leads to a place of new confidence, healthier living, and renewed wisdom for successful living.

> Those things that hurt, instruct.
> Benjamin Franklin

REFERENCES

1. D. Byrd, *Rise and Walk,* Harper Paperbacks, New York, 1993.
2. C. Jung, *Stages of Life,* Modern Man in Search of a Soul, Harvest House, New York, 1933.
3. J. Gray, *Men are from Mars, Women are From Venus,* HarperCollins, New York, 1992.
4. J. Sanford, *The Kingdom Within,* Paulist Press, Mahwah, New Jersey, pp. 33-34, 1970.
5. T. Golden, *Gender and Cultural Differences in Grief,* 10400 Connecticut Ave., Suite 514, Kensington, Maryland, 20895, 1994.
6. W. Frey, *Crying: The Mystery of Tears,* Winston Press, 1985.
7. Rosenblatt, Walsh, and Jackson, *Grief in Cross-Cultural Perspectives,* 1976.
8. C. Gorman, Sizing Up the Sexes, *Time Magazine,* January 20, 1992.
9. *Newsweek Magazine,* Gray Matters, March 27, 1995.

10. Reverend Miller, Creative Action and Ritual, in *Grief Quest*, Abbey Press, St. Meinrad, Indiana, pp. 143-168, 1995.
11. D. Levinson, *Seasons of a Man's Life*, Ballantine Books, 1986.
12. J. Robertson, *Death of a Hero, Birth of the Soul*, Tzedakah Publishing, Sacramento, California, 1995.
13. C. Jung, *Memories, Dreams, Reflections*, Vintage Books, New York, 1965.

CHAPTER 11

The Female Patient

Reverend Karrie Oertli

I write this chapter as a unique person, a middle-class, white, hetero-sexual, divorced, remarried female who is a stepmother to six young men and women, an ordained Christian minister, a chaplain, a pastoral educator, and a friend. As I am unique in my offering, so are the many females who account for more than half of the world's population. Concurrently, the care of the female patient is as varied and unique as each woman to whom care is offered. Of primary importance in providing health care and in seeking to support the spirituality of these wondrous women is the ability of the health care provider to render three services: listening to the women, assessing the women, and caring for the women.

LISTENING TO WOMEN

Of the support which can be provided to women, listening to women is of utmost importance in health and spiritual care. Unfortunately, the art of providing an open ear and heart to those who have information to share can be absent in the busy world of health care. By listening—preparing ourselves to be ready to hear, looking for signals, clues and nuances, and responding with openness and understanding—we can hear more than words. By remaining available to that which is spoken and unspoken, we can know how to offer physical and spiritual care to those whom we encounter.

We know too well the often repeated stories of how health care providers have disregarded or disbelieved the information that female patients have recounted about their own bodies, because the information did not necessarily fit the traditional medical model. Not long ago, pre-menstrual syndrome (PMS) was thought to be "all in a woman's head." Now we know that women with PMS can benefit from medical intervention. When women insist long enough, their words are sometimes considered and acted upon and, very often, they are found to be correct. Even in these more enlightened days, women are often disbelieved or disregarded until the medical model is changed.

In the same way, women have experienced a silencing of their spirituality over the years, since, for many women, their feelings about it did not fit the patriarchal model presented by conventional faith traditions. Some women, in finding the standard spiritual models lacking, have chosen to seek different avenues for spirituality. For example, some women have found the freedom to conceive of the divine with feminine pronouns. Others, being unaware of different possibilities, have chosen to subvert their own expression to that of the traditional model.

This disregard for women's voices and the need for changing models are at the heart of the writing and research which have magnified the reality that women have not always been believed and, thus, have not always been heard. Voices stifled over generations have begun to speak and are speaking in many different ways. Some speak the only way they know: in stories, myths, and fantasy. Some speak with strident voices, so strong and so loud after years of being muffled that they are difficult to hear, calling forth the anger that comes after being silenced for so long. Some speak with this fury, and some speak with the fear that surrounds it. Some speak confidently, having been heard and finding their own voices. As these voices have been heard, more physicians and pastoral caregivers are making changes in the way they offer care. The medical model is changing as women are not only speaking their minds, thoughts, and opinions, but also being heard. The spiritual model is also changing as women speak and act and live.

Women must first know that their voices can be heard, even if they do not recognize their voice or cannot speak because of the way in which they have kept quiet or been kept quiet over the years. For some women, even being able to access the silenced parts of themselves is a task that some cannot imagine beginning.

Betty, an older woman who never had to take responsibility for her health care, came to the hospital because she awoke one night gasping for breath. For the forty-seven years that she and her husband had been married, her spouse had spoken with her doctor about every health care decision that affected her body. She had quietly followed his decisions, because she was loyally following the tradition of her family and her husband's faith tradition by acceding to his direction. Her husband died of a heart attack three years before this personal health experience, and she was diagnosed with severe cardiac dysfunction which her cardiologist discovered after two days of inpatient testing and monitoring. The nurse, social worker, chaplain, and the new cardiologist assigned to her case met to discuss the situation since the patient declined any input into decisions about her health care. She seemed to have no regard for her health, yet she called for an ambulance and came to the hospital for help. At the very least, these actions spoke that she did not want to die.

With Betty, the question is not, "Why doesn't she take responsibility for her own health?" but rather "How can she speak with words she has not used in many years or never at all?" After so much time in silence, she needed new tools and new words to be able to express herself more clearly. As the time for her discharge from the hospital loomed on the horizon, she was faced with the reality that she might have to spend her remaining years in a nursing home. Her tears began, and a stream of jumbled, confused words came forth. She felt afraid and puzzled. Soon she was with the chaplain, and long periods of silence ensued. In time she was able to say that she felt angry deep within herself for the freedoms of her voice which she sacrificed long ago. She feared she would have to forsake all she had held dear to make such a monumental change. Slowly, however, she was able to participate in the direction she wanted her health care to go, and she moved to rehabilitation with a plan for recovery and living independently. She chose to remain connected with her traditional faith group, and she chose to remain vocal about her health care choices.

What Betty had been unable to say with her mouth she said with her body. Her heart was broken, and she knew she needed help. She came to the hospital to find healing, and her own words coupled with the responsiveness of her health care team provided healing for her spirit as the medical therapies and interventions provided by her health care team provided healing for her body. With a group of people waiting long enough to hear her story, as metaphorical as it was, and in that way hearing her to speech,[1] she began to find new strength to care for her body as she found words for a voice that had been quiet for so many years.

Seeing the body as a metaphor in health care and spirituality can bring a new understanding to the care of this woman and the thousands like her who seek care each year. Because of the pressure some women

---

[1] See [1]. This book is a wonderful tool to understand the process of "hearing to speech," that is, empowering women to come to and speak their present and innate knowledge of themselves by giving support and encouragement through listening and hearing.

have felt to act according to societal and religious rules and to keep silent, some women learned to speak through their bodies instead of or in addition to speaking with their mouths. Just as a woman may cross her arms over her breasts to deliver a message in body language, so also may a disease process in her heart, kidneys, uterus, or skin speak of other realities about pain and lack of health. This was the case with Betty: her heart was not working well physically, but this was only one part of her health problem. That her heart has lost its spiritual and emotional path in the journey of life is another part, the part which listening with ears and eyes can discover.

Central to a vibrant and healthy person's spirituality is the power of the communication between a human and the essence of what that person believes to be holy. However a person may view the divine— whether through traditional models of major world religions or through less popular, less traditional models—the way that she can communicate that belief and draw upon it as a resource can lead to greater health and healing. Bringing a woman's voice to the center of health care, not only to hear but also to find that which is basic to her beliefs about herself and her health, can give the health care worker tools with which to care for her.

ASSESSING WOMEN

So how can a health care professional make sure she or he is really listening to women? When might a health care professional know that he or she needs to listen more closely to what some women may have to say? Knowing that a woman may speak through her body, the health care professional has a first insight to use. For what else can we look?

Medical history is not simply the purview of physicians and nurses. A person's medical history can be telling and insightful for the patient's spiritual care as well. Someone who has had a long history of chronic pain may have developed coping mechanisms that are unhelpful and that contribute to a sense of helplessness and disease and a mind set of hopelessness. Someone who is suddenly diagnosed with a disease unique in her family history may have more to tell.

Knowing a patient's spiritual history and understanding the way her family system works provide valuable keys in assessing the support a woman needs so that she may find wholeness and health. How many of us have seen women come to the hospital with vague yet valid symptoms only to find that, just a year ago, those women had experienced the deaths of parents, partners, or children? Perhaps a woman has also experienced a crisis of faith, a change in the way that she communicates with God, or the way she views a divine being. Asking a woman about the events of the last year or two of her physical, emotional, and spiritual life can often yield insights that otherwise would be lost and ignored.

I once met a woman who came to the hospital for tests and began to decline quickly. Her deterioration baffled all of us on her health care team: she had seemed to be in good health, but she was beginning to show signs of a severe disease process and no tests verified the disease. Through conversation with her over the course of several days, I found that many women in her family had died around a certain age and she was about to reach that age. As we began to work together around that issue, she experienced the grief of her family's history and her fear of repeating it. She confessed her struggle with her Christian faith over the past few months: she had found it more and more difficult to communicate with God, in the same way her family always had communicated with God. She had spent a great deal of time in therapy dealing with her relationship with her overpowering father who had died a few years before. As she had come to see her own power in a different way, she had difficulty viewing God through her family's traditional, patriarchal lenses. Even in her short hospital stay, she began to improve as she commenced a pattern of grief work that allowed her to mourn, and as she opened herself to the possibility of modeling God in unique and healthy ways. The second important part of this intervention was calling a care conference with her health care team, when we encouraged the patient to continue psychotherapy along with the home health care she would receive.

The health care team meeting is essential in the changing world of medicine and medical care. Though the thought of daily rounds on each patient is naïve, particularly in these days of shortened lengths of stay and increased outpatient care, the ability of any team member to call together a group of professionals for the benefit of the patient's health is essential. The sharing of information between professionals means that the patient can be understood in all aspects of her being.

CARING FOR WOMEN

When women are heard, they can know healing. Much of this healing may come in unusual and different ways, aided by pharmacology and therapy and under girded by a holistic sense of a woman as a human being with a mind, a body, and a spirit.

Making the connection between what happens in the head and what happens in the body is an old truth that is being rediscovered these days.[2] Once again, we are moving away from the dismissive assumptions that "it's all in her head" to a new understanding that our emotional and spiritual thoughts and beliefs have a physical effect upon our wellness.

Published studies detail the connection between spiritual wellness and healing [2]. These works indicate that folks who have a spiritual connection—some activity such as church/synagogue/mosque attendance or prayer—are healthier, fight off sickness more effectively, and are likely to recover more quickly after receiving a health care intervention. Work is being done to incorporate this sense of spiritual power into the healing process of people in different settings, including inpatient hospitals and mental health facilities.

Spiritual wellness contributes to physical wellness. Tending to a patient's spiritual wellness is essential to the entire healing process. Providing space for professionals certified to deal with spiritual and religious issues creates a good foundation for the care of women. Well-intentioned but inadequately trained folks attempting to offer spiritual support can be as damaging to a person's health as can be improper drug therapy or poor surgery. The employment of professionally trained, certified chaplains is essential if true health care is to be provided.

One last note to this chapter: please understand the biases presented herein, that of the white, heterosexual, Christian, middle-class, female perspective. Greater understanding and pastoral care for women can be given by accessing the myriad literature available about cultural differences that exist in our world.

REFERENCES

1. N. Morton, *The Journey Is Home,* Beacon Press, Boston, 1985.
2. H. Benson and M. Stark, *Timeless Healing: The Power and Biology of Belief,* Scribner, New York, 1996.

SUGGESTED READING

Balenky, Mary Field, Blythe McVicker Clinchy, and Nancy Rule Goldberger (eds.), *Women's Ways of Knowing,* 10th anniversary edition, Basic Books, New York, 1997.

[2]See the ever-growing field of the mind-body-spirit connection. Among the many authors who present work in this field are Andrew Weil, Bill Moyers, Larry Dossey, Joan Borysenko, Herbert Benson, and Caroline Myss, to name but a few.

Gilligan, Carol, *In A Different Voice: Psychological Theory and Women's Development* (reissued edition), Harvard University Press, Cambridge, Massachusetts, 1993.

Glaz, Maxine and Jeanne Stevenson Moessner (eds.), *Women in Travail and Transition: A New Pastoral Care,* Fortress Press, New York, 1991.

Goldberger, Nancy Rule, Jill Mattuck Tarule, and Blythe McVicker Clincy (eds.), *Knowledge, Difference, and Power: Essays Inspired by Women's Ways of Knowing,* Basic Books, New York, 1996.

Sue, David and Debra Sue, *Counseling the Culturally Different: Theory and Practice,* John Wiley & Sons, New York, 1990.

CHAPTER 12

The Gay-Lesbian-Bisexual-Transgendered Patient

Reverend Sue Jelinek

> By the rivers of Babylon we sat and wept,
> remembering Zion.
> On the poplars of that land we hung our harps;
> there our captors asked of us
> the lyrics of our sons and daughters,
> and urged us to be joyous:
> "Sing for us one of the songs of Zion!"
> they said.
> How could we sing a song of God
> while in a foreign land?
>
> (Psalm 137, verses 1-4)

At a hospital where I was previously employed as a staff chaplain, I stopped to make a note in a patient's chart. There, in the "patient history" section, was supposed to be the physician's dictation concerning the patient's past medical history and social supports. What I found was a long narrative concerning the person's sexual orientation. The physician included moral judgments about his sexual orientation and his illnesses, as well as comments about the person's partner. It was anything but a past medical history and identification of social supports. If it is true for most (if not all) people that navigating the health care system leaves them feeling to some degree anxious, separated, fearful, isolated, and hesitant just by the nature and structure of the system; then these feelings are magnified and multiplied when a lesbian, gay male, bisexual, or transgendered (lesbigate[1]) person is the patient. The verses sung by the people of Israel in Psalm 137 during their time of captivity strike a cord with lesbigates, whom already feel alienated when going about their daily lives in the places where they work and live, let alone in the "alien" setting of health care.

Let me begin by offering two definitions of terms that I will be using throughout this chapter. The first term *homophobia* was created in 1972 by Dr. George Weinberg. Homophobia is defined as the fear of homosexuals and homosexuality [1]. As Leanne Tigert writes,

> Homophobia is a form of prejudice (meaning "prejudgment") and discrimination. When people prejudge others, they hold certain attitudes, opinions, and beliefs about others without adequate knowledge. When these attitudes, opinions, and beliefs become actualized into behavior, the result is discrimination [2, p. 5].

Heterosexism is a term which means the system of belief in which heterosexuality is presumed to be the only acceptable life orientation [3]. Since heterosexuality is the assumed norm as the starting point in most health care settings, we would do well to be aware of the pitfalls this brings to bear concerning lesbigate persons. As Blumenfeld and Raymond suggest,

> Because this norm is so pervasive, heterosexism is difficult to detect. . . . Heterosexism forces lesbians, gays, (transgendered) and bisexuals to struggle constantly against their own invisibility. . . . Heterosexism is discrimination by neglect, omission, and/or distortion, whereas often its more active partner—homophobia—is discrimination by intent and design [3, pp. 244-245].

We know that a person's psychological health and well-being as well as their spirituality are tremendously influenced by one's ability to integrate their sexuality and sexual orientation, as well as their ability to be open and honest about who they are and who they love (in other words, one's ability to be "out"). Keeping secrets, whether to protect one's job, family, safety, professional standing, or for fear of losing one's health care provider is harmful. The internalizing of homophobic attitudes causes significant psychological and spiritual harm. The harmful effects of internalized homophobic attitudes touch not only lesbian, gay, and bisexual persons but heterosexuals as well [2, pp. xxiii-xxiv].

There are many unique issues facing the lesbigate patient and his/her health care provider. First, the basic social support systems

---

[1]The term "Lesbigate" is a composite word referring to lesbian, bisexual, gay, and transgendered individuals. It was originated by Dr. Rev. Mel White in an address to the National P-Flag (Parents, Families and Friends of Lesbians and Gays) Convention, Indianapolis, Indiana, October 1995.

assumed for heterosexuals may not be necessarily so for the lesbigate patient. Social isolation and therefore spiritual isolation are very real concerns. To assume, for instance, that the lesbigate person will have their biological family as support may be a mistake. Many biological families are not supportive of the lesbigate person, either by conscious decision or because of lack of information, since they may not know of the loved one's sexual orientation. Because of this, the lesbigate person may instead have "chosen family" or "family of choice" to surround them. Both the health care provider and health care institution need to be aware and sensitive to this.

Second, lesbigate persons are in a system that assumes heterosexist privilege. Therefore, the forced choice is between safety and security or support and community (not being "out"/honest about who they are at a critical time reinforces the lie). Added to this is the heterosexist benefit of the legal protection, privilege, and rights that come with marriage. The lesbian, gay, and possibly bisexual person (depending on whether or not their partner is of the opposite or same gender) is afforded no legal recognition or privilege by virtue of "marriage." That is to say a legally recognized process by which the state and federal governments automatically grant the person's partner or spouse certain legal rights. One of the ways in which this plays out is by automatic assumption that the spouse of a heterosexual couple will have visitation rights if their husband/wife is in critical care or other restricted visiting areas. In many cases, the only way a gay/lesbian/ bisexual partner of the same gender gets access is by showing legal documents that indicate the partner would be "allowed" to visit. Once again, the partner of the patient is forced to decide whether the risks outweigh the benefits in coming out to the staff.

The psychological split that this can cause for the lesbian, gay, or bisexual person and their partner is damaging. Because so much of American society functions in dualistic value judgment thinking, this leaves the lesbigate person dealing with shame and guilt. As Leanne Tigert argues,

> The psychological split into good and bad can easily collude with the theological split of dualism. In a dualistic theological construct, everything is divided into good/bad, heaven/earth, spirit/body, spirituality/sexuality, male/female, heterosexual/homosexual. Inevitably, the gay/lesbian/bisexual person becomes aligned with the "bad" object, which is somehow juxtaposed to all that which is theologically and psychologically "good." The act of aligning and being aligned with bad, earth, body, sexuality, etc., contributes to the experience of isolation both socially and individually. In other words, persons who fit this half of the dualistic equation, for whatever

reason, find themselves outside of relationship with the larger community . . . and relationships become polarized rather than integrated [2, p. 72].

As long as lesbigate persons are placed in the position of carrying the sexual shame for the institution (the theological term for this is scapegoating), then it is virtually impossible for their voices and therefore their concerns to be heard. The lesbigate person is invisible in the system and therefore has no authority or power. Scapegoats are objectified and not taken seriously. Shame that is projected also objectifies. As the shame is internalized, it prevents persons (lesbigate and straight) from speaking and hearing one another as valued individuals [2, p. 138]. As one of my buttons that I wear says, "No one is free when others are oppressed."

Visiting a lesbigate patient, the chaplain can elicit a variety of responses. The fear, stigma, anger, anxiety, guilt, shame, or depression that is felt may be great. If the person has had a negative experience with the formal religious community, I may become the scapegoat, carrying the sins of organized religion out the door with me into the wilderness.

Because there are so few individual communities of faith, let alone religions that are intentionally welcoming and affirming, many lesbigate persons have a spirituality that includes a God from whom they are feeling cut off, disconnected, judged, condemned, or abandoned. Because one of the ways we gather ideas about God, or our Higher Power, is through particular experiences with the communities and people around us, it is easy to understand how one's spirituality is formed, shaped, and influenced by our surroundings and past history. Therefore, it is particularly important that the interdisciplinary team who cares for the lesbigate person be as professional, open, and non-judgmental as possible. The type of hospitality (which is the same root from which the word hospital derives) which is offered is critical.

The chaplain on the team may have a very particular task as he or she is the official "representative" of God. One of the ways I try to model openness and support is by offering self disclosure when it seems appropriate. If I am lucky enough to know that a person is lesbigate by their own disclosure, I will often in the course of the conversation share the pronoun "we" in terms of me and my own partner. I also wear something with the rainbow symbol on it, which has long been the gay and lesbian code language for another who is "family," or at least "straight but not narrow."

I often find myself acknowledging and apologizing on behalf of organized religion for the ways in which we have mistreated, abused, and scapegoated lesbigates, often making them seem less than human. There is much we need to be concerned about in our listening, assessing, and caring for the lesbian, bisexual, gay, and transgendered person. It is important that all patients feel their concerns are being heard and taken seriously.

Suggestions for ways we as health care providers might increase our own awareness of the special needs and issues of lesbigate persons include: 1) Sensitivity/Diversity training for the staff—it could be worked in during part of the annual in-house mandatory education, or special teaching modules designed for meeting clinical ladder requirements; 2) Take a look at your policies and procedures for the rules regarding visitation of patients. How is the concept of "family" defined? Who has access to restricted units? How are the questions asked in admitting that concern the patient's partner/life partner/significant other or spousal equivalent? How does the non-discrimination clause concerning medical treatment of the patient read? In the list of things mentioned (e.g., race, gender, national origin, income, etc.) is sexual orientation mentioned?; 3) Take a look at how your policy and procedures are designed for the employees. How is "family" defined? How does your family medical leave policy read? How does your non-discrimination in hiring clause read? Does your bereavement policy and insurance coverage include the same sex partner of the employee? I would suggest there is a direct correlation between the attitude of care the lesbigate patient receives and the attitude of care toward the lesbigate employee by the institution.

Finally, I share with you two very personal stories. First, a story concerning me and my partner.

> At the time of this writing, I have been the Director of Pastoral Care at La Porte Hospital for five years. Three years ago in July 1994, my partner (who's name is also Sue) had an increasingly severe allergic reaction over the long fourth of July weekend. We were in the hospital emergency room (the same hospital where I work as the only full-time chaplain) every day from July 1-3. Finally on the third, she was admitted, because her throat had started swelling shut. From the admitting process on, we had to make decisions about how "out" to be. We did tell the admitting clerk that I was her partner and would be the "contact person," should they need someone. There was no way to list me on the face sheet as "partner" or "significant other." I was listed as "friend" and referred to as such while in the emergency room, even though we were up front about the importance of the relationship, and the staff as a whole knew who I was and called me by name.
>
> Once on the floor, with each change of shift, we once again had to decide how much to say, if Sue's nurse for that shift didn't already

know us (this is a small community of about 20,000). On more than one occasion, we needed to explain our relationship to staff who couldn't quite figure out why I was coming back in the evening with my casual clothes on to spend time with Sue. Our family doctor was well aware of our relationship and was very good about including me in the information loop when needed. The kicker came when one of the consulting physicians in asking about support once she got home, mentioned something about Sue's "husband."

It also happened that during the course of her hospital stay, there was a death in Sue's immediate family. The funeral happened to be scheduled the evening of the first day she was admitted. The attending physician would not authorize a few hours pass for her to leave and attend the funeral, for fear that her throat would swell shut, she was not yet stable. Jeanette and Dorothy, a lesbian couple who are dear friends of ours (who have been together 11 years), happened to be visiting from out of town at the time. They immediately suggested that they stay with Sue at the hospital, while Joe and Dave, also dear friends of ours (who have been together 19 years) who live in town, came and picked me up and went with me to the funeral. After the funeral was over, Joe, Dave and I came back to check in on Sue and our other "family of choice." Since it was an evening memorial service, we returned to the hospital after the front doors were locked and had to enter through the emergency department. After we said hello to everyone (Joe also works at the hospital—17 years), for security procedures we had to explain who we were going to see and why. Luckily I had already arranged with our family doctor to allow Jeanette and Dorothy to stay past visiting hours if necessary until we returned.

The second story involves two of our friends and family of choice mentioned above, Joe and Dave. Six months after Sue's and my experience, Joe was involved in a serious car accident on his way back into La Porte. He was brought to the hospital. Once again, Dave had to explain the relationship, so that he could get back to see Joe, since Dave would not automatically be listed as "immediate family." Once Joe was up on the floor (a different floor than Sue), he and Dave also had to explain to the staff why Dave was there so frequently, as well as his coming to visit when he finished work, which was after visiting hours. So once again, the Emergency Department went through another educational process, as the definition of family was broadened.

As I reflected on these two experiences, I realized all the explaining we had to do as people who "know" the system and are "known" well by those in the system. What must it be like for those who come to us who are not "known" and do not "know" the system?

If the goal of health care is the health and well-being of the individual as well as the community, then we will work with and care for those different from ourselves. Our challenge, task, and goal in our listening, assessing, and caring is to "work and struggle together with those whom we define as different from ourselves," to create "patterns for relating across our human differences as equals; we do not have to become like each other in order to work together for a future we will all share" [4, 5].

REFERENCES

1. G. Weinberg, *Society and the Healthy Homosexual*, St. Martin's Press, New York, 1972.
2. L. McCall, Tigert, *Coming Out While Staying In*, United Church Press, Cleveland, Ohio, 1996.
3. W. Blumenfeld and D. Raymond, *Looking at Gay and Lesbian Life*, Beacon Press, Boston, p. 244, 1989.
4. A. Lorde, *Sister Outsider: Essays and Speeches*, Crossing, Trumansburg, New York, 1984.
5. A. Lorde, There Is No Hierarchy of Oppressions, as cited in G. D. Comstock, *Gay Theology without Apology*, p. 109, The Pilgrim Press, Cleveland, Ohio, 1992.

SECTION 4:

Health Care and Spirituality: Patient Perspectives

Introduction

Reverend Richard Gilbert

Thus far we have looked at the wider stroke of the brush of health care and its interplay with spiritual and pastoral matters. Through this brush stroke we have been looking at others as they look at the patient, and then some general statements about "people types" and what these types, both ethnic and gender, mean for the person who enters the health care system.

Now we turn to specific patient situations and how life events, including dying and death, bring into focus the experience of spirituality in health care. We ask what the "system" must be and do to more effectively integrate spiritual matters and more intentionally offer "certified" chaplains who specialize in pastoral care in the health care setting.

The first group of chapters include the medical patient, the chronically ill patient, the gay-lesbian-bisexual-transgendered patient, and the HIV-AIDS patient, with the section drawn together around the poem *Variance*. Chaplain Laurel Burton, Chicago, and Past President, The Association of Professional Chaplains (The College of Chaplains) speaks powerfully and prophetically of the pastoral presence in the general medical patient, the person struggling not only against disease, pain, and emotional and sometimes social isolation, but often against the system that places a different set of values or priorities ahead of those of the patient, and yet still seeks something called dignity, purpose, value, and meaning.

Chaplain John Vander Zee, Bloomington (Indiana) Hospital, a well recognized expert in the care of the chronically ill patient and a noteworthy contributor to professional chaplaincy, pulls us quickly into the soul and struggle of chronic illness. He points out how the system (and maybe, at least by perception, God) backs away from the chronically ill patient because it is easier and faster than moving closer.

Dr. Inge Corless is a nationally recognized leader in nursing and nursing education and has taken on the rights, needs, and care of the HIV-AIDS patients in ways that have shaken the foundation of many of our postures, programs, and procedures to draw us closer to the patient that others would push away. She has some sharp words (spoken in love for the patient) to say to the religious establishment.

We have a brief pause with the poem *Variance*, by Chaplain Denise Ryder, and then continue our focus on particular patient experiences. Rabbi Earl Grollman, who has brought us an essay from his larger work on Alzheimer's, helps us meet the patient as well as the larger sphere of concern, the needs of the family. Cathi Lammert, R.N., director of the national support group SHARE, addresses two aspects of childbirth. First she speaks of the "routine" obstetric patient. We then discuss the death of a child during pregnancy or at birth, not only in ways that express its impact on the parents and family but how it also impacts on the staff.

Chaplain Paul Bierlein, who has done pioneer work in developing state networking for chaplains and continuing education opportunities, brings us his insights concerning the trauma patient and the disruptive flavor of trauma for the patient. Chaplain John MacDougall, from the respected Hazelden Foundation, speaks forthrightly about conceptions and misconceptions related to the addicted patient and the place for spirituality in the journey to recovery.

Two chapters are offered for our view of the dying patient. Sr. Frances Dominica, the founder of Helen House (the first pediatric/adolescent hospice), discusses how dying impacts on a child and his or her family and also how the system can be as oppressive as the death sentence. Rev. Jon Nyberg, a board certified chaplain and formerly a hospice chaplain, now serves as a pastoral care minister in the parish. He addresses the concerns that surround the dying adult patient.

This section concludes with a rare look at the spiritual side of domestic violence and victimization, offered in the context of health care. The chapter is a joint effort by Sharon Gilbert, the executive director of The Caring Place, which provides intervention, advocacy, and education related to domestic violence, sexual assault, and date rape, and her husband, editor Richard Gilbert.

A third contribution by Chaplain Denise Ryder closes the book.

CHAPTER 13

The Medical Patient: Compassionate Listening and Spirit-Mind-Body Care of Medical Patients

Reverend Laurel Arthur Burton

> They shall come and sing aloud on the height of Zion, and they shall be radiant over the goodness of the Lord . . . their life shall become like a watered garden, and they shall never languish again.
>
> (Jeremiah 31)

THE NEED TO LISTEN TO MEDICAL PATIENTS

Too many of the medical patients I see are languishing. I can hear it in the words they speak. Their distress can also be determined from the way they use health care. Herb Benson, M.D. says "Anywhere from 60% to 90% of visits to doctors are in the mind-body, stress-related realm . . . traditional modes of therapy—pharmaceutical and surgical—don't work" [1]. Gallop Polls have consistently shown that more than 90 percent of Americans say they believe in God and more than 80 percent report that they pray on a regular basis. Another poll, this one conducted for *USA Weekend,* revealed that 79 percent of Americans say that spiritual faith can help people recover from illness, injury, or disease. This same poll indicated that 64 percent of those surveyed believed that physicians should pray with those patients who request it. However, studies of clinical psychologists suggest that health care professionals are not comfortable with the topic of spirituality or religion, let alone engaging in prayer with patients. This leads one to wonder just how well patients are being listened to by health care professionals.

In 1993, David Eisenberg, M.D. published an article in *The New England Journal of Medicine* claiming that $10.4 billion was spent out-of-pocket by Americans seeking alternative forms of health care [2]. Some have suggested that the reason so many Americans are willing to spend their own money on alternative medical care is because alternative practitioners take the time to listen.

Managed care has touched the lives of most Americans in some way. Pressures to decrease the cost of health care have led to a variety of new delivery forms—such as Health Maintenance Organizations, Point-of-Service plans, Physician Hospital Organizations, and more. The point of each is to cut the cost of health care, with the promise that quality will not diminish. While the ethical issues associated with the changes evoked by managed care continue to be debated, one thing is clear: more and more health professionals are being driven to treat more patients in a briefer time. At many HMOs, for instance, the amount of time scheduled for an appointment has shrunk from thirty minutes to fewer than seven minutes. Fewer and fewer health professionals can "afford" the time to simply listen to the patient.

However, listening is perhaps the chief tool of the chaplain's art. A spiritual teacher of mine once said, "To listen is to hear through all the noise and discover the quiet place where both pain and promise wait to speak their healing words." When people are not heard, when others do not listen to them or pay attention to their being, they are diminished. Yet, through being heard patients can experience their own sacredness and thus enter into a process of healing.

In the new health care system, healing is a powerful focus. Aging and chronicity do not lend themselves to cures, but physician practice and hospital intervention still focus on the physical dimensions of diagnosis and treatment, with little attention to listening and drawing out the sacredness of persons. Yet one physician, David Baughan, says "I consider health problems as dysfunctional relationships between biopsychosocial-spiritual systems, not as molecular abnormalities in skin-encapsulated organic chemistry stew-pots" [3]. Assessing and healing this dysfunction requires compassionate listening.

In this chapter, in the context of the emerging spirit-mind-body connection, we will examine a definition of compassionate listening and illustrate that definition through a case study.

A CALL FOR COMPASSIONATE LISTENING

The only light in the room came from the green-glow of the clock radio. My pager insisted that I return its call. "I'm sorry, Dr. Burton," said the nurse at the other end of the phone. "It's a new patient, Mrs. Holmes. (The names have been changed, obviously, to maintain confidentiality.) She's having a bad night and nothing seems to make a difference. You're the only one I could think of to call. Will you come and talk with her?" For the on-call chaplain, the answer is always "Sure! Be right there."

I dressed, knotted my tie, put on my lab coat, and headed to see Mrs. Holmes. She was located on the CCU, being monitored after a possible coronary episode. After a brief consultation with the nurse during which I learned that Mrs. Holmes had been anxious and agitated since her arrival, I entered Mrs. Holmes's room. She gave the OK to sit with her a while. She had no specific complaint other than her inability to sleep. A few minutes of conversation revealed that her husband had died less than a year ago. "I guess I'm just not used to sleeping by myself," she said. "Maybe that's why I can't sleep." I asked about her husband and she told me story after story, moist eyes sometimes giving away to either laughter or sobs. Her only child had died while still a child and Mrs. Holmes lived alone, now. Taking her hand, I observed that it sounded like she felt a little lonely and maybe was afraid. "Yes," she responded tearfully. "That's it exactly."

After a little time I asked if she considered herself a religious or spiritual person. "I used to go to church, but not since Frank died." Then I asked if she could describe a time or a place where she felt safe and secure. After a moment's thought Mrs. Holmes said, "That's easy, in my garden." She painted a beautiful picture of her garden with a profusion of roses and a winding path lined with impatiens. And there was a bench, just big enough for two, where she had sat with her husband on summer evenings. It was no surprise that, when I asked if she had a favorite hymn, it was "In the Garden." "What is it you especially like about that hymn," I asked. She answered, "I know it must sound silly, but there was a time when I felt more peaceful when I sang that song." "Would you like to sing it right now?" Mrs. Holmes looked at me skeptically. "Here?" I nodded and began to hum the tune then we sang the chorus together; then the verse and another chorus. I noticed that Mrs. Holmes had closed her eyes and that her breathing was becoming more regular and her physical agitation had quieted. Mrs. Holmes smiled. "It's almost like being in my own garden again, I feel so peaceful." We had been quiet for a while when Mrs. Holmes said, "I feel like I can sleep now. Thank you for coming. Will you come back?" I said I would. We prayed and I left.

COMPASSIONATE LISTENING DEFINED

Mrs. Holmes responded positively to compassionate listening. Compassionate listening is a process where we hear with the heart the story of the other, while withholding judgment and maintaining appropriate boundaries.

Hearing With the Heart

Compassionate listening does not begin with the medical patient. Rather, it begins with the heart space of the listener, the caregiver. Heart space is a way of describing the chaplain's ability to create a safe and hospitable space where both the chaplain and patient may find sufficient sanctuary for the patient's story to be told. Creating a safe and hospitable space requires that the chaplain have an awareness of her/his own issues and an ability to set them aside in order to be present to the patient. This is the primary reason that Clinical Pastoral Education is so important to the training of chaplains.

Heart space is always hospitable. Parker Palmer once described hospitality this way: "Most of us from experience know what real hospitality feels like. It means being received openly, warmly, freely, without the need to earn your keep or prove yourself. An inhospitable space is one in which we feel invisible—or visible but on trial. A hospitable space is alive with trust and good will, rooted in a sense of our common humanity. When we enter such a space we feel worthy, because our host assumes we are" [4].

Often medical patients have come to believe they are not worthy. Shame, blame, and self-doubt often accompany illness. The common phrase "I don't know what I've done to deserve this," is only one indicator that at some level patients believe that they are somehow the cause for their own suffering. So-called "new age guilt" places responsibility for illness squarely on the shoulders of the sufferer saying "you brought this on yourself." Shame is the unconscious acceptance of blame for one's illness, and the sense that one's internal flaws—responsible for the illness—are being exposed. Patients, blamed for something they could not control, now experience themselves alone, exposed, and vulnerable. Aaron Lazare, M.D. has written:

> In the medical setting, patients may experience physical or psychological limitations as defects, inadequacies, or shortcomings that assault various treasured images of the self: youth, beauty, strength,

stamina, dexterity, self-control, independence, and mental compe-
tence. This sense of inadequacy further jeopardizes social roles that
give meaning and self-respect to patients' lives . . ." [5, p. 147].

With shame there is less and less room for patients to share and explore
their feelings and experiences. Instead, they often come to live from a
position of "should" and often experience judgment from health care
professionals, family members, and religious authorities. I discovered,
for instance, that Mrs. Holmes had been told by some members of her
church that she "shouldn't feel sad about the death of her child because
the child was in heaven with God." She had stuffed her grief and anger
around her child's death for many years. When her husband died she
simply dropped out of the church, rather than stuff that grief and anger
too. Her physician had apparently not helped much, either. Though he
was an excellent cardiologist, he had suggested to Mrs. Holmes that she
was responsible for her heart condition because she hadn't been "taking
proper care of herself." All of these messages constricted the emotional
space around Mrs. Holmes much as plaque can constrict the space
though which blood flows in the human body.

I don't for a moment believe that anyone "deserves" to be sick. Nor
do I think that informing someone of how they should have dealt with
life better is helpful. I do believe, along with many others, that how
we respond to life events may contribute to disease states. Therefore,
healing hurtful ways of being—like shame—can promote greater well-
being. Stephen Sinatra, M.D. says,

> . . . just as atherosclerosis can close arteries and result in heart
> attack, I believe that closing your heart to love can have an equally
> devastating effect. I also believe there is a strong link between a
> closed, guarded heart and the driven unconscious struggle for love,
> which can also result in heart disease [6].

Hospitality is the experience of spaciousness. Instead of constricting
healing space, hearing with the heart actually creates and expands the
space for healing. The hospitable heart space of the chaplain provides
a sanctuary for the patient, where the oughts and shoulds may be
temporarily suspended and where the story may safely be told. It is
through the telling of the story that healing can begin. A patient once
said to me, "I don't quite know why or how, but this room always seems
larger, brighter and safer when you've been here." I think that is a
description of healing, heart space.

The Story of the Other

Stories are the way most people communicate. According to psychologist Dan McAdams, ". . . the story appears in every known human

culture. The story is a natural package for organizing many different kinds of information. Storytelling appears to be a fundamental way of expressing ourselves and our world to others" [7]. Medical patients tell a variety of stories. It is my experience that these stories fall into three types:

Stories about Power and Authority
Stories About Connection
Stories of Explanation

Stories about **power and authority** reveal a person's beliefs about who is "in charge." Psychologist David Kantor says that power is the freedom to decide what we want and the ability to get it [8]. When I listen for these stories I sometimes hear a voice that tells of the rage of feeling powerless in the face of devastating disease. Other times I hear about despair or bargaining in the face of deep sadness at anticipated losses.

One of the things that happens to many people when they get sick is a feeling of being less and less in control of life. Power often shifts to others: physicians, nurses, therapists, and, increasingly, to health plan administrators who may determine the patient's access to certain dimensions of treatment and care. Patients may lose their voice in terms of participating in their own care as others—and organizations—take over. Ironically, this loss of voice may make it difficult to hear stories about power and authority, and consequently caregivers must exercise particular sensitivity and care to listen for what stories patients are telling about their own sense of power and authority.

Another dimension of stories of power and authority is that of religion. When the voice is one of confidence, acceptance, faith in God or a Higher Power, the results can be profound. McAdams says, "Apparently, expectations that things will work out well in the end, support positive and life-affirming strategies for coping during difficult times" [7]. Research reported by Shelly Taylor indicates that "when we believe that life is relatively good and that we are in control of our fate to some degree, we tend to cope better with adversity and meet challenges with confidence and hope" [9].

Drawing on the work of Kenneth Parmagant from Bowling Green State University in Ohio, we find that religious people may tell us that they prefer to exercise their power and authority by *deferring* to God, *collaborating* with God, or by being *self-directing* [10]. Deferring patients are likely to turn-over their power to medical as well as religious authorities and may need someone to serve as their advocate and intercessor. Initially, collaborating patients may need encouragement in expressing their questions, opinions, and preferences in conversation with health care providers and family members. Though self-directing patients may appear counter dependent and even aggressive in their efforts to take care of themselves, they too need support during a medical crisis.

University of Chicago historian Martin Marty [11] has identified models of healing that fit nicely with Parmagant's research. Monergistic healing, which relates to the deferring way of problem solving, ascribes all agency to God. The self-directing folks are more likely to think of healing in terms of autogenesis, or self-created. Empathy and synergism relate to the collaborative model. Empathy has to do with suffering in/with and synergism describes a kind of cooperative action.

As she found her voice, Mrs. Holmes told stories that revealed a diminishment of personal power and tendency to defer her authority to others. If she were going to be healed, it would be from outside her (either by the actions of medical professionals or God). She experienced God as the source of power and potential healing, but God was distant and uninvolved. These themes were related to the stories she told about a diminished sense of connection.

Stories about **connection** tell of the degree to which one feels related to and loved by others, experiences safety in a situation, and the amount of intimacy experienced in a relationship or situation. Hearing these stories is important in assessing both the interpersonal supports of a patient, and the patient's relation to God or the universe. Albert Einstein is supposed to have said that the most important question a person can ask is this: "Is the universe a friendly place?" Stories of connection are answers to that question.

Many patients express this story in words of woundedness, cries of being cut-off, cast out, and isolated. Others find comfort and confidence in being cared for, supported, and accompanied. "As long as my wife is with me, I'll be OK," said one patient to me recently. Another, referring to more overtly religious images, said, "the way I figure it, God never abandoned Moses in the wilderness. He won't abandon me either."

Mrs. Holmes clearly did not feel safe nor well connected. The loss of her child, and more recently her husband, had left her with a deep sense of loneliness which was exacerbated by the disconnection she experienced from her church and volunteer work. It is here, particularly, that I began to wonder about the degree of depression Mrs. Holmes had been carrying.

There is evidence of some link between depression and heart disease. One study at the Montreal Heart Institute, found that of 222 patients who had suffered heart attacks, those who were also depressed were four times more likely to die in the next six months. A researcher at Washington University in St. Louis found that patients with newly diagnosed heart disease who were depressed were twice as likely to have a heart attack or require heart surgery in the next year. Mrs. Holmes' loneliness and lack of connection, as revealed in her stories, was significant information and crucial to her care. It is possible—even likely—that when people begin to experience diminution of religious faith and practice, they may believe in God, but not be able to build on that belief in a health-producing way. Hearing stories of connection can be a key to effective treatment.

Stories of **explanation** tell us what the patient believes an illness means and, beyond that, what life itself means to the patient. They reveal the degree to which things do or do not cohere for the patient. Associated with these stories of explanation are epistemologies or ways of explaining how we know what we know. In his book *The Heretical Imperative*, sociologist Peter Berger identifies three ways of knowing. The first is by deduction. The facts are given, from generation to generation, and we deduce our explanations from those "facts." The second method is by reduction. Berger says that if the motto of deduction is "Deus dixit" (God says), the motto of reduction is "Homo modernus dixit" (modern people say). Without reference to the past or anyone else, reductive knowing relies on the individual's experience alone. The third method is inductive and integrates both historical knowing and experiential knowing [12]. These epistemologies are usually evident when we listen to patient's stories of explanation.

Shelly Taylor's research with women diagnosed with breast cancer shows that most of the subjects developed a story about their disease and its origins, ranging from stress, heredity, diet, exposure to carcinogens, or even an accident. These stories are a way of giving meaning to the event, a way of making sense and gaining some control. Taylor says,

> By formulating personal stories about the past (cause of illness) and future (mastering the illness), these women were able to assimilate the cancer into their own personal myths. Furthermore, some of the woman were able to bolster their self-esteem, further enhancing their ability to cope with the disease, by concentrating on positive images [9].

In a subsequent visit to Mrs. Holmes, I asked her if she had a theory about her physical problems. She thought about it for a while and then said, "God broke my heart when he took my child, but I still had my dear husband. Then when God took him, it was too much." Mrs. Holmes explained her heart problems by referring to her belief that God was responsible for the death of the two people who were most important to her. This was consistent with her deferring use of power and her sense of disconnection. Stephen Sinatra, M.D. writes:

Hold Until: 11/27/2023
Requested For: Di Vito-Thomas, Pamela

Hold Shelf Request Slip Letter

11/15/2023

Please note: A specific item is specified in this request.

Item Barcode:

Requested For: Di Vito-Thomas, Pamela

Title:
Health care & spirituality : listening, assessing, caring /
By: Gilbert, Richard B.

ISBN: 9780895032508

Imprint: Amityville, N.Y. : Baywood Pub Co, ©2002.

Location: Second Carrel

Call
Numb
291.1'
G4658

Destination: Jessie C. Eury Library

Request Type: Patron physical item request

Although usually relegated to the realm of psychiatry, an increasing number of medical specialists in other fields—psychoneuroimmunologists (who examine the relationships among the nervous, endocrine and the immune systems) and cardiologists, to name a few— are studying what happens to the body when a vital connection between two human beings is threatened or even broken. What these medical specialists have in common is their increasing belief that the loss of love or a vital connection can contribute to disease, especially heart disease [6].

When patients, like Mrs. Holmes, feel more-or-less powerless and disconnected, and they tell stories that reveal their sense of being victims of the universe, the results can very well be deadly. However, when these stories can be shared, examined, and revised, healing can result.

The stories we have explored can be placed in a master grid under three generic headings: traditional, negotiating, and individualistic. I have written about these in much greater detail in *Models of Ministry*, published by The Alban Institute [13].

The traditional story teller relies on hierarchy to structure her/his life, avoids new information, and relies on the familiar and proven. The negotiating storyteller prefers a more democratic structure, welcomes new information, and integrates the familiar into changing ideas and ways of operating. The individualistic storyteller prefers a kind of anarchy, avoids tradition, and embraces what is new and personal. Table 1 shows what these master story types look like in chart form.

WHILE WITHOLDING JUDGMENT

When the listener is busy making judgments, s/he has ceased to regard the patient in a way that is compassionate. By "judgment" I mean forming opinions about the morality, wisdom, motivations, etc. that place the listener in a one-up position and the patient in a one-down position. The reason for withholding judgment is that we cannot truly hear the patient's voice when we are busy listening to our own.

Withholding judgment is a way of enacting love. Leonard Laskow, M.D., is former Chief of OB/GYN at the Community Hospital of the Monterey Peninsula in Carmel, California. He is the author of *Healing with Love: A Breakthrough Mind/Body Medical Program for Healing Yourself and Others*. Dr. Laskow says,

Unconditional love, for self as well as others, is a crucial element of [my] method. Love isn't just the stuff of poets and mystics. It is also a profound tool for facilitating the body's natural healing processes. I have done laboratory experiments which suggest that focused, loving

Table 1.

	Traditional Master Story	Negotiating Master Story	Individualistic Master Story
	Deferring	Collaborative	Self-Directing
Power and Authority	God is Source and Cause of all.	Things happen and together we'll work it out.	Things happen.
Connection	"I feel alienated from those I need."	"I feel powerless to connect with sources of healing."	"I feel disconnected from people and stories that give my life meaning."
Explanation	Meaning is based on what has come before.	Meaning is derived from a conversation between past and present.	Meaning is reduced to what the individual is experiencing right now.
	Healing comes only from outside me.	Healing is the result of empathic and synergistic relationships.	Healing comes strictly from within me.

energy can create results not dreamed possible . . . it may affect bacterial growth in test tubes, unwind and entwine DNA molecules, and inhibit the growth rate of tumor cells in tissue culture [14].

Usually, when a caregiver moves away from listening into judgment, s/he has touched on some personal, unresolved issue. Emmet Miller, M.D. says,

Notice the statement "Love thy enemies. . . ." Of course you need to love your enemies as well as your friends. They're also a part of you. Perhaps they're the part that you fear, that you don't like about yourself, that you refuse to accept in you, that you don't want any one to know about, including yourself. If you don't like what you see in others, take a good hard look at yourself. Mirrors don't lie. When you start to accept yourself the way you are, you'll allow others more freedom to be the way they are. When you focus on aspects of yourself that you don't like, you continually create those same aspects in others until they are resolved within you. Once you're able to allow other people to be who they are and realize that you are the "cause" of your relationship with them, then you can stop complaining about the fact that people are exactly the way they are. Then maybe you can start to communicate with them [15].

Maintaining Appropriate Boundaries

Boundaries are those invisible fences that define our space and personalities as well as the space and personalities of others. These fences can be high, wide, and rigid or they can be virtually nonexistent, allowing one person to "flow" into the other. It may sound romantic to imagine this merging of personalities, but it isn't very helpful when it comes to listening. Even at its best, merged boundaries can lead to a kind of mind reading where one person continually intuits the wants and desires of the other and seeks to fulfill them. Of course this kind of boundary-meshing leaves little room for individual distinctiveness. At the worst, merged boundaries are highly reactive, often judgmental, blaming, and angry.

Merged—as opposed to clear—boundaries may appear compassionate, but they seldom are. That is because unclear boundaries allow us to identify with patients in the sense that we take on—and sometimes take over—their pain. This is sympathy: when I can identify with your pain so that it is my pain, too, and now there is only our pain together.

Clear boundaries allow for individuals to be themselves in the presence of the other. One of the fathers of family therapy, Murray Bowen, M.D., described this as being "differentiated." Compassionate listening requires this kind of boundary. That is because empathy, rather than sympathy, is at the heart of compassionate listening. Empathy hears the pain, accurately reflects the pain without, and is able to stand beside the pain. But the pain still belongs to the sufferer. The caregiver—who may have her/his own pain—recognizes that the experience is unique and personal, but it is now shared and mirrored. Now pain can be explored, perhaps understood, even discharged, and the promise of healing has begun.

A Healing Realized

Let me finish telling you about my time with Mrs. Holmes. She remained in the hospital for several days and I went to see her on a regular basis. Each time we talked more about both her losses (there were others about which I had not known) and we began to explore her faith. We read favorite psalms and Bible stories. Mrs. Holmes had ceased all connection with the church when her husband died and had dropped-out of volunteer work. At one time, both of these activities had been important to her, so I asked her to tell me stories about what had been important and fulfilling about each. Then we explored the possibility of her returning to church and perhaps becoming involved in volunteer work once more. At the end of each of our talks we would "visit the garden" and visualize being in that peaceful and healing place. And I prayed not just with Mrs. Holmes, but for her as well.

The nursing staff said that Mrs. Holmes always seemed "better" after these talks. "More optimistic" or "more peaceful," they said. Her cardiologist, a man I knew only slightly, reported to me that he thought maybe our talks had done more for Mrs. Holmes than anything else. Finally, just before she was discharged, Mrs. Holmes gave me permission to contact the pastor of her church. He came to visit and a new relationship was begun. I didn't see her again for some time. Then one day in late spring, she was back; not as a patient, but as a visitor. It was good to see her and hear that she had, indeed, returned to her church and volunteer work. She had planted a garden, too. "I have my life back," she said.

Compassionate Listening and the Spirit-Mind-Body Connection

Why might compassionate listening with Mrs. Holmes have been effective? Emerging understandings in spirit-mind-body point to several possibilities.

1. Perhaps it was the singing, the restoration of the voice. Music therapy has long been associated with the reduction of stress. British physician Christine Page uses music and "toning" as part of her treatment for certain stress-related disorders. Michele George, who is associated with the C.G. Jung Foundation in Toronto, says

> The voice is an actual, organic instrument within the body which can reach to other human beings, which can reach out to the divine, which can reach out to nature. Your voice is there to be worked with and played with to give you a renewed sense of self, of vibration; an inner massage that can wake up all your systems. When you start sounding in your body, you're waking up all your systems: your immune system, your neurological systems, your circulation . . . all these systems are waking up [16].

2. It is likely that the images of the garden, evoked both by the music and the guided imagery meditations, were helpful as well. Health care professionals such as Emmett Miller, M.D. and Belleruth Naparstek, LISW have been pioneers in the use of guided imagery as an adjunct to treatment for a wide variety of medical problems. Dr. Miller writes:

> We have the capacity to be more than simply aware, we can operate at a still higher level; we can carefully choose the thoughts and images that will be the focus of awareness. This is the level we refer

to as the philosophical or spiritual level. Activities that reflect functioning at this level include prayer, meditation, contemplation, deep relaxation, and guided imagery [16].

3. The stress of unresolved losses suffered by Mrs. Holmes may have contributed to her heart problems, and the bereavement conversations may have helped reconcile some of the unfinished grieving. Stephen Sinatra, M.D. speaks of a "feeling connection" that exists between bonded people.

> When this connection (at least the physical connection) is broken, as in the case of a partner who dies after 50 years of marriage, the survivor may be left with a heart that is damaged, broken or closed. The sudden loss of a loved one is particularly hard on the survivor. Often the heart breaks very slowly, or the heart may even "shut down" completely, causing the wounded one to withdraw from contact with others [6].

Healing requires a telling—and retelling—of the wounded story and a reworking of that story until healthy connection returns.

4. Finally, as startling as it may seem to conventional scientists, the chaplain's prayers for and with Mrs. Holmes may have helped. A recent poll commissioned by *Time*/CNN found that 73 percent of Americans believe that praying for others can help cure their illness. Randolph Byrd, M.D. is a cardiologist in San Francisco. He took almost 400 patients in the coronary-care unit and randomly assigned them to two groups. One was prayed for the other was not. Neither group knew of the experiment. Those who were *not* prayed for (the control group) were five times more likely to need antibiotics and three times more likely to have complications.

5. Mrs. Holmes returned to a regular practice of her faith as well as to her work as a volunteer in the community. Positive beliefs and practices—whether maintained or restored—seem to make a difference in health and recovery. A Dartmouth study of 232 patients who had elective open heart surgery found that the patients who said they received no strength and comfort from religion were almost three times more likely to die within six months than those who said they receive at least some strength and comfort. There are other studies which show that folks who attend church on a regular basis cut their risk of dying from coronary-artery disease in half! The Dartmouth study discovered that the patients who felt strengthened and comforted by religious faith *and* who participated in social groups (such as the local church or volunteerism) were fourteen times more likely to be alive six months after surgery than those who found no strength and comfort and had no social involvement.

6. Finally, Mrs. Holmes began to feel loved and to give love again. A relatively new area of study is called psychoneuroimmunology or PNI. This mind-body approach focuses on the immune system. Dr. David McClelland was curious about the healing power of love, so he conducted an experiment. Having measured the levels of immunoglobulin A (IgA) in their saliva, he showed a group of medical students at Harvard a brief documentary about Mother Teresa. He measured the IgA levels afterwards as well. IgA is an antibody that fights viral infections such as colds and is one measure of immune function. IgA levels went up after seeing the documentary. McClelland went further. Discarding the film, he simply asked the students to think about two things: past moments when they felt deeply loved and cared for by someone else, and a time when they loved another person. The results were the same. McClelland said, ". . . all of us can learn . . . that being loving to people is really good for [our] health" [17]. This echoes Parcelsus who long ago wrote that "the main reason for healing is love."

Janet Quinn, Ph.D., RN, one of the foremost proponents of therapeutic touch, has defined healing as "the emergence of right relationship at or among any one or more levels of the human experience." Right relationship, she goes on to say, "at any level, body, mind or spirit, increases coherence of the whole; decreases chaos/disorder in the whole; maximizes energy available to the whole to do the work of the system; and maximizes freedom, choice and the capacity of the whole to creatively unfold" [18].

A CONCLUDING STORY

In the final analysis, compassionate listening and the healing it empowers is about grace. One time when I was on call at the hospital, it seemed that all hell had broken loose. I was on the run all day, through the evening, into the night. By early morning all I wanted to do was crawl into bed for a few desperately needed moments of sleep. As I headed for the on call room I realized I was near a patient I had been following for a couple of weeks. He had been in serious condition and fighting for his life when he came in. Now it looked as if he had turned a corner, but it was still touch and go. I wondered, "should I go past and check on him? It's a terrible hour. He's probably asleep. I shouldn't disturb him." Wrestling with my conscience I decided to stop by. If he was asleep then I would go on to bed. That would settle it. As I stood at the foot of his bed I saw his eyes were closed. Feeling some relief, I turned to go.

"Chaplain?" came his voice. "Yes, it's I," I answered. "I can't talk . . . too tired . . . thanks for coming . . . would you stay a while?" I said that I would and moved to the side of the bed. I was sure that I was as tired of the struggle as he must be. I dropped into the chair next to his bed for a few moments of grateful silence. He reached for my hand and we were both quiet. After some time—I may have even been asleep—the man said, "Would you sing to me?"

"Sure," I said wearily. "What song did you have in mind?" He replied that he wanted to hear "Amazing Grace." So softly, and only a little self-consciously, I began to sing. As I got to the words ". . . and grace will lead me home . . . ," I noticed that he was smiling. He was soon asleep.

I stayed a few minutes longer and then left to get some sleep myself. As I walked away from his room toward my own, I thought how grace, that unexplainable, always available, always bountiful gift of God's unfailing love, can lead us through pain, sleepless nights, fear, exhaustion, bad news, and good. Grace, that wonderful gift of God's endurance, can taken any journey and make it home.

That is the task of compassionate listening: to give voice to the pain of the journey and accompany that pain until it is transformed into the healing promise of home.

REFERENCES

1. H. Benson, *Timeless Healing,* Scribner, New York, 1996.
2. D. Eisenberg et al., Unconventional Medicine in the US—Prevalence, Costs and Patterns of Use, *The New England Journal of Medicine, 328*:4, p. 246, 1993.
3. D. Baughan, personal communication, 1990.
4. P. Palmer, source unknown.
5. A. Lazare, Shame and Humiliation in Medical Encounters, *Archives of Internal Medicine,* p. 147, September 1987.
6. S. Sinatra, Taken from plenary address at 8th International Conference on The Psychology of Health, Immunity and Disease (NICABM), December 13-14, 1996.
7. D. McAdams, *Stories We Live By: Personal Myths and the Making of the Self,* Guildford Press, New York, 1997.
8. D. Kantor and W. Lehr, *Inside the Family,* Jossey-Bass, San Francisco, 1975.
9. S. Taylor, Positive Illusions, Basic Books, New York, 1989.
10. K. Parmagant et al., Religion and the Problem Solving Process: 3 Styles of Coping, *Journal of the Society for the Scientific Study of Religion, 27,* pp. 90-104.
11. M. Marty, *Second Opinion,* Vol. 7.
12. P. Berger, *The Heretical Imperative,* Anchor, New York, 1979.
13. L. A. Burton, *Models of Ministry,* The Alban Institute, Washington, D.C., 1988.

14. L. Laskow, *Healing with Love: A Breakthrough Mind/Body Medical Program for Healing Yourself and Others,* Harper, 1992. This quote is copyrighted by Dr. Laskow, 1992 in lecture notes.
15. E. Miller, Taken from workshop notse: 8th International Conference on The Psychology of Health, Immunity and Disease (NICABM), December 13-14, 1996.
16. M. George, Taken from workshop notes: 8th International Conference on The Psychology of Health, Immunity and Disease (NICABM), December 13-14, 1996.
17. D. McClelland, source unknown.
18. J. Quinn, On Healing, Wholeness and the Haelan Effect, *Nursing and Healthcare, 10*:10, pp. 553-556.

CHAPTER 14

The Chronically Ill Patient

Reverend John Vander Zee

WHEN ILLNESS DOESN'T GO AWAY

A thirty-seven-year-old woman, let's call her Jane, is admitted to your hospital for a particularly severe exacerbation of a chronic bowel disease. To relieve Jane's symptoms, her internist puts her on I.V. pain medications, makes her nothing by mouth (NPO), and orders some diagnostic tests to determine the extent of the disease. Wanting to avoid surgery, her doctor opts for a conservative approach: maintain her on I.V. fluids and pain medication, allow the bowel to rest and heal itself. However, Jane complains that her current level of pain medication is not giving her relief, and so more is ordered. The nurses wonder whether Jane is more eager to get her "meds" than she is in getting a handle on her disease. Jane picks up on the unspoken judgment of the staff and further isolates herself, becoming depressed.

The social worker and the chaplain are called to help with Jane's emotional state. Jane's own pastor tries to call on her but always finds her in a drug induced sleep or in too much discomfort to talk. As Jane gradually improves and the pain subsides, the pain meds are moderated. After several days the crisis seems to have passed and Jane is gradually put on oral fluids and eventually real food again. The dietician is called to reinforce with the patient the importance of maintaining her highly restricted diet and encourages compliance. The social worker follows up to see about discharge planning needs. Finally Jane is discharged and the staff quietly celebrates.

Sound familiar? For those who work day to day in a hospital, this is quite commonplace. Whether it be Crohn's disease, obstructive lung disease, congestive heart failure, diabetes myelitis, or a host of other conditions, what they share in common is frequent and severe exacerbations and considerable suffering. We see people like Jane come into our hospitals month after month, year after year. Most seem to cope with their disease, the ubiquitous pain, the emotional pitfalls, some do not. Many are compliant with their treatment regimens, others are not. A few of them will be fortunate enough to live reasonably functional lives. The majority will enter their senior years requiring long-term care or labor intensive home care.

People who have been diagnosed with chronic illness are living much longer than they would have even fifty years ago. Widespread use of antibiotics, better immunology, and life-saving medical and surgical interventions now make it possible for people to survive acute opportunistic illnesses and infections.

As we begin a new century of progress, caring for the physical, psychosocial, and spiritual needs of the chronic sufferer will present one of the greatest tests for not only health care centers and research institutions, but faith communities as well. It is a situation fraught with irony: even as medical care advances, a growing number of people will continue to join the ranks of the chronically ill.

Combine this phenomenon with the demographics of an aging baby-boomer generation, and we have the makings of a huge health care quandary. The present generations will witness a profound change in the way health and illness are understood and managed. Future fears notwithstanding, it is the reality of present suffering that hopefully will move health providers and caregivers to accommodate the rising tide of chronic illness.

Up to now neither the medical nor the pastoral care community has risen to the occasion. The "biomedical model" of disease warfare still prominent in Western medicine perpetuates the myth of body/self dichotomy that separates disease from the human experience of illness. Still fixated with an acute-care-slanted medical system, and a "fix it" approach to psycho-social-spiritual care, we do not seem to know what it takes to faithfully minister to the holistic needs of the chronic sufferer.

There will be times, as with Jane, when the chronically ill person will surely test our pastoral skills, resourcefulness, and patience. How can we be steadfast in our ministry to them and help them see their value within the human community?

BEYOND RECOVERY TOWARD RENEWAL

In his wonderful book *At the Will of the Body*, Arthur Frank writes about his own experience with a heart attack and cancer [1]. He draws the helpful distinction between "disease talk" and "illness talk." Disease talk, which is what you hear from most health care professionals, reduces the body to physiology which is measured and organized. So they talk about body temperature, and the presence of infections, and components of the blood, and organisms and tumors and lesions. Disease happens when there's a breakdown. And disease talk refers to objective measurements about how things break down and what it will take to get things right again.

"Illness," on the other hand, says Frank, "is the experience of living through the disease." Illness begins where medicine leaves off, where I recognize that what is happening to my body is happening to my life. My life does consist of temperatures and circulation, but also of hopes and disappointments, joys and sorrows, none of which can be measured. . . . Illness talk is a story about moving from a perfectly comfortable body to one that forces me to ask: "What's happening to *me*? Not it, but *me*" [1, p. 13].

We in pastoral ministry are no less short-sighted than the health care industry in responding to the growing *chronicity* of illness. For the most part, we continue operating under the same kind of acute care mind set. We are prone to think of illness as a single acute crisis experience in which we are called to provide spiritual support, counsel, and encouragement. Like most other crises, we usually perceive illness as having a beginning, a turning point, and a conclusion. People either get better or they die, and for the most part we can handle that within our pastoral and theological grab-bag.

Chronic illness, however, has the power to alter all our predictable patterns of care and counsel. In the words of the Chrysler truck commercial, "the rules have changed." Cheri Register, from her own experience, writes,

> Chronic illness does not fit the popular notion of how illness proceeds: You get sick, you go to the doctor and get some medicine, and wait to get better. If there is no remedy for what ails you, you die. An illness that drags on for years, defying diagnosis, treatment, and/or cure is an intolerable anomaly [2, p. 3].

Eventually the chronic sufferer will come to the frightful realization "that illness has become your normal condition" [2, p. 3].

When the crisis of illness repeats itself in never-ending cycles of aggravation and torment, we the helpers struggle for a foothold from which to leverage some kind of support. Troublesome theological issues are raised when no end to suffering is in sight and healing is not on the horizon. Even when death might provide a merciful finale, it does not seem to come soon enough.

Troubling pastoral problems are raised. How does one deal with those constant fluctuations in the chronically ill person's condition, and when frequent flare-ups lead to yet another hospitalization? Enormous strains are placed upon our other pastoral responsibilities. Sometimes we even find ourselves identifying with the same feelings of helplessness and hopelessness that afflicts the sufferer. We develop behavioral patterns of avoidance and even begin to resent their demands on our time and energy.

It is important that we as pastoral care providers reexamine from time to time the way we understand and respond to illness. Each of us will be called upon to build on clinical skills that reach beyond crisis intervention and death bed ministry. As people live longer with progressively disabling forms of illness, we will be spending more time sitting with them in nursing homes, sub-acute care units, and other long-term care facilities. Persons who are chronically ill will look to us—pastors, chaplains, and counselors—to care for their spiritual needs over the long haul.

In his ground-breaking book *The Illness Narratives*, the psychiatrist Arthur Kleinman challenges his medical colleagues to be what he calls "empathetic witnesses" with chronically ill persons [3, p. 54]. That means talking with them about what it is like to be sick and helping them to somehow integrate this experience with the rest of their lives.

Kleinman's cogent expression has much to teach us. We ministers should also be empathetic witnesses with the chronically ill. Unlike the physician, however, the resources at our disposal will be the biblical witness, theological reflection, and a deliberate pastoral presence. Our task will be to minister to the suffering in their hopes, in their fears, in their strengths, and in their vulnerability.

Arthur Frank, after his illness, made some observations about the relationship between sickness, recovery, and renewal. Recovery is the ideal, but "recovery is worth only as much as what you learn about the life you are regaining." Then what about those for whom recovery is but a distant dream? How is it possible to find value in interminable illness? Frank maintains that "the answer seems to be in focusing less on recovery and more on *renewal*" [1].

For the chronically ill and their families, learning to live with a sickness that is not going to go away involves ongoing adjustment, adaptation, realignment of their values and beliefs. If illness affects individuals in their totality of body, mind, and spirit, all of these will be employed in the journey toward renewal.

The complex physical and emotional factors of chronic illness are well documented in the literature. What is less understood and researched are the intense spiritual struggles for which many chronic sufferers are ill-equipped.

It is fundamental to the human condition to look for meaning and purpose to prolonged in the midst of prolonged suffering. "Why is this happening to me? "Why must I endure this pain for so long?" "How can my life have purpose even while I suffer?" "Where and how can I see God working in my life?" Anyone who has experienced long-term illness— or witnessed it closely—has pondered such matters. The task of the pastoral caregiver is to hear their questions, sometimes to gently raise the questions for them, but always to walk with them on this perilous journey.

In *Ministry to Persons With Chronic Illnesses* I offer the paradigm of "negotiation" adapted from family systems theory as a way of engaging the person who is chronically ill in a healthy relationship [4, p. 97]. Negotiation is pertinent in three areas of engagement: in the physical environment, in human relations, and in religious discourse.

Theological negotiation is especially applicable to the role of the pastoral caregiver. The pastor can assist the chronic sufferer in integrating their illness experience with their spiritual journey. This may mean helping the person who is ill stake claim to their faith even when they are questioning long held beliefs. "The goal of pastoral care is to empower those who are chronically ill to live as fully and faithfully as possible within the constraints of their illness" [4, p. 97].

IMPLICATIONS FOR PASTORAL CARE

In caring for those who suffer long with chronic illness, the pastoral journey is treacherous and risky. The temptation is to scramble for familiar pastoral interventions and resort to trusted biblical truths. However, offering a faithful ministry that truly makes a difference involves a ministry of mutuality and a real presence.

First, I enter into a relationship of mutual trust with the patient. The path to a trusting pastoral relationship is found in my allowing the patient to tell his/her own personal story. This illness experience will become a dominant factor in the shaping of his/her narrative. Helping the patient explore the rich meaning of his/her experience of illness is a demanding but essential function of pastoral care. The process of "narrative pastoral care"—listening to the sufferer's story—creates a "hospitable place" (Nouwen) for the hurtful experience to be accepted and integrated into the self.

Increasingly, we will encounter people who have been sick for so long that they will have a hard time disassociating themselves from their illness. They will be tempted to see themselves as part and parcel of their malady. They will have a tough time imagining what it means to have an existence that is not defined by their pain. The pastoral challenge is to help the person who is ill reflect upon what it means to be an image-bearer of God, wounded as they are. To do that we must begin to discover with them who they are unbounded by their disease. This authentic self will be revealed as we sit and listen to the unraveling of their life stories.

When a significant level of mutual trust is reached, I may explore with the patient his/her own beliefs, values, and commitments. This "spiritual assessment" may include questions that examine the person's concept of and relationship to God, the sources of hope and strength from which s/he draws, the values to which s/he feels committed.

Secondly, as the patient's story begins to unfold, I endeavor to connect the patient's narrative with my own spiritual journey and faith tradition. In this way, narrative pastoral care becomes a meaning-making and transformational process for both the patient and myself. I discover that as I receive their story, I also accommodate myself through their story.

This too is not an easy process. This is certainly part of what makes caring for the chronically ill so onerous: it is bound to remind me of my own embodied frailty. As the person who is ill opens to me his life of pain, dependence, and grief, I may discover that my soul trembles under the strain such extremity. I may bracket it with professional self-control, but if I continue to ignore it and do not speak of it, I may be rendered, sooner or later, pastorally impotent. Often too, I inwardly acknowledge that my own spiritual journey, compared with the sufferer's, is tempered with such paltry hardship. Would my own faith survive such a brutal test? As I minister to the chronically ill and their families, how do I authenticate in my own life the biblical challenge to "choose life," while living faithfully in the "valley of the shadow?"

Thirdly, as a participant on the health care team, I have the responsibility of interpreting the patient's illness narrative and spiritual journey to the other disciplines. I become an advocate for and a trustee of the patient's inner life and meaning-making endeavors.

As one who will witness a patient's emotional and spiritual heights and depths, I can help the rest of the team understand the relationship of the patient's faith and values to his/her approach to living with illness. Consequently, the ill person's behaviors and attitude's will be understood within a context of associated meanings and relationships. The extent to which these meanings and relationships can be re-focused toward healing or renewal will determine how well the pastoral care-giver's goals keep pace with the rest of the team.

Fourth, I will offer the patient and family religious rites, rituals, and other "means of grace" (Scripture, prayer, sacraments) as a way of giving symbolic recognition of the patient's present existence. Scripture, prayer, and sacramental rites may be especially significant at these times. For one such patient I recall, daily readings from the Lectionary helped to transpose order from chaos, and intercessions we offered for her family and faith community helped distract her from her physical limitations.

Pastoral care is often an activity of "being with" more than an act of "doing for" the suffering person. There may come a point in my relationship with the chronically ill when conversation is limited if not altogether impossible because of extreme suffering, reduced awareness, or the limitations imposed by invasive medical procedures. At those moments all I can do is "stand by" and be decisively present.

The pastoral task then is nothing more or less than "in the journeying, befriending, and companioning" [4, p. 87]. This is a precarious undertaking. To sit with someone on this "long day's journey into night" requires the kind of consistent caring that often clashes with our own tolerance for human misery.

Lastly, in a prophetic role, I attempt to raise or clarify the religious, moral, and ethical concerns that may limit the healing institution's effectiveness in caring for the chronic sufferer. For example, I may observe that the community lacks the supportive infrastructure that makes it possible for families to care for their loved one at home. I may do what I can to help point out the persistent problem of limited access to people with special needs in our churches.

But the real challenge for my ministry with chronic sufferers is the extent to which I will patiently accompany them—however long it takes—on the road to renewal. Erika Schuchardt expressed it well,

> In our crises, we need partners who have lived out forms of human-ness that we have repressed, who can accept limits and wait, who persevere where there seems to be no way out and in so doing develop abilities that make it possible to be human together [5, p. 110].

There is a certain ambiguity in Schuchardt's quote that conveys a richness of meaning for me. Does the sufferer need a partner who has lived out forms of humanness and can accept limits, or is it the helper who needs such qualities in the person s/he pastors? Intended or not, this double entendre expresses for me the kind of mutuality that is required when ministering on the boundaries of human existence.

WHEN CHRONICITY EXTENDS TO DYING

Although another colleague will be contributing a chapter on ministering to the terminally ill, I would like to briefly comment on what I can only describe as the chronicity of dying.

As medical technology becomes more adept at prolonging life, even the terminal stage of illness seems to manifest a loathsome chronic character. People with end stage kidney, heart, or lung disease may suffer for months or even years before finally succumbing to the disease. Even when a person who has cancer is judged incurable, the end may still be a long time coming.

We, in hospital ministry, witness routinely what Ivan Illich termed death "under intensive care" [6]. It is a relentlessly prolonged and often painful disintegration, guarded by medical professionals bent at averting or deferring what even they acknowledge to be inevitable. You and I have been at those bedsides where ventilators, profusion pumps, lines, tubes, and glaring lights construct physical, emotional, and spiritual barriers between patient and concerned others.

Bonnie Miller-McLemore is correct in asserting that "death tests our resilience as care givers and the community itself as a network of care" [7]. The stakes are raised when the process is stretched over months and even years. How we pastorally manage these situations is dependent, at least in part, upon the lessons we learn in ministering to the chronic sufferer in the earlier stages of their illness.

Chaplains, parish pastors, lay care givers will need to work together in and outside of the clinical setting to provide a full continuum of pastoral care for persons who are chronically ill.

REFERENCES

1. A. Frank, *At the Will of the Body,* Houghton Mifflin Co., New York, p .13, 1991.
2. C. Register, *Living with Chronic Illness: Days of Patience and Passion,* 3, The Free Press, New York, 1987.
3. A. Kleinman, *The Illness Narratives,* Basic Books, New York, 1988.

4. J. Vander Zee, *Ministry to Persons with Chronic Illnesses,* Augsburg, Minneapolis, 1993.
5. E. Schuchardt, *Why is This Happening to ME?—Guidance and Hope For Those Who Suffer,* K. Leube (trans.), Augsburg Press, Minneapolis, 1989.
6. I. Illich, *Medical Nemesis,* Pantheon Books, New York, 1975.
7. B. J. Miller-McLemore, *Death, Sin and the Moral Life: Temporary Cultural Interpretations of Death,* Scholars Press, Atlanta, 1988.

CHAPTER 15

The HIV-AIDS Patient: Holier Than Thou

Inge B. Corless

In June 1997, The Southern Baptist Convention called upon its members to boycott the Walt Disney Corporation. The reason given for the boycott was the gay-friendly stance of the Disney Corporation. This attempt to boycott a major company attracted media attention. It also underscores the antipathy expressed toward gays and lesbians both directly and indirectly. That such condemnation occurred in 1997 suggests that many of the discriminatory forces present in the early days of the human immunodeficiency virus (HIV) and acquired immunodeficiency syndrome (AIDS) pandemic are still active.

The condemnation of the gay lifestyle, as well as the fear of a strange new disease, resulted in a non-welcoming attitude, if not outright hostility, toward HIV-infected persons on the part of many religious denominations in the 1980s. The proclamation by the Southern Baptists notwithstanding, not all religious groups are as rejecting and unwelcoming to individuals of varied lifestyles.

Although negative attitudes toward gays and lesbians have been transposed and integrated with the attitudes toward HIV disease by some individuals and groups, it behooves us to maintain the conceptual distinction between attitudes toward specific behaviors and lifestyles and attitudes toward those infected with the human immunodeficiency virus.

This chapter begins with a brief examination of the attitudes and beliefs of faith communities toward HIV infected and affected persons. The notion of illness as punishment as well as the punishment of illness—i.e., stigma—will also be addressed. Thereafter, the attitudes of HIV infected and affected persons toward religion and spirituality will be discussed. The last section of this chapter will explore the impact of religion and spirituality on well-being and end with an exploration of the impact of the new AIDS therapeutics on well being and spirituality.

ATTITUDES AND RELIGIOUS BELIEFS OF FAITH COMMUNITIES

Shallenberger, in a study of fifteen gay men and lesbians, observed "it is important to acknowledge that most gay men and lesbian women have been and continue to be very uncomfortable with traditional religious organizations. Virtually every one of the 75 participants in this research experienced some sort of break with his or her church after coming out" [1, p. 92]. The reason for this becomes apparent in the work of Ayers, who found negative attitudes in a survey of evangelical Christians in New Jersey [2]. "The evangelical community takes an irrevocable position against homosexuality, for abstinence and a life-long monogamous relationship within the boundaries of marriage" [3, p. 203]. It is interesting that some homosexuals too would like a life-long monogamous relationship within the boundaries of marriage. The latter, often prohibited for homosexual couples, has been replaced with a ceremony of commitment. This ceremony, however, has no legal standing.

Many of the above mentioned evangelical teachings are similar to those enunciated by Sepulveda in outlining Pentecostal beliefs [4]. Premarital sex and sex outside of marriage are considered sinful. Only total abstinence, and not the use of condoms, is considered "safe sex." A respondent to Burnard's study of the psychosocial needs of HIV-infected persons says "Fundamentalist sects of the church have difficulty with it. They feel it to be a moral issue and that AIDS people are sinners" [5, p. 1784]. Individuals who are HIV positive and homosexual thus suffer a double burden. Fortunato argues that such individuals will not seek spiritual sustenance within organized religion given the discrimination prevalent in some churches [6].

The missed opportunity for reaching out to the HIV infected and affected is characteristic of some church and religious groups and is noted by Ayers who states "The church has had the chance to set the pace and be on the cutting edge of ministering to people with social problems. Generally speaking, the church has not risen to the challenge nor capitalized on its opportunity" [3, p. 206]. Ayers continues "In my opinion, the church's responsibility in the midst of this epidemic disease is not in question. The initial failure of the church to offer a comforting presence ought to be admitted and forsaken" [31, p. 210]. Noting that the church "has fallen short of God's intended purpose," Ayers suggests that this has created what he calls "an integrity question" for those affected by HIV disease [3, p. 210]. Ayers, however, feels there is a Christian responsibility to provide "physical care, emotional support, financial relief and spiritual assistance" to the HIV infected [3, p. 209].

Some clergy and churches have been involved in locating housing for visiting parents and siblings of HIV-infected persons [7]. Other clergy have played a vital role in supporting the family members of dying men. In particular, some African-American pastors have sought to provide counseling and support to the mothers of sons who are dying [8]. Sepulveda notes that the Pentecostal Church is involved in counseling, home and hospital visiting, and helping people not to feel guilty about HIV disease transmission to spouse or children [4]. The Pentecostal Church also has a focus on prevention in keeping with the previously mentioned beliefs. Other pastors, like the representatives of other religions, have not reached out to the HIV infected and affected.

Moragne, in a study of fifty-six African-American churches, states "Many African-Americans are church involved, but few of the institutions are involved in the provision of services to people with AIDS. Assumptions abound regarding the attitudes of Protestant fundamentalist A-A churches" [9]. (Abstract) A formative evaluation showed that 42 percent of the 115 respondents viewed AIDS as a punishment from God while 53 percent thought that persons living with AIDS (PLWA's) have not lived right [9].

Don Hawley, in a Web page, is clear about his stance as a Christian toward homosexuality, namely to "love the sinner, but hate the sin" [10, p. 2]. Hawley quotes Stanton L. Jones, chair of the psychology department of Wheaton College, as saying, "We must change the church so that it is a place where those who feel homosexual desire can be welcomed. The church must become a sanctuary where repentant men and women can share with others the sexual desires they feel and still receive prayerful support and acceptance" [10, p. 8]. The emphasis by Hawley is on the repentant. He clearly disdains any behaviors which might expose the individual to the human immunodeficiency virus. Hawley states "No, God didn't send the AIDS virus to punish homosexuals. However we forget at our peril that certain natural laws do exist in our present world. . . . homosexual practices tend to dangerously expose one to the AIDS virus, and homosexuals in particular (heterosexuals who are promiscuous are also going in harms way) end up with the AIDS disease" [10, pp. 7-8].

Note that homosexuals and promiscuous heterosexuals are at risk. This misses the point that it is promiscuity which engenders risk and not gender or sexual orientation. Winget, of the United Methodist Urban

Ministry, makes the same point when he states "the real issue about sexually transmitted disease is not sexual orientation, but promiscuity" [11, p. 2].

ILLNESS AS PUNISHMENT

The notion of illness as punishment for promiscuity and other behaviors is widespread among both HIV-infected and uninfected persons. Somlai and colleagues examined the attitudes of sixty-five HIV positive (HIV+) and twenty-seven HIV negative (HIV–) persons [12]. These investigators explored alternative spiritual practices, formal religion, spiritual beliefs, illness as punishment, emotional distress, and coping. The items on the punishment scale were: "AIDS is the result of divine retribution"; "AIDS is the result of sinful behavior"; and "Illness is a divine punishment for sin" [12, p. 191]. Emotional distress and coping were measured by the Beck Depression Inventory, the UCLA Loneliness Scale, the State-Trait Anxiety Scale, and the Suicide Scale.

For HIV+ Christians, strong ($P = .01$) relationships existed between the belief that illness and AIDS are a result of religious punishment and retribution and measures of emotional distress. For those who were HIV+ and non-Christian (i.e., Buddhist, Unitarian, Muslim), "a negative relationship (.05) existed between Punishment and all of the emotional distress measures" meaning that the less the sense that illness is a result of punishment, the greater the distress [12, p. 187]. It is also of significant interest that "HIV+ respondents believed less strongly than HIV– participants that HIV/AIDS is a form of divine retribution ($F(1,90) = 9.3, P < .002$)" "... or that "AIDS is a punishment from God or a divine being" [12, p. 188].

A Haitian woman living in Boston, however, had an illness-as-punishment explanation for her HIV disease. She said "It is a malediction. God sends sickness to people who do bad things" [13, p. 47]. She attributed the malediction, namely HIV disease, to the fact that she had had a premarital sexual relationship, was living with someone to whom she was not married, and had had an abortion.

An explanation other than illness as punishment is that it is black magic or sorcery. This explanation was also given by the Haitian respondents living in Boston [13]. Supernatural origins encompassed acts "caused by angry spirits, neglected ancestors or by malicious human beings" [13, p. 48].

God's will as a relief from suffering rather than as a punishment was the belief espoused by African-American mothers of individuals dying as a result of HIV disease [8]. The sense of these women was one of the direct intervention of God to release their sons from suffering. This provides an account for the dying but not for the disease itself. It portrays the role of God as merciful rather than vengeful. In this perspective the emphasis is on mercy and not illness as punishment.

THE PUNISHMENT OF ILLNESS

Whether illness is viewed as divine punishment or not, the end result can still be in the punishment of illness. Self-inflicted illness resulting from behaviors which are voluntary are subjected to such punishment. There are gradations however. Injury incurred as a side effect of sport does not incur punishment. Injury sustained as a result of marginal behavior is punished to varying degrees depending on the gravity of both the deviance of the behavior and the extent of the illness. The same behavior with different illness outcomes will incur different degrees of disdain or punishment. For example, sexual intercourse which results in Chlamydia or HIV infection incurs different responses and certainly different degrees of punishment.

One form of such punishment is stigma. Goffman refers to a deeply discrediting attribute as characterizing the stigmatized person. The individual is considered "blemished and to be avoided" [14, p. 1]. The result is that the individual so blemished often manages his or her environment by attempting to hide the stigmata so as to avoid the avoidance of others.

The response to HIV infected persons, particularly in the first decade of the epidemic, has been one of ostracism and discrimination in the family, workplace, and community. Unfortunately, such discrimination continues, as is evidenced in the following quotation of a man who told his brother and sister he had AIDS: "Since then, there have been bad words between us. I do not have contact with other relatives. Sometimes my phone goes eight days without ringing" [13, p. 48]. This isolation has been called by the respondent to another study as the "process of leperization" [5, p. 1782]. "He felt that AIDS was akin to a new form of leprosy and a condition which could isolate people from each other and from themselves" [5, p. 1782]. Not surprisingly this fear of contagion brings historical memory not only of leprosy but of plague—the fear of the infected by the uninfected.

Smith, in *AIDS, Gays and the American Catholic Church,* states "AIDS would likely have been stigmatized regardless of whom it first infected. A mysterious and terminal disease . . . AIDS would inevitably disrupt the stable identity of any given culture. It would forcefully confront the noninfected with the reality of death . . ." [15, p. 79].

But what of the fears of the infected. What are their concerns? "The Church" along with stigma, life insurance benefits, questions about transmission, hemophiliac issues, concerns about traveling, who to tell, and problems with health care facilities are components of the outer world or "how the (HIV+) person experiences his or her environment" that are described by Burnard [5, p. 1785]. Who to tell is clearly a question which emanates from the stigma attached to HIV disease. "The Church" along with health care facilities are part of the environment of the HIV infected. That environment becomes problematic if not hostile to the degree that HIV disease is stigmatized and those infected suffer discrimination.

A different environment is experienced by those with "people being present, unconditional loving relationships, a strong spiritual or religious base and a disease ideology of social activism" [16, p. 87]. This environment is perceived as less stigmatizing than in the past. And indeed it is.

THE ATTITUDES TOWARD RELIGION AND SPIRITUALITY OF HIV INFECTED AND AFFECTED PERSONS

A strong religious base was observed to be helpful to African-American mothers who, in addition to prayer, had daily conversations with God about the care problems they were experiencing [8]. Strong spiritual beliefs have been similarly helpful to Haitians. "A central belief of spirituality is people can reach out and call upon a higher power for solutions to their problems" [13, p. 49]. Other spiritual practices include church attendance, singing in a choir, participating in a charismatic prayer group, having a prayer group visit at home, bible study, and listening to tapes of religious prayers or songs.

Spiritual issues become more salient for some people as the end of life becomes palpable. Finding meaning in one's own life and dying provides a coherence that is absent when such meaning is not identified. In a study of twenty-nine HIV-positive persons encompassing the range of illness from asymptomatic to terminal, Kendall coined the term wellness spirituality to represent the complex of views expressed by these research participants [17]. "They perceived wellness spirituality as making sense out of one's life and living life connected to that which was the most meaningful, whether that meant being religious, learning to love, giving to others, working in one's garden, finishing a book, or being a parent and partner" [17, p. 31]. Wellness spirituality was achieved by the research participants "through their ability to experience emotional intimacy with others, discover meaning in life, and attain some level of self-understanding and inner peace" [17, p. 31].

Wilson, Hutchinson, and Holzemer describe a similar process as "They engage in spiritual and religious reflection, treasuring the gifts in their lives; accepting and surrendering to the approach of their death; facing the part they may have played in their own demise; and dwelling on a sense of connectedness with others, all of life, or with God" [16, p. 94]. Spiritual issues are resolved with the use of a number of strategies such as "consolidating a spiritual belief system, emphasizing connectedness with the larger community and leaving a legacy" [16, p. 94].

Obstacles to attaining spiritual wholeness have been identified by Doka [18]. These obstacles include a "lack of structure, lack of access to clergy, lack of privacy, and reluctance on the part of caregivers to address spiritual issues" [19, pp. 72-73]. The lack of required ritual or spiritual practices concerning dying and death in some religions is what is meant by a lack of structure. Lack of access to clergy should read lack of access to compassionate, understanding clergy.

Spiritual reflection requires quiet and privacy. Dying individuals may find themselves in environments where such private time is difficult to obtain or the environment itself is not conducive to reflection. Medical care facilities are often so congested with activity, people, and noise that the only time for reflection is at night when some attempt at providing a quiet environment is made. Unfortunately remaining awake can be perceived as a problem rather than a choice. The problem is identified as sleeplessness and pharmaceutical cures are provided, further eroding the opportunity for spiritual reflection.

The pharmaceutical cure is indicative of the reluctance of some care providers to acknowledge the deeper issues giving rise to the need for spiritual reflection. Spiritual concerns of persons living with AIDS identified by Flaskerud include exploration of self-identity and the meaning of life, as well as questions about adversity, destiny, and existence [7].

THE IMPACT OF RELIGION AND SPIRITUALITY ON WELL-BEING

The call to the pastoral care person does not end the caregiver's responsibility to the terminally ill person [20]. As Flaskerud states, "Spiritual care involves strengthening the person's sense of meaning, purpose, worth, dignity, and identity" [7, p. 417]. The respondents to a study by Carson and Green "viewed spirituality as a source of comfort and a way of understanding and ordering the AIDS experience" [21, p. 211]. Peri notes the importance of love, compassion, and support for the person living with AIDS [19]. An aspect of compassion is open and honest communication, an important part of which is listening [19].

Being present without speaking conveys a powerful caring and compassion. Then when the individual is of a mind to speak, listening to the sharing of deepest concerns is an intervention that any individual can provide. The intervention here is one of being rather than one of doing. In some circumstances, to be is to do.

Other interventions include prayer, meditation, and life review. The latter permits the terminally ill person to put his or her life into perspective. Some individuals may find it useful to make an audio or videotape for younger persons in the family. Bailey describes the use of art works in helping dying persons achieve closure [22]. All of these approaches assist the individual to bring closure at the time of the ending of his or her life.

Somlai and colleagues make a similar observation about people living with HIV/AIDS, noting that "a blending of spiritual traditions and mental health approaches are needed to facilitate . . . coping" [12, p. 181]. In effect, spirituality, religion, and mental health processes, to a greater or lesser extent depending on the individual, are all approaches to coping with living and dying.

In an intriguing study, Carson investigated whether spiritual activities, health-promoting behaviors, and AIDS related activities (participation in clinical studies and activism) were related to hardiness [23]. Prayer, meditation, exercise, and use of special diets were all significantly related to hardiness. AIDS-related activities, however, were not correlated with hardiness. The latter is a surprising finding. And yet, in the context of stress reduction, prayer, meditation, and exercise might all be construed as stress reducing. The use of special diets, like involvement in AIDS-related activities, involves an activist stance. Perhaps the AIDS-related activities are stress enhancing.

Carson and Green also found spiritual well being and hardiness to be significantly related [21]. The spiritual well-being scale had two subscales: religious well being and existential well being, both of which were significantly related ($p = < .05$ and $p = < .001$) to hardiness. The investigators state, "The ability to believe and to act on the belief that life is meaningful is essential to hardiness and its components of challenge, control and commitment" [21, p. 217].

The belief in God as protector and in particular as their protector from HIV disease was characteristic of some of the mothers studied by Boyle and colleagues [8]. This gift of faith is a strong bulwark against the voices of discrimination. Not everyone is so fortunate.

Writing prior to the consciousness of an AIDS epidemic, Norman Cousins averred "Death is not the ultimate tragedy of life. The ultimate tragedy is depersonalization—dying in an alien and sterile area, separated from the spiritual nourishment that comes from being able to reach out to a loving hand, separated from a desire to experience the things that make life worth living, separated from hope" [24, p. 133]. Clearly this statement is applicable to those infected with the human immunodeficiency virus; indeed to anyone.

THE IMPACT OF THE NEW AIDS THERAPIES

The reality of HIV-infected persons suffering from the isolation of discrimination as well as from the infection of a virus, unfortunately still is true in some communities. What has changed dramatically is the impact on well-being produced by the introduction of protease inhibitors and combination antiretroviral therapy. The Lazarus-like phenomenon of recovery of some semblance of normal daily activity from a prior terminally ill status has been nothing but miraculous. The "miracle" is the result of the dedicated work of scientists, health care providers, clinical trials participants, and others who have sought to find a cure, therapy, and preventive vaccines.

The "miracle" is not all encompassing. Some individuals, given triple combination therapy, have not responded and are continuing their downward trajectory. Other individuals who seemingly responded to therapy, have done so in a time-delimited fashion and now find themselves in an inexorable decline. "It's a roller coaster," said Mark Baker, editor of the *Provincetown Positive* newsletter [25]. Baker started one protease inhibitor a year ago but his condition deteriorated again after six months. He immediately started another one and gained some weight and energy. But he is not sure how long the positive effects will last." "'Then once again, he will be perceived as 'failing therapy.' "

The finger pointing inherent is such medical phraseology as "the patient failed therapy" continues in common parlance. A brief but necessary digression. "The patient failed therapy" has the implication that if only the patient had done his or her homework, he or she would have passed the test and succeeded with therapy. What nonsense! This places the responsibility on the patient rather than the efficacy of the physician. This is not to imply that the physician has failed or committed some error. The truth of the matter is that current therapies for a number of diseases are not adequate to the task of resolution of pathology.

The current combination therapies are complex requiring pill taking before, with, and after meals several times a day. Strict adherence to such a regimen is a daunting challenge. And yet such adherence is required to prevent the onset of drug resistance. And even with strict adherence there is the suggestion that drug resistance may be occurring.

There is great concern in the medical community about "compliance" with the antiretroviral regimen by the patient. Indeed some individuals have not been given access to such therapies because there are concerns about the fidelity with which pill-taking will occur. Substance-abusers and homeless persons in particular have been the recipients of medical triage. In some instances where substance abusers are given combination therapy, their adherence has been impressive.

Why the concern? If virus resistant to these latest wonder drugs occurs in a number of individuals, the danger is that this drug resistant virus will be transmitted from person to person creating a nightmare for treatment. In essence, if protease inhibitor resistant virus becomes prevalent, the gains of the last years will have been for naught—if not totally, at least considerably. This is why there is such a concern about adherence to therapy. And because there are individuals whose infections are not susceptible to the triple combination therapies, there is a chasm between those whose health has been regained and those whose decline continues. The latter must watch while others who were passengers on the same sinking ship are being rescued. Still others, as noted above, never gained access to the life boats.

THE IMPACT OF THE NEW AIDS THERAPEUTICS ON WELL-BEING AND SPIRITUALITY

What has all of this to do with spirituality? For some individuals, nothing has changed. The new therapies, if attempted, have not proven beneficial. Their lives have not improved nor have their deaths been forestalled. These individuals will require support and acts of compassion as their health continues to fail. For some fortunate individuals, there has been a resurgence of health and well-being. The issue here is quite different. Individuals who had prepared for death have been given a new lease on life. There is the hope for a longer life span and with that questions about work, finances, and even relationships.

Individuals who have recuperated are returning to work. They are finding they have to repay the debts that were incurred when life looked bleak. And they need to think about the quality of their lives. For faith communities this may mean being confronted with sexual behaviors that did not occur when the individual appeared to be languishing. Will Christian charity embrace the rejuvenated gay person as readily as it has those who were dying? It may be that the mercy and compassion shown to those about "to pass" is not rendered those who aren't in any hurry to go anywhere and, in fact, are rejuvenated. If the Southern Baptist Convention could call for a boycott to a corporation friendly to gays, what actions are being suggested by the convention against individuals: gay persons and those living with AIDS?

What is encouraging is the response given by Arkansas Governor Mike Huckabee to the question as to whether or not Christian communities should boycott corporations friendly to gays. His response would appear to be a more positive and healing Christian response. Perhaps it is Governor Huckabee who is literally holier than thou. He was quoted as saying "I have enough trouble keeping up with my own relationship to Jesus Christ that I really don't have time to keep up with someone else's relationship to Mickey Mouse" [26]. Amen.

REFERENCES

1. D. Shallenberger, Companions on a Gay Journey: Issues of Spiritual Counseling and Direction with Gay Men and Lesbian Women, *The Journal of Pastoral Care, 50*:1, pp. 87-95, 1996.
2. J. R. Ayers, *The Attitudes of Evangelical Christians toward Persons with AIDS* (D.Phil dissertation, Graduate School), 1992.
3. J. R. Ayers, The Quagmire of HIV/AIDS Related Issues which Haunt the Church, *The Journal of Pastoral Care, 49*:2, pp. 201-210, 1995.
4. W. Sepulveda, How I View the HIV Epidemic as a Pentecostal, *Journal of Community Health, 20*:2, pp. 171-175, 1995.
5. P. Burnard, The Psychosocial Needs of People with HIV and AIDS: A View from Nurse Educators and Counselors, *Journal of Advanced Nursing, 18*(11), pp. 1779-1786, 1993.
6. J. Fortunato, *AIDS: The Spiritual Dilemma,* Harper & Row, San Francisco, 1987.
7. J. H. Flaskerud, Psychosocial and Neuropsychiatric Care, *Critical Care Nursing Clinics of North America, 4*:3, pp. 411-420, 1992.
8. J. S. Boyle, J. A. Ferrell, D. R. Hodnicki, and R. B. Muller, Going Home: African-American Caregiving for Adult Children with Human Immunodeficiency Virus Disease, *Holistic Nursing Practice, 11*:2, pp. 27-35, 1997.
9. T. Moragne, *African American Churches—Evaluation Utility and KAB Collection,* paper presented at the VII International Conference on AIDS, 1992.
10. D. Hawley, Homosexuality—A Christian Perspective, http://www.sabbath.com/hawley.htm (pp. 1-8).
11. G. Winget, *United Methodist Urban Ministry, 13*:11, November 1996, http://www.lovverture.com/umumum/novnewsletter.html
12. A. M. Somlai, J. A. Kelly, S. C. Kalichman, G. Mulry, K. J. Sikkema, T. McAuliffe, K. Multhauf, and B. Kavantes, An Empirical Investigation of the Relationship between Spirituality, Coping, and Emotional Distress in People Living with HIV Infection and AIDS, *Journal of Pastoral Care, 50*:2, pp. 181-191, 1996.

13. M. A. Martin, P. Rissmiller, and J. A. Beal, Health-Illness Beliefs and Practices of Haitians with HIV Disease Living in Boston, *Journal of the Association of Nurses in AIDS Care, 6:6*, pp. 45-53, 1995.

14. E. Goffman, *Stigma: Notes on the Management of Spoiled Identity*, Prentice Hall, Englewood Cliffs, New Jersey, 1963.

15. R. L. Smith, *AIDS, Gays and the American Catholic Church*, The Pilgrim Press, Cleveland, 1994.

16. H. S. Wilson, S. A. Hutchinson, and W. L. Holzemer, Salvaging Quality of Life in Ethnically Diverse Patients with Advanced HIV/AIDS, *Qualitative Health Research, 7:1*, pp. 75-79, 1977.

17. J. Kendall, Wellness Spirituality in Homosexual Men with HIV Infection, *Journal of the Association of Nurses in AIDS Care, 5:4*, pp. 28-34, 1994.

18. K. J. Doka, The Spiritual Needs of the Dying, in *Death and Spirituality*, K. J. Doka and J. D. Morgan (eds.), Baywood, Amityville, New York, 1993.

19. T. C. Peri, Promoting Spirituality in Persons with Acquired Immuno-deficiency Syndrome. A Nursing Intervention, *Holistic Nursing Practice, 10:1*, pp. 68-76, 1995.

20. International Work Group on Death, Dying, and Bereavement, Assumptions and Principles of Spiritual Care for the Terminally Ill, Corless, I. (Chair), *Spiritual Care Work Group, 14:1*, pp. 75-81, 1990.

21. V. B. Carson and H. Green, Spiritual Well-Being: A Predictor of Hardiness in Patients with Acquired Immunodeficiency Syndrome, *Journal of Professional Nursing, 8:4*, pp. 209-220, 1992.

22. S. Bailey, Creativity and the Close of Life, in *Dying, Death, and Bereavement: Theoretical Perspectives and Other Ways of Knowing*, I. B. Corless, B. B. Germino, and M. Pittman (eds.), Jones and Bartlett, Boston, pp. 327-335, 1994.

23. V. B. Carson, Prayer, Meditation, Exercise, and Special Diets: Behaviors of the Hardy Person with HIV/AIDS, *Journal of the Association of Nurses in AIDS Care, 4:3*, pp. 18-28, 1993.

24. N. Cousins, *Anatomy of an Illness*, Norton, New York, 1979.

25. S. Leung, Keeping Death at Bay, *The Boston Globe*, p. B01, July 14, 1997.

26. M. Huckabee, Quotes of Note, *The Boston Globe*, p. A15, June 21, 1997.

Variance

Reverend Denise A. Ryder

Taught to manage money
then taught to manage time.

Taught to manage people
then told to manage care.

Productivity not proclivity
Measures outcomes for stats concern.

Variances are variations
different from the norm.

Authenticity validates humanity
compassionate living word.

Revelation on Revelation
Variance is Lord.

Reprinted by permission, *Healing Ministry,* 5:5, pp. 35-36, September/October 1998.

CHAPTER 16

The Alzheimer's Patient

Rabbi Earl A. Grollman

A PROPER DIAGNOSIS

I keep forgetting things:
Important dates,
Appointments,
Where I left my glasses,
People's names, my closest friends,
I sometimes think, I'm losing my mind.
I'm so afraid that I have Alzheimer's.

The part of life we live as elders is a gift. Very few species live as long beyond the reproductive years as humans do. Perhaps we have this relatively long life span because elders serve such important roles in human society: as repositories of wisdom, keepers of history and family memories, and backup caregivers for the young. The feeling of joy that comes from filling these roles—the joy of grandchildren, the joy of allowing others to benefit from our experience—is built into the design of human life.

Lives that conclude without that final chapter, without the time to grow old and gain perspective, often seem bitterly incomplete. But the greatest loss, the greatest dehumanization, is to grow old without possession of your mind. *That is Alzheimer's disease.*

Studies indicate that 10 percent of the population aged sixty-five and over suffer from this disease. The incidence of Alzheimer's increases with age. Twenty percent of individuals aged seventy-five to eighty-four, and nearly half of all people eighty-five and older are afflicted. No race, gender, or socioeconomic class is exempt.

United States President Ronald Reagan demonstrated great courage when he revealed that he had been stricken with Alzheimer's disease. He called it "a journey that will lead me to the sunset of my life." Despite this image, Alzheimer's disease is not a pleasant twilight stroll. It is a progressive brain disorder, fatal, but slow. Patients often linger through years of increasing decline and dependency. Professionals are called upon to help caregivers during this long and rough journey and understand their questions in order to assist them to face each new challenge and decision with courage and compassion.

WHEN AN AGING PERSON FORGETS, IS IT ALZHEIMER'S?

Because Alzheimer's disease is common among the elderly, many people live in fear of this illness. Every time they forget a name, miss an appointment, or neglect to pick up a particular item from the store, they fear that the disease is beginning to affect them. But the tendency to falter a bit over recalling names and other details is nearly universal among elders and is not related to Alzheimer's disease. Physicians call mild memory loss in people over fifty "age-associated memory loss." People who feel some decline in their memory function and are formally tested may show a very small impairment. This condition is to be gracefully accepted as a normal part of life.

WHAT IS THE DIFFERENCE BETWEEN NORMAL FORGETFULNESS AND ALZHEIMER'S DISEASE?

Everyone forgets. We could not function if our minds did not screen out the forgettable, like the temperature on this day last year or the color of the socks we wore one week ago.

Sometimes, though, under the most ordinary circumstances, we forget things we should remember. For example, dashing out the door your spouse says, "Don't forget to stop for a loaf of bread on the way home." Moments after you return empty-handed, the memory of that reminder comes rushing back. This is called "failure of registration": you simply weren't paying enough attention for the request to register. Paying attention is a prerequisite to the formation of any memory. In this instance, the inability to pay attention made the memory fragile so that you could retrieve it only when cued by the original text, the return home. Alzheimer's disease does not cause this kind of memory loss.

The ability to recall, say, a list of words after a few minutes is called "short-term memory." Short-term memory is basically equivalent to learning. This form of memory is the most affected by Alzheimer's disease. The inability to recall over the short term is why Alzheimer's patients often repeat themselves over and over again.

The ability to recollect past experiences and feelings is called "long-term memory." The effect of Alzheimer's disease on long-term memory is complex. Even when the mind is working normally, memories retained over the long term may seem like a disconnected patchwork. Alzheimer's patients retain many of their long-term memories, but sometimes the distant past inappropriately intrudes into the present. For example, when asked about his occupation one patient mentioned a job he had held several decades ago for a brief period, overlooking the work he had been employed at for most of his adult life. When asked the name of her spouse, another patient mentioned the name of her high school sweetheart. When an inquiry was made of a woman who had been married for more than fifty years, she recalled only her maiden name.

Mild short-term memory loss represents only age-associated memory loss. Alzheimer's disease differs in that it is progressive and affects other brain functions besides memory, such as thinking processes, personality, and perception.

HOW DO WE KNOW THAT IT'S ALZHEIMER'S DISEASE?

Often, by simply talking to the patient, performing a physical examination, checking the patient's cognitive abilities, and doing a few laboratory tests, a trained physician could make a diagnosis of Alzheimer's disease with a confidence level of approximately 90 percent (meaning that the diagnosis will be correct in 9 out of 10 cases). Because conditions of Alzheimer's patients deteriorate over time, the doctor would increase the certainty of the diagnosis by seeing the person at six-month intervals.

Testing for Alzheimer's disease involves a few blood tests, often a brain scan, and sometimes a neuropsychological evaluation, testing a person's memory, problem-solving ability, and use of language. None of these tests prove conclusively that a person has Alzheimer's disease, although recently some tests have become available which more accurately suggests the diagnosis. One of the most important reasons to evaluate a person with dementia is to discover whether a diagnosis other than Alzheimer's disease might explain the symptoms and, if so, whether the dementia can be treated. The doctor may discover that the dementia is caused by the patient's medications; side effects from a surprisingly large number of drugs can result in dementia.

The medical evaluation for Alzheimer's disease is not time-consuming, not painful, and relatively easy for the doctor to perform. If someone in the family is worried about having the disease, it is worth getting the few tests required. Their fears may well be laid to rest.

As a professional, you can contribute greatly to what the eminent psychiatrist, Dr. Karl Menninger, told his students was the most important part of the treatment process: **a proper understanding and diagnosis.**

THE PATIENTS AND THE CAREGIVER'S JOURNEY

Before, the husband said:
"My wife hasn't changed.
(Not much anyway)."

So my father stumbles once in a while.
(Probably needs new glasses).

My Mom forgot to turn off the stove.
(Everybody makes mistakes).

All kinds of excuses are made by the patient and the family. If they don't admit what is happening, then it may not be true. It's a way of saying, "I don't want to think about it. Not now, anyway."

Disbelief is often a first reaction to change, a denial of painful events, a defense against emotional involvement. But pretending that nothing is wrong prevents the client and family from seeking available help. A Jewish expression states, "Believe in miracles but be prepared for alternatives." William James said it differently: "Acceptance of what is truly happening is the first step to overcoming the consequences of misfortune." They need to know: "What happens to the brain?" "What is the progress of the disease?" "Will other family members be more vulnerable to the illness?" Finally, "Is there a cure?"

WHAT HAPPENS IN THE BRAIN OF A PERSON WITH ALZHEIMER'S DISEASE?

Years before the onset of any symptoms, as much as one or even two decades before there is the slightest hint of the disease, a small peptide (a combination of amino acids, the building blocks of proteins) called B-amyloid accumulates within the brain. Now, all of us have exceedingly small amounts of this peptide circulating in our bloodstream and spinal fluid. However, in Alzheimer's disease B-amyloid molecules clump together to form first a loose mesh and then an increasingly dense mesh of filaments that insert themselves among the many delicate nerve endings of the brain. These deposits are called *senile plaques* and represent one of the hallmarks of the disease. After death, pathologists might look for these microscopic structures during the post-mortem examination. But senile plaques alone are not sufficient to make possible a diagnosis of Alzheimer's disease.

The other change in a brain affected with Alzheimer's disease and the other microscopic structure for which pathologists search is the *neurofibrillary tangle*. Neurofibrillary tangles form when a highly resistant protein becomes concentrated within the nerve cells. Eventually nerve cells choke as the tangle crowds out the cells' contents. The tangle itself sometimes remains behind once the cell around it dies, earning the eerie names "tombstones" or "ghost tangles." Not surprisingly, the parts of the brain most affected by the tangles are those that deal with *memory* and *emotion*.

HOW DOES THE DISEASE PROGRESS?

The long journey between the diagnosis and the more advanced stages of the disease usually lasts about ten years but will vary greatly. A decade is the average time from diagnosis to death. In the later stages, patients usually become bedridden and highly susceptible to pneumonia, which is the most common cause of death in Alzheimer's patients. By the time pneumonia sets in, patients are often completely unable to care for themselves.

Before that final stage, Alzheimer's disease extends its destruction beyond a failed memory. Patients may lose their ability to find their way around, first in unfamiliar settings and later in their own homes. They lose nearly all sense of time: they may prepare breakfast at dinner time, or assume it is time for breakfast regardless of what time they awake. They may wander outside in the middle of the night. They lose the ability to recognize objects and so may no longer be able to use a key or a fork. A wastebasket or a fireplace may be mistaken for a toilet. Their ability to use language, particularly names, begins to fail, and the words they speak may seem empty and devoid of meaning. They lose interest in hobbies and events going on around them. They may stop participating in conversations and even become disinclined to speak at all.

Their personality may also change. Alzheimer's patients often get angry, although their outbursts are usually brief. They may become paranoid and accuse others of stealing their possessions. Suspicion leads to a vicious circle in which an Alzheimer's patient hides money or valuables, forgets where the objects are hidden, and becomes convinced that the belongings are stolen.

As the disease progresses and Alzheimer's patients may require help with feeding, bathing, and going to the bathroom, certain physical symptoms develop. Patients may hold their arms, legs, and neck very tightly; they seem unable to relax their muscles. Sometimes they will make quick jerking movements over which they have no control and possibly no awareness. At this point, when the peaceful sleep of pneumonia ends the ordeal, it is clear why pneumonia has been called "an old person's friend."

DOES ALZHEIMER'S DISEASE RUN IN FAMILIES?

Some forms of Alzheimer's disease do run in families. Among these inherited forms, we know the most about the extremely rare type of Alzheimer's that begins as young as age forty or fifty. Less than 1 percent of all patients with Alzheimer's have this early-onset disease. Because many of these patients carry on mutation from birth, a blood test could detect the mutation before the disease begins.

The more common older-onset variety of the disease is usually not inherited. If one or more members of the family have the disease, it may be because Alzheimer's is common, not because the disease is in the genes. Even among identical twins, one twin may get the disease and the other may not. Except for the rare inherited form of Alzheimer's, genes are only one of several factors that determine whether one will contract the disease. If clients are concerned about inheriting Alzheimer's disease, they must raise this topic with their physician.

IS THERE A CURE?

As of this writing, Alzheimer's disease is incurable. As scientists learn more, piece by piece, about how the disease inflicts its ravages on the brain, optimism that a cure is possible is growing. What no crystal ball can predict is when that effective treatment will emerge. Unfortunately, the powerful desire for a cure can lead to a less than critical judgment about current treatments. As with any incurable disease, patients, families, and even medical professionals tend to grasp at all manner of passing treatments, whether folk remedies or medications that have not been proven effective.

It may be difficult to ignore anecdotal reports about remedies that were said to have helped a neighbor or a friend, although keeping an open mind about new treatments openly takes advantage of the consumer's longing for a cure. It's the job of the physician, usually a neurologist, to provide the family with current information and treatment. Staggering scientific advances are at least bringing reassurance and hope for a cure.

Until then, it is the role of professionals to become more knowledgeable about this devastating disease in order to help patient and families confront the ravaging physical, emotional, and *spiritual* challenges that lay ahead.

Unfortunately, studies show that spiritual concerns of Alzheimer's families are often overlooked in health care literature. Spiritual beliefs are often challenged during unbearable crises. Spouse, children, and relatives may feel: "What did I do to deserve this?" They may look inward to justify this agonizing event as a divine chastisement: "Dear God, why me?" Anger may be directed against God: "If God is all-powerful, why won't He answer my prayers?" Great philosophers have felt this way: "My God, my God, why hast thou forsaken me?" (Psalm 22).

The long journey of the Alzheimer's patient caregivers alters life's meaning. Listen to their arduous journey but don't impose your own theology. If they choose to seek spiritual responses to profound issues concerning God, good and evil, sickness and health, they may begin to release feelings of helplessness and guilt and find comfort and renewed strength even in the mystery of darkness and impending death. Faith may not take away the heartache, but it may help them to live and accept the unacceptable. Faith communities and support groups validate crushing despair as normal and natural reactions to life-threatening disease. Sharing is healing, and oh, how you help when you share the ordeal of a fatal, progressive brain disorder.

RESOURCES

Alzheimer's Association. 919 Michigan Avenue, Suite 1000, Chicago, IL. 60611-1676. 800.272.3900.

SUGGESTED READING

Aronson, M. E. (ed.), *Understanding Alzheimer's Disease*, Scribner's, New York, 1988.
Callahan, S., *My Mother's Voice,* Elder Books, Forest Knolls, California, 2000.

Grollman, E. and K. Kosik, *When Someone You Love has Alzheimer's: The Caregiver's Journey*, Beacon, Boston, 1996.

Mace, N. L. and P. V. Robins, *The Thirty-Six Hour Day*, Johns Hopkins University Press, Baltimore, 1991.

Wright, L., *Alzheimer's Disease and Marriage*, Medical University of South Carolina, 1993.

CHAPTER 17
The Obstetrics Patient

Cathi Lammert

A few days before I started writing this chapter, I was asked by a fellow nurse to work a six-hour shift on the mother-baby unit. Because the previous few months had been filled with my ministering to bereaved parents whose babies had died, I agreed and was excited to return to active nursing if only for a six hour shift. Little did I know that the evening would be so indicative of the challenges health care workers face constantly as they provide physical and spiritual care for their obstetric patients.

When I arrived for my shift, the unit was not in order and there were no nurses present at the nursing station. After changing into my scrubs, I understood why. When I was given report, I knew why it seemed to me that this had not been a good day. Three patients were in the final stages of discharge. One, a college student who had decided to relinquish her baby to a family friend, was saying her good-byes while waiting for social services to take her baby to foster care. Another patient's baby, with the possible diagnosis of hypoplastic left heart syndrome, was being transferred to a children's hospital several miles away. The last patient, who was "normal," was to leave shortly after a stay of less than twenty-four hours.

As I helped the family whose very sick baby was being transferred, a flood of feelings filled my heart. I had walked in their shoes with two of my babies. It was so difficult for the mom and dad to see their baby in the transport incubator as they kissed him tenderly and said good-bye before he was taken to the helicopter. I shared with them that I had "been there" and I understood their pain and fear. They were so frightened and desperately hoped that their baby would make it. I simply

211

said that I would pray for them and their baby. I explained the policies of the children's hospital and they were grateful for the information. I silently prayed that our brief visit was meaningful as we hugged good-bye when she was discharged.

When I returned from the discharge, the college student who had just said good-bye to her baby was ready to enter the elevator. Even though I had no contact with her, my heart ached as I saw the tears in her eyes and her mother's. I looked at her tenderly and told her to take care of herself as she left the division with my colleague.

As I discharged the third patient, I thought to myself, "These family members have not had time to adjust to their new baby physically, let alone emotionally and spiritually. Mom is moving so slowly and looks so tired." I was startled by the father's warm compliment, "Thanks for caring so much, this hospital is wonderful." I accepted the compliment, but all I had done for them was to give them my best wishes as I placed their child lovingly and securely in their car.

Back on the division, I received notice from *Admitti*ng that we were receiving a new patient. Her baby had died at nineteen-weeks gestation and she had complications following a D&C. I was concerned about her being placed on the OB floor so I checked with the Out Patient Department. They verified that the patient chose to be on this floor because she had received wonderful care after her two other babies were born. A few minutes later, Labor & Delivery called because they needed a bed for a stabilized patient whose membranes had ruptured prematurely at nineteen weeks. They also advised me that they just had three admissions, one of which was an imminent delivery.

In addition, there were other patients who were already on the OB floor and had needs as well. A single mom who had relinquished her first baby was unsure if she would keep this baby. A mother from Mexico had just delivered her fifth baby and spoke very little English; her husband served as interpreter. Another new mother was recovering from a C-section with no major problems. A single mom had developed a high fever during labor and was waiting for the results of her baby's septic work-up. She had just been involved in a major screaming match with her sister and mother. Besides another single mom whose support person was her sister, a new mom was recovering fairly well from a C-Section.

As I tried to meet the many needs of my patients, I could not remember ever having such a diverse and challenging evening. Somehow we made it through the evening and my patients received the best of our care. However, the morning after this shift, it became obvious to me that we had barely touched the surface of these patients' spiritual needs. Pastoral Care was involved earlier in the day with some of the patients but there had not been an "official crisis" so they were not called during our shift. So I shared the many spiritual needs of those patients with a member of Pastoral Care who had been unaware of their needs. Even though that shift was unusual for our small unit, it reflected the diverse challenges faced daily by caregivers at many health centers.

Care for obstetric patients has changed dramatically. Some changes have been positive and others have tested caregivers' tolerance. The concept of Mother-Baby Care emphasizes that the baby remains with the mother and father throughout the hospital stay. The nursery is used only for sick infants or is available at night for baby's care. The nurse assesses and cares for the baby in the patient's room. Obstetrical nurses are now trained to care for both mom and baby and are assigned to three or four couplets. Many seasoned professionals have had trouble adapting to this concept but are beginning to see the value in providing continuity of care for the family unit. Care has become so much more family oriented by providing warm, beautiful surroundings, complete with the many comforts of home such as bigger rooms with a bed for dad, whirlpool baths, and VCRs. This family centered concept includes not only prenatal classes but also sibling and grandparent classes. Now, expectant parents are more involved with decisions that affect their labor and delivery. Some even choose to develop a written birth plan. Patients have the assistance of their partner and may experience the additional support of a Doula, who assists with labor, delivery, and postpartum care. These changes address physical and even some emotional needs.

Other changes in Obstetrical care present frustrations with which health care professionals struggle on a daily basis. Budget cuts have increased the patient-caregiver ratio, challenging all aspects of care: physical, social, emotional, and spiritual. Shortened, predetermined hours of care may not allow a patient's needs to be completely addressed in the hospital setting. Even though legislation that allows a minimal stay of forty-eight hours for patients who have delivered vaginally and ninety- six hours for a C-Section has been enacted.

In addition, chaplains and Pastoral Care staff can be overwhelmed with an increased number of patients, only part of whom are on the OB floor. Some minister to as many as 200 patients each day. After helping patients through varied crises or meeting sacramental needs, chaplains who attempt to visit non-crisis patients may be deterred by feedings, OB teaching, and the many visitors that fill a new mom's room. Caregivers, whose time is often filled with taking care of physical, emotional, and social needs of the family, may feel that they have no time to assess patients' spiritual needs. However, the chaplain's time is even more limited, and, as a result of the changes in health care, a new, multi-disciplinary approach to meeting patients' spiritual needs is necessary.

This new approach requires the health care staff to learn how to listen for, assess, and address the spiritual needs of their patients. They cannot supplant the role of the chaplain or clergy but rather screen, complement, and augment pastoral care. This requires a knowledge of spirituality and successful strategies as well as skill in using these strategies to meet a patient's spiritual needs in the absence or presence of pastoral care staff.

Spirituality is difficult to define. It involves understanding one's relationship with a higher power and other people. It is based on beliefs and values. Spirituality is as unique as each individual. An individual's spirituality impacts his or her reaction to events and people. It is not static but changes with a person's life experiences. A person may be spiritual yet not particularly religious. Active participation in an organized religion is not always required for some to have a deep sense of the meaning of life and understanding the importance of his or her relationship with others. Another person may be very religious but not very spiritual. Involvement in a faith community may not be commensurate with spirituality. Also, a person may very well be both spiritual and religious. Such an individual may be active in a chosen faith while completely in touch with his/her inner being.

The key to meeting the spiritual needs of a patient is the acceptance that each individual is unique. A person's response to a positive outcome or an unexpected crisis is also unique and may reflect or provide for spiritual growth. This precludes assuming that a person will react to an experience in the same way as others or in a prescribed manner. James Lockhart, who specializes in OB pastoral care and is Director of Pastoral Care at Missouri Baptist Hospital in St. Louis, Missouri, adds, "The most significant thing we can offer to our patients is a safe place. If they feel secure with you, they will trust their soul with you." This sense of "spiritual security" comes from the caregiver's restraint in making assumptions about a person's beliefs. People may be members of a specific faith congregation and not totally embrace all of its teachings.

Reserving judgment is essential to providing a sense of spiritual security. Many families who are in crisis are forced to reexamine their beliefs. They may find that the religious beliefs instilled in them as children no longer seem to make any sense. They may be confused because their faith community refuses to allow their expression of anger and they do not know how to cope with the rage they feel. While they may hesitate to share these feelings with their minister, pastor, or rabbi, the chaplain often serves as a sounding board to help resolve their conflict.

Individuals in a mixed faith marriage may be forced to recognize what they truly believe when they face a crisis involving their baby.

Many couples do not believe that having different faiths is a problem and as a result do not attend church or talk about their religious views. If the couple has talked about their beliefs before a problem arises, they can be more confident that their decision in a crisis situation is consistent with their beliefs and a crisis within a crisis can be averted. The chaplain is a neutral, objective person with whom the parents can discuss these differences. Most of the time the couple is able to reach a decision or at least meet each other half way. If both parents are very active in their different chosen faiths, points of conflict often can be resolved such as having *her* pastor perform a blessing of the baby at the hospital and *his* pastor officiate at the baby's funeral.

Other families have involved both of their clergy with important roles at their child's funeral service. Health care professionals also now serve as spiritual caregivers and must be careful not to assume anything. If the mother is very active in the Catholic faith, for example, and the dad does not attend a church, the assumption cannot be made that they will want the baby to be baptized, if the need arises.

In our multicultural society, people come into these traumatic situations with a wide diversity of perspectives, feelings, needs, and how they approach others (if at all) for care and assistance. If one parent belongs to a faith tradition that opposes pregnancy termination under any circumstances and they are faced with prenatal decision making, the option of termination should still be discussed. Gently, these issues can be addressed by beginning with "I know you and your husband are of different faiths, one of which is against termination. Would you like to share your feelings regarding this?" Other helpful phrases are "Have you considered . . . ?" or "What are your thoughts about . . . ?" By allowing the family to explore their options and reflect upon them, they can grow in their own spirituality. This can only occur when the caregiver does not restrict discussion because of assumptions about the parents' expressed beliefs and also remains open to exploring the previously unexpressed beliefs or practices.

The spiritual aspect of giving birth to new life invokes many reactions from parents and those who support them. The miracle of new life is awe-inspiring. Caregivers who are also parents bring a special sensitivity as they share the reactions of many of the families. As patients go through labor, many are frightened and are not sure about how they can endure the entire process. After the baby is born they are amazed and proud of themselves because they safely delivered a healthy baby. This is a sacred moment. Bonding occurs between the couple and with the baby. To see dads bonding with their child in their arms is a true privilege. New moms often begin to feel spiritually connected to other women and mothers.

Many new moms and dads are able to share some of their inner feelings at the time of their baby's birth, while others, in awe, are more quiet and reserved. It is a wonderful time to celebrate and share. They are proud that they were able to create such a wonder, their own child. If a couple has endured the death of a previous baby (or even babies) and have given birth to their first living child, they experience indescribable joy. Many thankful tears are shed and disbelief expressed that they finally were able to have a living baby. But another reaction such as the refusal of a mom or dad to bond with a baby may indicate that there is an underlying reason such as rape, a previous trauma, or depression. Sometimes the father of the baby is not overjoyed by the arrival of this new person and feels uncomfortable. This may occur with a question of paternity or when the couple's relationship is not solid. Often these reasons are not disclosed to the caregiver.

Sacred, spiritual moments may occur at the time the cord is cut, when the baby is placed in dad's arms for the first time, or as mom is assisted with the baby's first suckling at her breast. Although not formally addressed, they are tender moments. Many caregivers have shared hugs and tears with families at these special times.

Also, in the course of the physical care of the OB patient, moms may be tearful. It is best to ask them if they would like to share the reasons behind those tears. The complexity of their feelings may seem overwhelming. Often they worry about how they will be good parents or how they can love two babies as much as they love one. Many couples wonder how they will adjust to the baby and all of the changes that will occur once the baby arrives. By acknowledging these concerns, caregivers provide an opportunity for the individual to grow personally and spiritually.

Most parents do not fully experience the spiritual impact of their child's birth until a few days, even months, later. Since their time at a hospital is limited, caregivers can assist as needed and hope that the spiritual growth of these new parents will continue to be nurtured by their loved ones, friends, their pastors, and community of believers. Some faith communities are blessed to have the special assistance of a Stephen Ministry Program, Elizabeth Ministries, or parish nurse program.

The daily test of caregivers is to decide what needs can be met and discern how to meet those needs best. This is true for spiritual needs as itis for those that are physical, emotional, and social. Corinne Biehl, an OB chaplain at St. John's Mercy Hospital in St. Louis, emphatically agrees with Reverend Joseph J. Driscoll, Executive Director of The National Association of Catholic Chaplains, and follows his model of spiritual care. Rev. Driscoll believes that ". . . *spiritual care* can be defined as discovering, reverencing and tending the spirit of another person." One must listen in order to discover. The chaplain stands on sacred ground, in the midst of the person's journey, not knowing the beginning nor the end, but hopefully with a posture of reverence. Tending the spirit can come only after discovering and reverencing [1]. This is also true for caregivers as they assess a patient's spiritual needs and determine if a chaplain should be called or how they themselves can assist the patient. Often, the support that is needed by a patient is that the health care professional acknowledge and embrace the sacred moments as they occur.

These basic principles can provide guidance to caregivers as they work with the obstetric patient in a variety of situations. Pastoral care is often crisis oriented, while other health care professionals work with patients in a variety of situations. If the family is trying to cope with uncomfortable, unexpected, or even tragic events, sensitive support from caregivers can still provide a tender, positive experience. Some specific types of OB patients may have additional spiritual needs that are best addressed by the health care provider at a time other than delivery. These may be undelivered patients, adolescent parent(s), single moms, parents facing difficult decisions, and parents who experience the loss of their babies.

THE UNDELIVERED PATIENT

Many prenatal patients struggle on the OB unit. These patients may be very sick or required to stay in the hospital because of problems with their pregnancy. They share feelings of loss of control of their lives, helplessness, and anxiety about the health of their babies. They may feel like a ship without an anchor as they are buffeted by circumstances beyond their control. They may struggle physically as well as spiritually because they are unsure that they will be able to endure what lies ahead.

One of the biggest challenges is a mom with hyperemesis. One patient, whose vomiting persisted into the second trimester, lost more weight than usual. The staff was very concerned with her care and began to wonder if there were psychological issues to be addressed. Her physician ordered hyperalimentation for several weeks and she was discharged, only to be readmitted in the same twenty-four-hour period. She feared for the health of her baby. Refraining from judgment, the staff acknowledged her feelings, graciously accepted her request for prayers and were supportive through her ordeal.

Some undelivered patients may express feelings about termination because they do not believe that they can continue. Some may pray for God to take the baby so they can obtain some relief but then struggle with guilt. Caregivers need to support the patient by listening to their anguish, pain, and exhaustion rather than to their words. Often, by allowing the patient to verbalize these fears and by providing assurance that they are accepted, caregivers can help the patient explore their inner strength and beliefs. Although some staff members may not consider this to be a crisis, the chaplain may be able to provide additional guidance and support to the patient.

The patient who begins premature labor early in the pregnancy may be faced with many weeks or months of bed rest. Some of these patients are treated at home but occasionally complications may require they remain in the hospital for the duration of their pregnancies. They may feel a loss of control because their life seems to be put on hold. Often these patients are very concerned about little ones and husbands at home. The focus often shifts to the baby and the mom may not feel as important as she may have felt earlier in her pregnancy. During this time, her spirituality may be challenged and tested or explored and expanded. Feelings such as guilt over not wanting the pregnancy may arise. If there had been previous loss(es), this could be the only pregnancy to progress and both parents may be willing to do anything for the baby. Meeting each patient where she is at a given moment allows each to explore individual feelings.

Writing thoughts and feelings in a journal is a wonderful way to reflect on one's own spirituality. If a patient is anxious and has trouble resting, meditation tapes, music, and guided imagery may be very helpful. Support services of local and/or national organizations like Sidelines provide understanding, peer support, resources, and wonderful suggestions that help these patients get through a very difficult time. These moms need to be reassured that, as helpless as they may feel, they are truly important to their unborn baby.

Daily visits from the pastoral care person can be breaths of fresh air and provide hope to the bedridden OB patient. During my fourth pregnancy, when I was struggling with severe preeclampsia, I valued the acknowledgment of my overwhelming fear that my baby and I would die. I do not remember any specific words, but I am still thankful for the consistent visits of my pastoral care person, for her warm hugs and sincere simple prayers that flowed from her heart. I clearly remember my own spiritual crisis that occurred in the middle of one night. I was very sick because my blood pressure had climbed even higher that night. My nurse was caring for me and I began to cry. I told her, "I am too sick to pray and I feel I need to; tomorrow is my C-Section and I'm not sure we are going to make it." She listened as she continued to rub my back and said, "Cathi, your pain is your prayer." She accepted me as I was and addressed my spiritual need at that moment in time. I was able to feel God's presence and endure that frightening night. She did not retreat from giving me spiritual support and I have never forgotten her because she provided both physical and spiritual care to me.

THE ADOLESCENT PATIENT

The situation that the teenage mom finds herself in may be challenging for her, her family, and her caregivers. "Chronological age does not always correspond to maturity level. An adolescent may be at one level cognitively and another level psychosocially, so it is important to base the plan for care on the level of development" [2]. This has implications for spiritual care as well. A number of years ago, teen mothers chose adoption whereas now the trend seems to be that more teens are keeping their babies. More and more teens are becoming very young parents.

As hard as it may be, caregivers must reserve personal biases and judgments. Teen pregnancies may occur as a result of a first sexual encounter or rape, not necessarily from promiscuity. However, some adolescents believe that becoming pregnant is a ticket to freedom and adulthood. They may believe that a baby is a guarantee that someone will love them. To them, a baby can be a symbol of self-worth and accomplishment. They may not have considered all of the challenges of parenthood and how this baby will alter their lifestyle and responsibilities. Instead, they may hold an idealized vision of motherhood as a child with a doll.

Some teen parents may be hostile or sarcastic as a way of coping with an unwanted pregnancy. Many are still searching for an identity as an individual. Adjustment to becoming parents, determining what their relationship to each other may be, how their relationship to their own parents will change, and what their new responsibilities will involve can be overwhelming.

Very young moms need to be treated with respect as do other moms. As patients, these moms should be questioned directly. If the father of the baby is involved, he should be included in the conversations as well as the guardian/parent present. Many teenage moms are frightened by the labor and delivery process and need reassurance and empowerment that they will make it through the birthing process.

Caregivers can maintain perspective by asking teenage parents what the baby means to them. By assuming nothing and taking time to listen, caregivers can better meet the physical and spiritual needs of teen moms. These young moms may not have much insight into their situation and may not be able to explore their spirituality at the time of their pregnancy. Caregivers have valid concerns and frustrations with the immaturity and lack of experience of these moms and dads, so follow-up and post-natal education is essential for the physical care of the baby and the mom. If caregivers strive to meet the needs and fears of these moms, without being condescending, one day they will be able to reflect on their own personal growth from the experience.

Emily, a thirteen year old, became pregnant as a result of rape. She decided to give up her baby for adoption. She had tremendous support from her family and social services. Her labor was very long and difficult; she was not able to progress without intervention. After the doctor finally performed a C-Section, she delivered a healthy baby. She held her baby for the longest time and shared how she knew this baby was meant for parents who were unable to have children. She had prayed that the hurt involved in conceiving this baby would be resolved and that this baby would bring her adoptive parents much happiness. This innocent eighth grader showed unbelievable maturity and spiritual growth. By being open to her as an individual, her caregivers provided her with tenderness and affirmation so that she was able to express her inner-most thoughts and feelings and they were able to share a very sacred, spiritual moment.

THE SINGLE PARENT

These moms are beyond adolescence and the baby's father may not be involved in the pregnancy. Several years ago this occurrence was rare, but in recent years the numbers have increased. According to 1999 Vital Statistic records 30 percent of all live births are to single moms. Acceptance of a couple who have a baby out of wedlock is fairly widespread today. It may not be viewed by the couple or single mom as a problem. The parents may be in a stable relationship, but more often the father is not present or supportive of the pregnancy. Furthermore, artificial insemination may mean that there is no recognized father and surrogacy may mean that other individuals will be involved in the pregnancy and birth.

Casey, a single mom, was twenty-nine years old, educated, and in a relationship with an older man who was not involved with her pregnancy or her labor and delivery. She was very hurt by his choices and lack of involvement but conveyed her love for her baby and her intense desire to be a mother. Her relationship with her baby became her focus along with the caregiver's. Affirmation of her as a prospective mom allowed her to get through the pregnancy and begin her new role. She felt so blessed to have her healthy son and was able to move beyond the hurt of the father's absence to experience all the wonders and joys of becoming a mother.

Susan was approaching her fortieth birthday with sadness and regret. She had not met the person of her dreams with whom she would share her life and still wanted to be a mother. Because this was so important to her, she underwent artificial insemination. The procedure had been challenging but successful. When Susan arrived on the OB unit in labor, she was full of excitement and anticipation. She shared that she was a single mom whose support for her decision was minimal but she had no regrets. Her caregivers were open and made no judgments as they assisted her. They were able to share a very special, spiritual moment as she became a mother.

Occasionally, sometimes with poverty stricken, single women, blissful joy may not be expressed when a baby is born. If the father provides no support, the mother may be overwhelmed as she faces caring for this baby and perhaps several other children at home. She may express anger at God and everyone in her path for her predicament. These women may not be open to any spiritual direction during their short stay because their primary concern is basically financial and physical survival. These moms present a tremendous challenge to caregivers.

DIFFICULT DECISIONS

With today's advances in medical technology, physicians are able to diagnose birth defects or other potential problems or risks early in a pregnancy and parents are faced with decisions few feel prepared to make. Parents are given the choice of continuing or terminating a pregnancy when there is a life threatening or fatal defect. New treatments, such as intrauterine surgery and other prenatal procedures, present difficult decisions for prospective parents. Fifteen years ago these options were neither available nor presented to families.

No situation has a clear-cut right or wrong solution. As families make these heart wrenching decisions, their spirituality is often challenged because most of these decisions involve faith beliefs and moral ethics. Parents may be torn between previous beliefs and their feelings about intervention procedures and their baby.

Mike and Eve learned at twenty weeks that their baby had several severe birth defects that would result in death. Their physician suggested they consider interrupting the pregnancy. This was very difficult for both of them because of their religious beliefs but they were afraid to continue the pregnancy. They read literature on these defects and researched the procedure for the termination. They spoke to their religious leader and other parents who had been through a similar situation. Their doctor presented their case to the ethics board and the termination by induction was approved at the hospital. Their son Samuel lived for an hour after his birth. The couple had the opportunity to see and hold their baby, name him, and have a farewell ritual. They grieved the loss of their baby but were at peace with their decision.

Carolyn and John were given the prenatal diagnosis of anencephaly at sixteen weeks. They were faced with continuing or terminating the pregnancy. They struggled for several agonizing days before they decided to continue the pregnancy, even though they knew that the baby could only live for a few minutes. Carolyn cherished the time that she carried her baby but it was not easy. They prepared for the hellos and good-byes they knew they would face during those four long months. Their daughter Hilary lived for twenty minutes and died in her parents arms. Saddened, yet at peace, they buried their little girl.

Both of these couples loved their babies deeply and grieved their deaths. Yet each grew spiritually during this difficult time. It is imperative that caregivers give these families support without judgment and provide the resources they need to explore all of their options so that the parents are secure in knowing that they made the best decision at the time. This helps parents avoid a spiritual crisis at a later time, although guilt and "second-guessing" will still probably occur. All options need to be presented to the parents regardless of their religious affiliation so that they themselves affirm their own beliefs. "Care must be taken to provide the options—the needed information for decision making—without making the parents feel guilty about their choices. Sensitivity and respect for the individual are paramount in this highly emotional and vulnerable time" [3]. These parents need time to decide what is best for them and their baby. Many health centers who work with families facing these challenges have a multidisciplinary team of physician, nurse, social worker, and chaplain. With this approach the physical, social, emotional, and spiritual needs of the parents can be addressed.

THE DEATH OF A BABY

In the last twenty years, caregivers have gained great knowledge in ways to minister and assist bereaved parents at the time of their loss. Yet, even the most experienced caregiver begins anew as another family faces such a tragic loss. Grief is as individual as the footprint each special baby leaves on his/her parents' hearts. Sr. Jane Marie Lamb, OSF states, "The grief experience is universal, yet each person has his or her own personality, history and coping style. Hospital guidelines regarding perinatal deaths must be based on respect for privacy and individual needs and responses" [3].

Most parents do not anticipate a perinatal loss. "Perinatal death, whether it be from miscarriage, ectopic pregnancy, stillbirth, or neonatal death, is a devastating crisis for parents. Most parents are unaware of their own needs and the options available to them at the time of their loss. After they have gone home, however, parents begin to regret opportunities with their baby that were lost to them in the hospital" [4]. Table 1 offers sample rights for parents and babies that caregivers can give to parents and use in establishing the policies and procedures of their own institutions. These rights originated when parents and professionals contacted the National SHARE Office for understanding and support of their many needs. SHARE Pregnancy and Infant Loss Support, Inc. is a not-for-profit organization that has worked for twenty years as a resource for bereaved parents and for caregivers as well. The original work of The Perinatal Bereavement Team at Women's College in Toronto was expanded to include choices that bereaved parents should be able to make when their baby dies and the result was "The Rights of Parents."

It is important that the doctor, nurse, pastoral care, social worker, pastor, funeral home (if involved) work together with the bereaved parents and other family members, whether as a formal or informal team, to provide the optimum care during this most challenging time. It is imperative that caregivers communicate the parents' needs and wishes so that there is a continuity of care. Also, it is important that the caregivers understand how to present and explain the rights and choices families have with compassion and sensitivity. There are many resource articles and books that can increase the caregiver's sensitivity when presenting these rights. Each family chooses that with which they are most comfortable. Many times their choices will depend on their religious or cultural background and must be respected. The more time the family has to consider their alternatives, the easier it is for them to make decisions and the less regret they tend to have.

Many times while working with these patients any member of the team may be called upon to outline and present the parents' rights. This may occur during the questioning and natural flow of the situation. The chaplain may not be readily available and the patient or a family member may have immediate emotional and/or spiritual needs. It is very difficult to define where each caregiver's job ends and begins in terms of emotional and spiritual comfort. Ideally, when spiritual

Table 1. Parents' and Babies' Rights

Rights of Parents When a Baby Dies

- To be given the opportunity to see, hold, and touch their baby at any time before and/or after death within reason.
- To have photographs of their baby taken and made available to the parents or held in security until the parents wish to see them.
- To be given as many mementos as possible, e.g., crib card, baby beads, ultrasound and/or other photos, lock of hair, foot and hand prints, and record of weight and length.
- To name their child and bond with him or her.
- To observe cultural and religious practices.
- To be cared for by an empathetic staff who will respect their feelings, thoughts, beliefs, and individual requests.
- To be with each other throughout hospitalization as much as possible.
- To be given time alone with their baby, allowing for individual needs.
- To be informed about the grieving process.
- To request an autopsy. In the case of a miscarriage, to request to have or *not* have an autopsy or pathology exam as determined by applicable law.
- To have information presented in terminology understandable to the parents regarding their baby's status and cause of death, including autopsy and pathology reports and medical records.
- To plan a farewell ritual, burial, and cremation in compliance with local and state regulations and according to their personal beliefs, religious, or cultural tradition.
- To be provided with information on support resources which assist in the healing process, e.g., support groups, counseling, reading material, and perinatal loss newsletters.

Rights of the Baby

- To be recognzied as a person who was born and died.
- To be named.
- To be seen, touched, and held by the family.
- To have life-ending acknowledged.
- To be put to rest with dignity.

Source: Parents and Babies Rights, *SHARE Newsletter,* p. 15, January/February 1992.

issues arise, they must be addressed by the professional caregiver who is present.

Caregivers have a responsibility to explain these rights to patients who experience the death of a baby due to miscarriage, ectopic pregnancy, pregnancy interruption, stillbirth, or neonatal death. When compassionate caregivers openly discuss such options, bereaved parents can say hello and good-bye to their babies. They are able to cope and integrate their loss better than those who are not given choices. When caregivers establish an atmosphere of compassion and respect at the time of the loss of a baby, they open the way for a sacred moment to occur. Because of these efforts, parents will be able to look back on that moment with gratitude and love rather than with anger and despair. The different circumstances of perinatal loss require some specific strategies but all instances call for sensitivity, openness, and tender compassion on the part of the caregivers.

Miscarriage
(the death of a baby in utero under 20 weeks gestation)

Parents almost never expect a miscarriage to occur. If the miscarriage occurs early, they may still be adjusting to the pregnancy and must then face adjusting to the loss of their baby. The mom may or may not have felt movement, but often has already bonded to the baby she carries. The dad is often more concerned with her well-being. The mom may be in pain or believe that she did something to cause the miscarriage to occur. A sense of helplessness, loss of control, and fear are strong emotions that these parents often feel. Quiet reassurance and explanation that the miscarriage usually occurs as a result of the death of a baby and often does not cause the baby's death helps parents in terms of guilt and blame. The sudden onset of a miscarriage can bring about many strong, even conflicting, emotions and irrational thoughts may be expressed. When caregivers acknowledge that losing a baby may be one of the hardest things that they will ever have to face, parents feel that they are given permission to grieve, even though many people will discount their loss. When caregivers encourage verbalization of feelings by bereaved parents, healing can begin to occur.

Angela entered the Out Patient Department for a D&C. She and her husband Carl had struggled with infertility for three years. Even though she was just in her fifteenth week, she had bonded with her baby. Carl did not understand her emotional pain; he was more concerned with her physical condition. Angela gratefully chose to see her baby even though the baby was very tiny. It really helped her to see the respect her caregivers gave to her baby. Her only regret was that they were unable to determine the baby's sex. However, she chose the name Joey, which could be for a boy or a girl.

Abby was not excited when she discovered she was pregnant because she had two other children and, at first, she was relieved when she began miscarrying her baby at eleven weeks. But, a few hours later, she began to feel guilty about her thoughts. Abby began bleeding heavily and her doctor told her it was necessary to perform a D&C. Her husband Ron, in the surgery waiting room with another caregiver, felt helpless. He lashed out, "It is making me sick knowing our baby is being torn into pieces during the D&C. Why is this happening to us? I am so angry at God!" It was very important that he was not alone and that a caregiver was with him to listen. He was able to express his feelings of disgust, disappointment, and anger, to cry and lash out at God. His feelings were acknowledged and accepted without judgment by the caregiver. He did not really want answers as much as he wanted his baby. But as he verbalized his feelings, he was able to let go of some of the anger and move toward healing.

Early pregnancy loss is a time of crisis for these parents as they arrive at the hospital. Caregivers may not truly know what the parents are feeling. It is very important to refrain from making any assumptions. Caregivers can gently ask, "Can you tell me what this baby has meant to you?" The answers vary tremendously. The parents may have considered the pregnancy an answer to prayers after many years of infertility. This could be their first baby who was anticipated with joy and love. The couple could have delayed having children because of careers. The pregnancy may not have been planned or wanted. They may be confused about their feelings and sense of loss or view the pregnancy loss as punishment from God. Or, their only concern may be about the physical aspects of a procedure. The answer to this question gives the caregiver valuable information so that s/he can proceed with an explanation of the parents' choices and their rights.

Some families find great comfort in seeing, holding, and naming their tiny babies while others choose not to do so. For some, the baby is so small, that it is not recognizable. Some bury their baby privately and choose a farewell ritual or blessing ceremony while others are thankful for the hospital burial policy for babies under twenty weeks. Most importantly, printed information regarding choices and the grief process are essential for bereaved parents to process their loss in a way that promotes healing. Follow-up and information about bereaved parent support groups help these parents as they cope with their loss.

Unfortunately these families have very few tangible mementos of their babies. Often, they are not given the understanding, compassion, and acknowledgment that they need. These parents want their baby and their grief to be acknowledged. To a very large number of parents who experience a loss before twenty weeks, this is a baby, not a fetus or tissue. They are grateful for compassionate caregivers during and after their losses as they question their beliefs and the meaning of this early loss. When caregivers perceive the touching and separation of the baby's and parents' lives as sacred moments, the respect that is so sought after by parents is gratefully acknowledged. Most faiths do not have a ritual for miscarriage, nor do they consider people who have no living children as parents. Jim Cunningham, Director Of Pastoral Care at Fairview General Hospital in Cleveland, Ohio, has challenged clergy to plan a service in remembrance of babies who died in utero and asks them to take note of the large number of parents who attend [5]. Faith communities do not always provide support for parents who have had an early pregnancy loss and may be insensitive to their grief.

Stillbirth
(the death of a baby in utero from 20 weeks to term gestation)

Usually, a few hours prior to admission to the hospital, most OB patients and their partners happily anticipate the wonders of being parents by planning and dreaming about the baby they are expecting. When parents go to their doctor's office for a routine checkup or ultrasound and no heartbeat is found, they move from blissful happiness to devastation when they learn that their baby has died in utero. Experiencing these strong, diametrically opposed feelings in such a short time is very difficult. So when they arrive at the hospital dazed and confused, they are in dire need of support, direction, and information from those who will care for them. These individuals still have a stake in their pregnancy and it is important to understand their anticipated relationship with their baby. The parents were ready to say hello to their baby but instead must say good-bye with overwhelming hurt.

Michelle and Harry entered the same hospital OB unit for the second time in less than a year. Both times they delivered a stillborn son at twenty weeks. Two years prior to his first baby dying, Harry's first wife and two children were killed in a car accident. Harry tearfully said, "I am doomed, I am not meant to have children. I must not be a good parent." In that moment of despair, Harry could not wait for his pastor to arrive. His spiritual needs had to be addressed. The caregiver gave them her tears, time, and validation and shared their hurt by allowing them to talk about their disillusionment, confusion with God, and their hurt. Later, their pastor did provide counseling but what they needed most was compassion and permission to question their spirituality at that moment. They did not feel abandoned or alone.

Carol and John, thinking they were to deliver their baby within the hour, came to the hospital in the transitional stage of labor. Upon arrival, a fetal monitor indicated that the baby did not have a heartbeat. An ultrasound confirmed the tragedy. Within the hour, Carol delivered her stillborn son Matthew. Both parents were overwhelmed by extreme grief. Their choices were sensitively and carefully explained, yet they really struggled with making any decisions. They spent just a few minutes with their son on the day of delivery. Carol was discharged a few hours later. The next day they felt differently when their caregiver talked to them in a follow-up call. Some of the initial shock had worn off and they wanted their choices to be explained again. They were so thankful that they could see, bathe, dress, and hold their baby at the funeral home. They also chose to have a beautiful farewell ritual with their pastor and their three-year-old son.

Hannah and Jim arrived from the doctor's office after finding out that their baby did not have a heartbeat. Hannah was not in labor and her induction began that evening. Hannah did not deliver for three days. During that time, the staff was able to explain the rights and choices several times before their baby Elizabeth was born. The entire team was involved, including both of the couple's pastors. Hannah and Jim spent hours with their baby and chose to have a naming ceremony for Elizabeth. They decided to have a viewing at the funeral home and a comforting grave side service.

Being supportive of bereaved parents' decisions is one of the most important ways that professional caregivers can meet their needs. Non-traditional rituals with country western music, charismatic services, or traditional funerals provide comfort to these parents, regardless of what a caregiver thinks. Every child is unique and by personalizing his or her service, a family affirms that individuality and the place of the baby in the family. Rituals are healing and even more so if the family plays an active part in the planning the ceremony.

Neonatal Loss
(birth to 28 days)

When a baby dies during this neonatal period, parents usually will be able to spend some time together during his or her short life. Sometimes the death is impending and other times the death is not expected. Having a sick baby who is still hospitalized in a neonatal care unit can be an emotional roller coaster. Parents become exhausted from the stress of the birth, their other responsibilities, and trying to spend what little time they may have with their sick infant. Often there are decisions that need to be made which involve extraordinary means such as surgeries, medications, therapies, and respirators. Parents can feel like their child becomes the caregivers' as the baby is evaluated, invaded with wires and tubes, or monitored by many machines. Many times they cannot even hold their child and may be cautioned against touching their baby because of possible transmission of harmful ineffective agents. Most NICU caregivers are aware of the parents' concerns and attempt, when possible, to involve the parents and grandparents in the baby's care. It is important to know that parents are frightened by all of the activity and equipment and feel quite helpless. Often, the mom may not be very mobile or is very sick herself or the baby may be hospitalized far from the family home. Multiple births, premature births, or congenital disorders further complicate how parents cope with an infant in the NICU and neonatal loss.

Our son Christopher was born prematurely at twenty-nine weeks and transferred to a children's hospital in the same city. Due to my unstable condition, I was unable to leave the hospital during his short life of four days. My husband Chuck visited each of us three times a day. He gave me support and updates on Christopher's progress. It was probably the most challenging week my husband has ever had. Both of us were asking, "Why God? Why does our son have to go through all of this and why are you allowing our hearts to be broken? Is God in this NICU?" We were fortunate to have very supportive caregivers at both facilities. Also, the communication between both facilities' caregivers was very good. There were no answers for many of our questions but their support and presence, hugs and tears helped us through our darkest hours and will always be remembered. God was present in that NICU and He worked through these caring individuals.

Suzie and Greg's daughter, Allyssa, was born prematurely with an unexpected diagnosis of Trisomy 18. The doctors felt Allyssa would only live for a short time. The couple decided to take Allyssa home and let her die peacefully in their surroundings and were assisted by hospice staff, family, and friends. Allyssa amazed everyone; she lived for four weeks. Even though at times it was challenging, Suzie and Greg were thankful for their time together and created some cherished memories. Suzie was a practicing Baptist and Greg was a non-practicing Catholic. During Allysa's short life, baptism was discussed as an option and even though infant baptism was not the practice of Suzie's faith, it was important to Greg and Allyssa was baptized. No assumptions can be made by caregivers; parents must be made aware of options they may not have considered and make the final decision for their family. To say their final good-byes, Suzie and Greg invited their family and friends to their home where they held a meaningful service under the trees in their back yard. Allyssa was buried in their small family cemetery on their property.

Parents who have babies who live and soon die are thankful for the moments they have during their child's short life. However, there is never enough time and their hopes and dreams for their baby are shattered by the finality of death. With Sudden Infant Death Syndrome, the death of their baby is totally unexpected. Many parents express disbelief that their baby died because they believed the child would survive. One couple's son had survived two surgeries and was progressing well. They were preparing to take him home when he took a terrible turn for the worse and died quickly. Others have shared that they had so many people praying for them and they believed that God would heal their baby. They just knew their baby would live. They may feel disillusioned and confused, even betrayed. Many feel they have failed as parents because they could not do anything for their baby. It is imperative that caregivers acknowledge these deep emotions and not use worthless platitudes such as "This is God's will, the baby would not have been normal anyway . . . or you went through this because you are strong and He only gives us what we can bear." Instead, caregivers can tenderly express sadness that this baby died, grieve with the parents, and explain that they have every right to their feelings. Only then can healing begin. Caregivers explain what to expect from medical procedures, but often fail to explain what bereaved parents may expect to go through as they grieve for their baby. Bereaved parents are not prepared to filter inane, trite phrases that people, even people of faith, will say to them and they are often quite hurt by these comments.

The mementos and memories caregivers create for families have a lasting impact on their healing. One family was so grateful their children were able to be involved with their dying baby. The two other siblings were able to hold and touch their baby. They took family pictures that they cherish. Often other family members are excluded with thoughts of protecting them. Only their parents know if excluding their other children will be more harmful or healing. This experience was a comforting, created memory that might not have happened if the option had not been discussed and the parents had not been open to the request made by their children.

Caregivers are becoming very creative by making permanent cast moldings of the baby's hand and footprints. All mementos, locks of hair, baby bracelets, crib cards, stuffed toys, baby's clothing, and blankets are so important to the bereaved parents. They are tangible reminders that parents can hold even though they can no longer hold their precious baby. These special items validate that *this baby was real, was present on this earth and is very much a part of their lives.*

CONCLUSION

The topics addressed in this chapter are not wholly inclusive of all of the spiritual challenges presented to OB caregivers. Other important, complex issues such as postpartum depression and adoption have not been noted. But in this chapter, many diverse spiritual moments in the obstetric setting have been explored. Personal stories have been shared for your enlightenment and enhancement of your knowledge base of the spiritual challenges an OB caregiver addresses daily. It is my hope that you will glean insights on ways of reaching out to mothers and fathers during their short stay. Caregivers need to move toward a multidisciplinary approach of caring for all of the needs of these special families.

There are many challenges that we, as caregivers, face personally in reaching out to mothers and fathers. My greatest hope is that you will be able to ride the waves of emotions and spirituality with these parents, from the crests to the troughs. By doing so, your heart will be opened to new dimensions of your own spiritually.

ORGANIZATIONS THAT PROVIDE SUPPORT TO BEREAVED PARENTS

Aiding Mothers & Fathers
Experiencing Neonatal Death
(AMEND)
Maureen Connelly
4324 Berrywick Terrace
St. Louis, MO 63128
314-487-7582

Anencephaly Support Foundation
Anne Andis/Cynthia Coates
30827 Sifton
Spring, TX 77386
888-206-7256
www.asfhelp.com
e-mail: asf@asfhelp.com

Abiding Hearts
(Continuing pregnancy after prenatal diagnosis of fatal/ non-fatal birth defects)
Maria LaFond-Budge
P.O. Box 904
Libby, MT 59923
406-293-4416
Fax: 406-587-7197
www.imt.net/~hearts
e-mail: hearts@imt.net

Bereaved Parents of the USA
Shirley Otman, Pres.
National Headquarters
P.O. Box 95
Park Forest, IL 60466
708-748-7672
www.bereaveparentsusa.org
e-mail: ro0002@jove.acs.unt.edu

Bereavement Service
Fran Rybarik
1910 South Avenue
LaCrosse, WI 54601
800-362-9567 Ext. 4747
608-791-4747
www.gundluth.org/bereave
e-mail: Berservs@gundluth.org
Fax: 608-791-5137

Center For Loss In Multiple
Birth (CLIMB)
Jean Kollantai
P.O. Box 91377
Anchorage, AK 99517
907-222-5321
www.climb-support.com
e-mail: climb@pobox.alaska.net

Assn. of Congenital Diaphramatic
Hernia Research, Advocacy &
Support (CHERUBS)
Dawn. M. Torrance
P.O. Box 1150
Creedmoor, NC 27522
888-834-8158 or 919-693-8158
www.cherubs-cdh.org
e-mail: info@cherubs-cdh.org
Fax: 815-425-9155

The Compassionate Friends
National Office
Diana Cunningham
P.O. Box 3696
Oak Brook, IL 60522
630-990-0010
www.compassionatefriends.org
Fax: 630-990-0246

Downs Syndrome
666 Broadway
New York, NY 10012
800-221-4602 or 212-460-9330

www.ndss.org
Fax: 212-979-2873

Heartbreaking Choice
(Pregnancy Interruption)
Molly Minnick
Pineapple Press
P.O. Box 312
St. John's, MI 48879
517-224-1881
www.erichad.com/ahc

In Loving Memory—
Support for Loss of an Only/
or All Children
Linda Nielson
1416 Green Run Lane
Reston, VA 20190
703-435-0608
Fax: 703-435-3111

InterNational Council on
Infertility Information
Dissemination (INCIID)
Nancy Hemingway
P.O. Box 6836
Arlington, VA 22206
703-379-9178 or 520-544-9548
www.inciid.org
e-mail: inciidinfo@inciid.org
Fax: 703-379-1593

National SIDS and Other Infant
Death
Program Support Center
1314 Bedford Avenue, Suite 210
Baltimore, MD 21208
800-221-7437
410-653-8226
www.sidsalliance.org
e-mail: sidshq@charm.net
Fax: 410-653-8709

Pen-Parents
Melissa Swanson
P.O. Box 8738
Reno, NV 89507
702-826-7332
www.penparents.org
e-mail: PenParents@aol.com
Fax: 702-337-0866

Pregnancy & Infant Loss Center
(PILC)
Donna Roehl/Charlene Nelson
1421 E. Wayzata Blvd., Suite 70
Wayzata, MN 55391
952-473-9372
www.pilc.org
Fax: 952-473-8978

Pregnancy Institute
(Cord Accidents)
Dr. Jason Collins
2250 Gause Blvd., Suite 200
Slidell, LA 70461
504-649-0492
www.preginst.com
e-mail:
  75563.72@compuserve.com

RESOLVE, Inc. (Infertility)
National Office
1310 Broadway
Somerville, MA 02144
617-623-0744
www.resolve.org
e-mail: info@resolve.org

SHARE Pregnancy & Infant
Loss Support, Inc.
Cathi Lammert, RN

National SHARE Office
St. Joseph Health Center
300 First Capitol Drive
St. Charles, MO 63301
800-821-6819 or 636-947-6164
www.nationalshareoffice.com
e-mail:
  share@nationalshareoffice.com
Fax: 636-947-7486

Sidelines National Support
Network
(Complicated Pregnancies)
Candace Hurley
P.O. Box 1808
Laguna Beach, CA 92652
949-497-2265
www.sidelines.org
e-mail: sidelines@sidelines.org

SOFT
Trisomy 18 & Related Disorders)
2982 S. Union Street
Rochester, NY 14624
800-716-SOFT
www.trisomy.org
e-mail: barbv@trisomy.org

Wisconsin Stillbirth Service
Program
Univ. of Wisconsin-Madison
Dr. Richard M. Pauli
Clinical Genetics Center
1500 Highland Avenue
Madison, WI 53705
608-262-9722
www.wisc.edu/wissp

REFERENCES

1. J. J. Driscoll, The Sound of Spirit Blowing, *Vision 6*:9, pp. 14-16, October 1996.
2. P. Drake, Addressing Developmental Needs of Pregnant Adolescents, *Journal of Obstetric Gynecologic and Neonatal Nursing, 25*:6, pp. 518-524, 1996.
3. J. M. Lamb, Parents' Needs and Rights When a Baby Dies, *Health Progress,* pp. 52-57, December 1992.
4. M. R. Primeau and J. M. Lamb, When a Baby Dies: Rights of the Baby and Parents, *Journal of Obstetric Gynecologic and Neonatal Nursing, 24*:3, pp. 206-208, 1996.
5. J. R. Woods, Jr. and J. L. Esposito Woods (eds.), *Loss during Pregnancy or in the Newborn Period,* Jannetti Publications, New Jersey, 1997.

CHAPTER 18

The Trauma Patient

Reverend Paul Bierlein

- The driver of a minivan falls asleep at the wheel, rolling the van onto the berm and injuring herself and six passengers in the vehicle.
- An electrician slips and falls from a scaffolding severely injuring his back.
- A thirty-year-old man attempts to kill himself after murdering his wife, their daughter, and his girlfriend.
- A young businesswoman, from out of state, passes out in her hotel room and is brought to the ER with indications of abdominal bleeding.

Trauma strikes in many forms—accidents, violent crimes, industrial injuries, and medical conditions which suddenly become acute. At times it involves a major disaster with both direct and indirect impact on the lives of many. More often it is an individual drama unfolding at the scene or in the emergency room, involving the patient and a small cadre of family and caregivers.

The word "trauma" means "wound," and carries the connotation of something external inflicting pain and injury on a person. Yet, as with the young businesswoman, the "wound" sometimes comes from within the body, from a disease process suddenly and acutely threatening the whole person. That, too, is trauma. In fact, trauma has come to be identified as much with the emotional, psychological, and spiritual impact or wounding as with the actual physical injury. Even post-traumatic syndromes are included within the scope of this concept.

Trauma encompasses a broad and diverse spectrum of painful and tragic human experience. The focus of this chapter is to "visit" with trauma patients—to listen with sensitivity and compassion, exploring the spiritual themes and issues which the sudden encounter with pain, injury, attack, or illness engenders within them. While these issues will be examined individually, they are, in reality, dynamically interwoven spiritual threads of a whole person in crisis. The reflections will not seek to be exhaustive but representative, hopefully providing windows that invite the reader to peer more intently into the spirit and soul of the person caught up in trauma.

PAIN

I hurt so bad I asked the Lord to die.

Beginning a survey of the spiritual concerns of trauma patients with pain may seem strange. After all, pain is physical. That reaction may well indicate how strongly dualistic presuppositions underlie our perspectives (and perhaps medicine's less than stellar record in pain management). A holistic perspective suggests that pain is indeed a matter of the spirit. Ask Brother Job about the anguish of pain, especially when his friends minimized it. Or ask the patient who shared the opening words of this segment.

Pain can be demoralizing and destructive of the human spirit, depending on one's interpretation. Is the pain a sign of God's disfavor or abandonment? Is it a judgment/punishment? Is it a testing to be endured? Is one's pain sharing in the pain of Jesus? Or is pain simply a human reality? The key focus in spiritual assessment is how the relationship to God or the divine is played out. Is the divine a partner, comforter, bearer with or for? Or is the divine viewed as the "enemy" or "ambusher"? Or is the divine simply an interested observer/bystander?

That is the territory of pain that invites "care-full" exploration, with the hope that the person might feel befriended in his pain rather than attacked, judged, or punished by it. In that context, efforts can and should be made to relieve or to ease the pain medically. If the nature of the trauma demands minimizing analgesics, if the necessary treatment will add to the discomfort, or if a patient out of his/her spiritual perspective chooses to endure the pain, then a supportive, reassuring presence and companionship becomes absolutely vital. That presence sees the groans and sighs of a person as prayers that words cannot express, and is comfortable in accepting and sharing those spiritual laments.

FEAR

I woke up and everything was flying around and upside down. My leg hurt and I couldn't move it. It was caught and I was afraid I would lose it.

For the trauma patient, fear—ranging from anxiety to sheer terror—is an immediate reality. Fear arises when the predictability and trustworthiness of our world is suddenly jeopardized and our very life and being is threatened. Add an "in-and-out," twilight level of awareness in which the pain of injuries, the discomforts of treatment, and flash-backs of the trauma merge in anxious confusion, and that fear grows more intense and overwhelming.

Fear, however, is more rooted in the person than the specific circumstances. Certainly, trauma can and often is life threatening and will trigger many fears. Yet, one patient will express overwhelming panic while another expresses fearfulness in more focused fashion. Or a non-critical patient will exhibit a frantic fear of dying while a patient in danger of dying may express fears about an imminent procedure.

Careful listening reveals that one factor behind the differing responses is that fear is really a collection of fears learned out of a person's experience with the world. Points where one's world has been untrustworthy or threatening in the past are triggers for present fears and often compound the intensity. If several close relatives have died in auto accidents, we may be more fearful if we are involved in an accident. Also, the fears shared by other significant persons may augment our own collection. The caregiving task is to help the person name the "terrors," identifying those that are most intense and weighing them against reality. Some fears may diminish and fade; some fears may prove appro-priate and intensify, thus demanding a supportive presence and a willingness to assist the person in facing them.

A more significant root underlying the varied fear responses is the patient's sense of the Divine Purpose's intention toward oneself. Is God or the divine perceived as desiring one's good? Or does ill will seem to predominate? That same collection of world experience that fashioned the fears also shapes the perception of divine intent. More significant than that collection, however, is the sense of divine love conveyed in the conduct and caring of significant persons in the patient's life. On that is built a foundation of trust that can outweigh much untrustworthi-ness and a sense of divine goodwill that provides courage in the face of the fear. As caregivers, our listening will search for such foundational encounters with the divine as well as provide such an encounter in our own relationship to the patient so that fears might be eased and a measure of peace restored.

HELPLESSNESS

I could hear someone saying, "We're losing her!"
I wanted to sit up and say, "No, you're not!" but
I couldn't do anything. I felt so helpless and alone.

Those words of a friend recounting her experience in ICU as she went into a second anaphylactic episode following a bee sting highlight the isolated and helpless feelings that can accompany the trauma experience. The patient, especially when response is limited by the injury or interventions, finds herself in the hands of strangers, aware of and hearing things said about her but unable to respond. It is as if one becomes a spectator of one's own life.

Two spiritual issues come into sharp focus. The first, already touched on in relation to fear, is the capacity to trust. Trauma often creates a situation where one is utterly dependent on others. Have others been dependable in one's life? Has the "Divine Other" been faithful? These become crucial, albeit unspoken, questions underlying a patient's ability to place herself into the care of others, to relinquish for the moment much of what she does for herself.

A second spiritual dimension is a sense of connectedness, a feeling of human and divine companionship. Trust rests on relationship and connectedness. The caregiver hopes that there is already a web of relationships supporting a person's life and listens carefully for evidence of that, e.g., family, friends, or clergy present; stories of sharing. If present, these familiar and vital companions are brought into the patient's medical world as soon and as much as feasible without jeopardizing treatment. At the very least, a chaplain or caregiver serves as a bridge between treatment and waiting rooms, bringing messages from those familiar companions. The caregiver also seeks to be a companion, especially if others are not available. Such a companion speaks *to* the patient, never *about* the patient (something all caregivers do well to remember in the presence of a patient). Companionship seeks by words and appropriate touch to reassure and encourage, to reach across that "curtain of isolation and separateness" and draw the patient back from spectator to participant, to remind a dear friend that she was not totally helpless, that the "No, you're not!" shouted in her mind and heart was an integral part of her healing and recovery.

Companionship seeks to connect the divine with the patient. Whether through pastoral presence, hope-filled words, or ritual actions, the goal is to signal the presence of divine love and care in those helpless moments.

GUILT/ANGER

I'm so angry with myself!
IIow could I fall asleep at the wheel
and hurt my family so?

Guilt and anger are two closely related answers to the same question: "Why?" Guilt mumbles in remorse while anger shouts in defiance. At their root, both seek to make sense out of the tragedy, to explain or to fix blame.

Sometimes the trauma is of one's own doing and so the anger and guilt are self-focused, as with the driver who fell asleep at the wheel. The anger is directed at self and there is overwhelming guilt. Often other remnants of guilt and self-judgment come cascading forth, like a relentless internal "prosecuting attorney." The caregiver must resist the urge of the quick objection that short circuits the confession and unburdening. Reflecting with the person on these perceived failures allows for acknowledging those where responsibility is fairly taken and challenging those where the burden has been assumed or projected unfairly.

Anger is a feeling that often makes those around most uncomfortable. Yet anger can be appropriate and its expression helpful. Indeed, anger stored as hostility and resentment becomes a danger to the person and to others. Providing a safe space to share such angry feelings is helpful.

The anger may be expressed at self, at others, at God, and often at all of the above. In an auto accident, the patient may be angry at self for not approaching an intersection more carefully, angry at the other driver for running a stop sign, and angry at God or fate for allowing it to happen. The person who ran the stop sign may be angry at himself, but also angry at the other driver and God for not making allowances for his irresponsibility. Allowing the expression of all the angry feelings not only defuses their intensity but allows for eventual clarification and sorting out. The person who was hit may be able to focus and express the appropriate anger he feels toward the person who ran the stop sign. And the diversionary anger of the other driver can collapse out of sheer hollowness so he can finally deal with the self-anger and guilt of his responsibility.

The key spiritual issue in dealing with the two sides of this coin is a sense of grace or forgiveness. Without this spiritual dynamic, the person will be enslaved by stifling guilt or all-consuming anger, and the individual's life will be undermined or derailed. With this gift, the tragedy of the trauma need not be compounded into lifelong tragedy, a path to renewed living is possible. Spiritual caring will explore the terrain of grace with the trauma patient and, if the vista is limited, will seek to expand the horizon. Forgiveness is not a proclamation but a process for us humans, not a singular event but a day-to-day dynamic. Forgiveness doesn't magically erase remembrance, doesn't make all the hurt or anger disappear. But it does diminish their power and control over life and allow renewal and new beginnings.

Others can be invited to share that gift and nurture that process. Indeed, their words of forgiveness will often speak with greatest authority. A young student was brought to our emergency room after having misjudged a left turn in front of an oncoming truck. The pain of his multiple injuries paled in comparison to the anguish he felt knowing that his best friend and his own brother had been killed in the accident. His guilt and self-anger were overwhelming. Suddenly, his best friend's mother came into the room, traces of her own tears still evident. When he saw her, he began to cry saying, "I'm sorry!" over and over again. She gently put her fingers to his lips and said, "Rob, I know you are and I forgive you—I want you to forgive yourself." With that she gently hugged him. Such grace!

PURPOSE

You have to get me through this,
I have a little boy to raise.

With those words to the vascular surgeon, a young woman from Oklahoma eloquently stated her calling, her purpose in life. Far from home and her family, she would soon undergo surgery for abdominal bleeding. The trauma unfolding within her suddenly brought the tentativeness and vulnerability of human life into sharp focus, and with that the search for meaning, as Frankl has called it [1]. That search for meaning and purpose in one's life becomes more urgent in the face of life-threatening trauma. The urgency arises for two reasons: to affirm the worth and value of one's life thus far, and to lay out the purpose which still calls one to live.

The affirming of life often includes both a celebration of satisfying accomplishments and joyful moments as well as a measure of making peace, of touching on unresolved issues or hurts in the person's life and relationships. Thus, as we awaited her surgery, this young woman shared some of the struggles and frustrations she felt in her marriage relationship as well as the joys of birthing a son after a difficult pregnancy and her success in business. The caregiver needs to allow and encourage such sharing. It can foster a spiritual healing process that both removes barriers to the body's battle to recover from the present trauma as well as allows a more peace-filled death if recovery proves impossible. Thus, both joys and sorrows, successes and failures are shared, from mundane matters to profound moments in one's life. They are all a part of one's life-weaving.

More importantly, such life review helps to clarify and affirm the calling and purpose which invites living and invigorates the battle for recovery. Without the will to live, even the most marvelous efforts of modern medicine can prove futile. The caregiver's task is to listen for and help lift out the strands in this person's life-weaving that bring special joy and satisfaction, or that provide a goal or mission still needing her attention. Many times they surface naturally such as in the woman's comment to the surgeon. Often they are focused in significant relationships with others or with the divine.

At times, however, the windows of hope are obscured and the search is difficult. Indeed, the caregiver's own willingness to love and affirm the patient in that moment may provide the needed window to revisualizing life and a sense of calling.

COMMUNION AND RITUAL

Pray for me, please!

How do we respond to these words? What feelings do they generate in us? Most importantly, what do we hear in such words? Perhaps some of us jump at the request; it's a chance to "do something," to provide a religious service. Others may be more skeptical, trying to analyze whether the request reflects "magical thinking" or questioning whether such religious actions are meaningful.

There is a tendency today to divorce spirituality from religious expression, as if the two were at odds with each other. Religious ritual, symbols, and words are embodiments of spiritual reality; they are vessels that can assist in sharing and celebrating our spiritual treasures with one another. To divorce them is to impoverish and severely limit our spiritual caregiving.

Returning to our initial questions, what do we hear in these words and how do we respond? Is not the request a search for spiritual connectedness, a sense of belonging to a spiritual "family," of being embraced by God or the divine. It is mystical rather than magical, a desire for communion that transcends the fear, isolation, guilt, and other forces of separation at work in the trauma. Prayer, ritual, and religious expression are tangible connecting points to the divine mystery that lies at the heart of human experience.

How do we respond? Neither "jumping at the chance to do something" nor skeptical, somewhat judgmental, aloofness are helpful responses. What is called for is careful attention to the cues and indications of the patient's religious framework and simple, forthright conversation as to what would be most meaningful. The familiar words of a psalm, scripture, or traditional prayer may best touch the heart of some patients, like the elderly woman who had been largely unresponsive for several days and yet began to mouth the words of the Lord's Prayer as we spoke them gathered around her bed. For others, reflective prayer, spiritual dialogue, readings, meditation, or rituals of special meaning may be most helpful. Whatever the vessel, the goal is that the patient might feel embraced within the healing presence of the divine, within a communion of caring love.

While our focus has been on the trauma patient, that person is not an island. Those who wait—whose lives are interwoven with the victim's life—are in trauma, also. Most of the same spiritual dynamics will be evident, but not necessarily in ways that synchronize with those of the patient. Exploring the impact of family systems in trauma situations is beyond the scope of this chapter. However, several basic observations may be helpful. Listening to and observing the interaction of the trauma patient with the family can help assess the measure of support they offer as well as identify points of conflict. In addition to responding to the spiritual needs of those individuals, we may well find ourselves in a mediating role.

There may also be a need to protect the patient from the family member or friend who has a "need" for the patient to have "a certain religious experience." Generally, however, family members and friends are vital and supportive. Responding to their spiritual needs will enable them to be a resource for healing and recovery to the trauma patient.

Our visiting and listening to the trauma patient has touched on several spiritual concerns and themes that commonly arise in such crises. They provide a framework, but it is our task as spiritual caregivers to hear the unique nuances of each person's spiritual concerns in trauma. They may even well nudge us beyond the framework, inviting us to explore new spiritual frontiers, challenging us to reflect with them in unique ways on the spiritual realities of life.

REFERENCE

1. V. Frankl, *Man's Search for Meaning*, Washington Square Press, New York, 1963.

SUGGESTED READING

Fitchett, G., *Assessing Spiritual Needs*, Augsburg Publishing, Minneapolis, 1993.

Hall, D. J., *God and Human Suffering*, Augsburg Publishing, Minneapolis, 1986.

Kumasaka, L., My Pain is God's Will, *American Journal of Nursing, 96*:6, pp. 45-47, June 1996.

Means, J. J., Hear No Evil, See No Evil, Speak No Evil: Learning from Our Work with Trauma Related Disorders, *Journal of Pastoral Care, 49*:3, pp. 294-305, Fall 1995.

Proctor, M. and K. Proctor, Sounds of Comfort in the Trauma Center: How Nurses Talk to Patients in Pain, *Social Science and Medicine, 42*:12, pp. 1669-1680, June 1996.

Pruyser, P., *The Minister as Diagnostician*, Westminster Press, Philadelphia, 1976.

Ramshaw, E., *Ritual and Pastoral Care*, Fortress Press, Philadelphia, 1987.

Smucker, C., A Phenomenological Description of the Experience of Spiritual Distress, *Nursing Diagnosis, 7*:2, pp. 81-91, April-June 1996.

Stevenson, I. and E. W. Cook, Involuntary Memories During Severe Physical Illness or Injury, *The Journal of Nervous and Mental Disease, 183*:7, pp. 452-458, 1995.

Sutherland, A., Worldframes and God-Talk in Trauma and Suffering, *Journal of Pastoral Care, 49*:3, pp. 280-292, Fall 1995.

CHAPTER 19
The Addicted Patient

Reverend John A. Mac Dougall

Spirituality consists of the quality of the relationships we have with our higher power, with others, and with ourselves. These three relationships are intertwined, and cannot be separated very far apart. It isn't possible to love God, be at peace with yourself, and treat everyone else like dirt. It just doesn't work out that way. Any deterioration in one of the three relationships pulls down the other two. Any improvement in one lifts the other two up. Addictions are spiritual diseases long before they are diseases of the body, mind, or emotions. The addict's spirituality fades away. Recovery is a spiritual process, as well as being physical, mental, and emotional. Any model of addiction and recovery that fails to include the spiritual is likely to bring only short term benefit.

Addiction is a state of body, mind, emotions, and spirit in which our primary relationship is with the focus of our addiction. It is characterized by loss of control over and preoccupation with its focus (the drug or experience of choice). As the addiction progresses, it replaces other relationships until they fall away, leaving only the addict and the addiction in a shrinking circle of friends, leading to death.

The addict gradually leaves behind all former relationships in order to focus on the addiction. Using the image of a wedding liturgy, it is possible to imagine the shifts that go on inside the addict over time, by imagining that the addict is marrying his or her drug, not a spouse. Instead of a pastor, we have a dealer asking the questions:

> Will you take cocaine to be your drug?
> Will you love it, comfort it, honor it and keep it,
> and, forsaking all others, be faithful to it as long
> as you live?

If so, then repeat after me:
I (name) take thee, cocaine, to be my wedded drug.
To have and to hold
For better, for worse
For richer, for poorer
In sickness and in health
Until death do us apart. Amen.

It is as if the addict has entered into a marriage to the drug without ever understanding what the vows were. Without help, he or she may never return to the world of the real human and divine relationships.

Addiction is a primary disease and a complete disease. It is primary because it is not caused by something else, and it is complete because it is a disease of the body, mind, emotions, and spirit. It is not the same as physical dependence and is not merely a habit or preference, no matter how passionately felt. In addiction, relationships change slowly and subtly until all relationships are with the object or event of the addiction. The body, the self, God, and other human beings are reduced to minor characters in stories, as the addiction takes center stage.

To be of help, we must assume that addictions are primary, and treat them first. A common error of people who want to help is to look for the underlying causes of addiction. We may mistake things that came before the addiction for causes. We may mistake symptoms and consequences of the addiction for causes. Do not be diverted. The active addict will offer all manner of reasons why the problem isn't addiction. Some of these reasons will be remarkably sophisticated.

Sometimes as pastors we have an agenda that alcoholics and addicts need what we have, and so we are prone to attributing addiction to a lack of religion. A national study group of my own denomination attributed the underlying causes of drug addiction and alcoholism to "racism and an undisciplined church." Because that was on the study commission's mind, that's what they concluded "causes" addiction.

Many people have first abused alcohol and drugs while trying to self-medicate for the relief of pain, either physical or emotional. Because it worked, and their pain was relieved, they stuck with it. This doesn't mean that pain causes addiction.

For example, many adult women alcoholics in recovery report being sexually abused as girls. Their alcohol use started then, and continued well into adulthood. This doesn't mean that sexual abuse causes alcoholism, but means only that these alcoholics got started drinking in that way.

The distinction is important, because without it, all helpers, from pastors and psychiatrists through friends, may become useless. If a woman has active alcoholism and an incest history, and we believe that her incest history is what is making her drink, we may guide her away from Alcoholics Anonymous and toward therapy for incest. Trying to deal with her incest history while she is still drinking won't work, because her real self isn't available for counseling or therapy, and because nothing is happening to stop the drinking. Because her addiction to alcohol is primary, it needs to be dealt with first, so the real person is present and available. When she stops drinking, all the pain may come back, and so appropriate therapy and support should be available, to help with the effects of trauma and to prevent relapse. There is also a twelve step group for incest survivors, which uses the tools of A.A. to help heal the trauma.

Addictions are diseases of the body, in that the human body changes. This is easy to see in the broken-down drunk, but all the addictions change the body. Alcohol and drug addictions include the development of tolerance, in which the addict needs more and more of the same chemical to get high. Later, as tolerance progresses, the doses must continue to increase, just to feel somewhat normal.

Those whose addiction is to a relationship or an experience, such as compulsive gambling, codependency, and sex addiction, also have a physical basis to their addiction. All addictions have in common the attempt to change how we feel by using an object or experience. Changing how we feel produces subtle chemical changes in the brain and body. Doing it over and over again can produce at least habituation, and perhaps physical dependency on these chemical changes. The workaholic who drops dead at his or her desk of a stress-induced heart attack can be as much the victim of addiction as the alcoholic who dies of an alcohol-induced heart attack.

In relationship or experience addictions, the physical component may not be so evident. For example, a talented emergency medical technician would feel a rush of excitement when responding to an urgent call. If able to do a great job under pressure, the EMT can often feel a high. The heart pounds, adrenaline flows, and it is a pleasurable experience. So far, everyone benefits. The patient gets the total dedication of the EMT, and the EMT gets a mild high. If, however, that EMT becomes cranky without emergencies, takes a second job to get more calls in, and has a home and family life that deteriorates, one can suspect that addiction to excitement has started to set in. He or she is "chasing the high" and seeking that chemical and physical change.

Addictions are diseases of the mind, in that the addiction has thought disorders. Mild forms of thought disorders consist of thinking things that are clearly not true. The basic, persistent, untrue thought in addiction is that "this time it will be different." The alcoholic sets out to have just two drinks and to be a social drinker this time, and cannot. The drug addict sets out to use just one more time, planning to quit tomorrow, and cannot. The spouse or child of the addict thinks that this time they will respond to reason, emotion, threats, tears, or manipulation, and they don't. No matter how many times the untrue thoughts have been entertained and found false, they recur as if this time they would be true.

More severe thought disorders can occur in the alcohol or drug addict as a result of prolonged chemical use. These can resemble classic mental illnesses such as paranoia, schizophrenia, and manic-depressive disorders (more recently called bipolar affective disorders). Alcoholics and addicts who go to counselors or therapists for help, and omit the information about their drug use, often end up with a mental illness diagnosis because they present all their thought disorders and hide their drug and alcohol use.

Addictions are diseases of the emotions, in that the addict's emotions are distorted. An old joke classifies drunks as "bellicose, jocose, lachrymose, and comatose." When drunk, for example, people may become romantic, belligerent, humorous, sad, or sleepy. An old belief is that their real personality is coming out, under the influence of a "truth serum." The reality is that it is their distorted personality coming out. Even though the addict may be distorted in a stereotypical way, and the distortion is the same each time, that isn't their real self.

It is widely accepted that people's emotions are changed while under the influence of alcohol or drugs, but in addiction, the emotions are also distorted when the addict is not using at the moment. A common distortion is a combination of grandiosity and immaturity, which A.A. called "his majesty the baby." This may be well disguised, but the feeling inside is "**I** want **what** I want **when** I want it." As the addict develops more to hide, emotions such as defensiveness and hostility become more prominent.

Fear gradually becomes the dominant emotion in the addict's life. Some of the fear is simple: fear of running out of one's supply; fear of being caught doing something illegal or shameful; fear of losing important relationships; or fear of going broke. There is another fear, which is often hidden even from the addict: the fear of death. Inside, the addict knows he or she is dying. The disease grows more unmanageable and, as one told me, "The drain radius is shrinking."

Addictions are diseases of the spirit, in that the human spirit becomes dormant to the point of being nearly dead. Our spirit is at the core of who we are. Many, myself included, see it as God-given. Addictions seriously distort, damage, or destroy the spirit. Our spirituality is simply the quality of relationships among ourselves, God, and other human beings. As people begin to drink or drug in a problematic way, the quality of their relationships fades. The beauty, truth, honor, comfort, compassion, and loyalty they enjoyed all weaken, even though the relationship is still present. The enjoyment of work and creativity fades, leaving drudgery. The appreciation of life fades, leaving the addict just "killing time." Because our spirituality is intangible, it is easily overlooked in a scientific age. However, anyone working in the field of addiction and recovery quickly learns how crucial a spiritual awakening is. Even those who remain firm agnostics will refer to "getting it" or "click." That's the time when the spirit starts coming back to life. It's a great moment, whether it is all at once or very slow.

A simple contrast between the spirituality of addiction and the spirituality of recovery can be found by spending some time with actively using addicts and also with recovering addicts. Talking with active addicts is tiring, but spending time with someone who has had a spiritual awakening is refreshing. Listening to an active addict tends to tear down our own spirit, and listening to someone who is waking up gives us hope. Perhaps because spirituality is so subtle, it is the first thing to go as addiction develops and is the last thing to return in recovery.

As addictions progress, spiritual health is the first to become diseased, followed by emotional health, mental health, and physical health. In recovery, the process is reversed: physical health begins to improve long before emotional or spiritual health. Some recovering people are abstinent, feel physically healthy, and stop their program at that point. Because their thoughts, feelings, and spirituality remain unchanged, they are called "dry drunks" because that is how they seem to others. The pastor or spiritual care counselor can encourage people to do a full twelve step program that includes healthy spirituality.

Addiction is not mere physical dependence. It is also the mental, emotional, and spiritual state of being addicted. If addiction were the same as physical dependence, then detoxification centers would be sufficient to treat all of our addicts. The difference can be illustrated with people who quit smoking. Some smokers, who have become physically dependent on nicotine, but not addicted, quit. They suffer withdrawal symptoms such as anxiety, irritability, sleeplessness, and nausea because they are in withdrawal. They hate the withdrawal and come to hate the cigarettes, too. They are likely to quit and stay quit. Other smokers, who have become physically dependent on nicotine, and have become addicted, quit, too. They also have the withdrawal symptoms, but long after the withdrawal is over, the obsession with cigarettes remains. They are unhappy without one and are likely to return to smoking under stress. The non-addicted ex-smoker looks at them in wonderment, and possibly with contempt. The difference in how they feel and the likelihood of staying off cigarettes is based on addiction, not character, will-power, or personality. Those nicotine addicts who know they are addicts and work a twelve-step program for nicotine addiction are likely to succeed.

In this complete disease of addiction, our relationships with God, ourselves, and other human beings gradually wither and die. In their place, relationships with the experience of addiction grow. Whether the addiction is well known like alcoholism or drug addiction, or lesser known, such as compulsive shopping, eating, gambling, and relationship addictions, the addict's "action" is with the addictive experience or high. Objects become real and people become mere objects.

I saw a T-shirt in a country store with the legend "ten reasons why a beer is better than a woman." This breathtakingly obscene shirt included the reason that "a beer is good when it's frigid." It was hanging by the cases of beer, and the clerk told me it sold well. The men who buy the shirt have a much stronger relationship with their beer than with any woman, and the women who buy the shirt for "their" men are so codependent that they won't notice that buying the shirt amounts to tearing themselves down.

In the addict's life, real people are replaced with caricatures: the boss, the "ball-and-chain" wife, the drinking buddies. Relationships are valued to the extent that they reinforce the addiction. Addicts seek the company of addicts at the same stage of addiction, so that they can feel normal. This way, when they look around, everyone they see drinks and drugs like they do, so they must be normal. Invitations to social events are judged by the availability of the drug of choice. Old friends drop away, and the addict never notices, believing that their new friends are the best friends in the whole world, and that the old friends never understood them, anyway. The caricatures become real, and the real people become discards. One barrier to recovery is the addict's belief that they will have no friends at all if they get clean and sober. They intuitively know that their new friends will not follow them into recovery, and they cannot imagine that clean and sober friends could be of any value at all. It is a time of great mourning.

Addiction is characterized by a belief that the addict can be best nurtured by the addictive object or event. (Objects include drugs, alcohol, food; events include compulsive gambling, shopping, and relationship addictions.) There are several reasons why addictive objects and events are more easily satisfying than relationships with people. They are predictable, at least at first. If you drink or drug, you will get high every time. It is only much later, after addiction is well established, that the drugs betray their user and fail to provide euphoria any more. Addictive objects and events have no wants or needs of their own, so the addict's needs can always come first. Relating to objects and events can give the addict a sense of control. If one is in relationships with friends, family, employer, and neighbors, they will all want some love, loyalty, work, or nurture in return. If one is in relationships with drugs, food, alcohol, gambling, and/or sex addiction, all they may ever want is to be paid for.

For addicts, controlling their own mood changes becomes a substitute for human nurture and the love of God. Alcoholics have mood changes while drinking. They may feel sad, angry, humorous, or romantic and believe that they are having an intense and genuine human experience. Drug addicts have mood changes while using. Sedatives distort and give a dreamy feeling, stimulants banish all of life's insecurities with feelings of power, opiates produce a welcomed numbness that banishes life's fears and pain, and nicotine simply removes a lot of feelings, leaving its users alert and edgy.

Food addicts have mood changes, whether eating or starving. Both compulsively eating and compulsively dieting can be mood altering. Binge eating, purging, inventing elaborate food rituals, and carefully maintaining body shape all can take the place of human and godly love and care. Many food addicts will obsess all the time about the next thing that they are going to eat, or their next exercise, laxative, or purging plan, and never notice that they are becoming more and more isolated.

Compulsive shoplifters have mood changes while stealing, and compulsive shoppers have mood changes while shopping, even if (or especially if) the object is unneeded. Sex addicts have mood changes just walking into a pornographic book shop. Workaholics have mood changes staying later than anyone else and getting all charged up to work in isolation. Religious addicts have mood changes during an intense religious experience, and will leave their faith community to go from place to place seeking new ones.

Relationship addicts have mood changes in the passion of new love or the turmoil of breaking up and making up. If they happen to be at any risk of developing actual relationships, they will quickly dump the other people as "boring." It isn't the relationships they want, it is the "action" of being in and out of relationships. This is similar to compulsive gamblers who aren't in it for the winnings, but for the "action." If compulsive gamblers hit a big win, they don't take the money and leave. Their pleasure comes not from winning, but from "action," the rush of excitement that comes from having money on the line. Now, with their winnings, they can afford more "action." They have the opportunity to have a higher does of excitement, represented by bigger bets and entrance into the coveted "high roller" category.

In the beginnings of the development of addiction, no one outside the potential addict can see anything happening. All of the person's relationships are intact. The only sign is within the person: he or she is coming to love his or her "drug of choice" (which could be any of the objects or events of addiction) just a little bit too much. The difference between a person who likes two glasses of wine with dinner, a person who *really* likes two glasses of wine with dinner, a person who *needs* two glasses of wine with dinner, and a person who needs to drink some wine alone *before* dinner because two glasses will not be enough, can be impossible for another person to detect.

After coming to love the drug of choice just a little too much, a subtle internal shift takes place. Developing addicts begin to have internal monologues of grandiosity and resentment, finding fault with everyone. This discontent fuels increased use of the drug of choice, which fuels more discontent, and the process is under way. The normal self and the addict self have some arguments of which the rest of the world is unaware, but in time, the addict self's monologue starts to leak out. The corrosive nature of this addictive grandiosity and resentment begins to become noticeable to others, and the next phase of addiction begins.

In the next phase, people who are close to addicts can notice an attitude slip. Usually this deteriorating attitude is blamed on something other than addiction, because no one is expecting the addiction to develop. For adolescents, a developing addiction is virtually impossible to detect at this point, because people expect that the attitudes of adolescents will deteriorate anyway, and that it is "just a phase." Parents who suspect that there is more than "just a phase" going on may find it hard to connect with others who will take their concerns seriously. Post-adolescent developing addicts have no shortage of external factors on which to blame any attitude slip. Often these are the consequences of the growing addiction, rather than the causes.

In this phase, some of the enduring character defects and behavior problems of addiction turn up: making excuses, placing blame, lying, hiding, isolating, and treating people with hostility and contempt. This phase can last for many years, enough time to carry on a career and raise children. These children are likely to have the symptoms of "Adult Children of Alcoholics" due to being raised in an atmosphere of hostility and contempt.

During this phase addicts will try magic and rituals to control their use. They may believe a certain brand of drink or drug will give them a happy experience (which is why even street drugs often have brand names). They may try to drink or drug only in certain ways in an attempt to stay in control and not be addicts. ("The sun must be over the yardarm somewhere.")

As people react to the addict's negativity with negative labels, the addicts take criticism as permission. ("If you're going to call me a drunk,

I'll show you what a drunk really is!") It is from this attitude and point of view that the defiantly illogical statement comes, "I've been thrown out of better places than this!" After all, if the addict has been thrown out of better places than this, than this must be a worse place, and so the addict is on a downward side.

The progression of the addiction is accompanied by an increase in tolerance, and so addicts must use more and more to get high or even to feel somewhat normal. Their energy is drained by trying to get the resources to both support their addictions and to carry on a normal life at the same time. Relationships with God are long gone, and human relationships are becoming empty or missing. Addicts are no longer in good company when alone. This is the stage when most people who are going to recover begin to recover. Enough has gone wrong so that they have the chance to realize what is going on, and they are not yet so mentally debilitated as to block recovery or so physically debilitated that they will die even if they stop using their drug of choice.

In the final stage of addiction, life collapses. The use of the drug of choice no longer satisfies. It is at this point that alcoholics encounter "misery drinking" in which they don't drink because they like it or want it, but just drink because they have to, with their misery unrelieved. Addicts' coping skills break down, and they can't handle new situations or new demands. They may be able to continue to do things they have done for years, but be quite unable to show up for outpatient treatment, simply because it is something new, and they can't cope. (People in this stage will need inpatient treatment in part because they cannot take on new tasks without guidance.)

Fear dominates the spirit; interactions with other people break down; relationships end. End stage addicts want to be alone because the rejection of others is painful, but are afraid to be alone, because they can sense that death is coming.

Outcomes include suicide or a semi-natural death from the medical consequences of addiction, loss of sanity, and a reduction of life to the homeless, mentally ill/chemically dependent model. Recovery can happen even at this stage, but the best opportunities for recovery have gone by.

The origins of addiction are unproved. There seems to be a genetic predisposition to addiction. People also learn drinking, drugging, and addictive lifestyles from their families of origin. It is likely that addiction results from a combination of genetic predisposition, learned behaviors, stress, and a high enough dose of an addictive drug, alcohol, food, or experience to trigger the addictive process. Those who are children of alcoholic or addicted parents may be the most at risk, and the most in need of good education and information on addictions.

In trying to understand the difference between an addiction and a habit or pattern, there are three key signs: loss of control, preoccupation, and continued use in spite of negative consequences. To illustrate, take an "addiction" that is usually just a habit or a passion: chocolate. Many people who love chocolate say, "I am a chocolate addict" or "I'm a chocoholic." They may be quite cheerful when they say this. They are using the term as a figure of speech. A chocolate fan might buy books on chocolate, attend exhibits of chocolates and candy-making, subscribe to newsletters, and order from catalogs of specialty chocolates. They might have souvenirs in their home of early chocolate making. They might stop to look at and buy samples of any new chocolates they see in their travels, and still not be addicts.

To identify a chocolate addict look for loss of control, preoccupation, and continued use in spite of negative consequences. Also look for specific, observable behaviors (the "SOBS") that demonstrate these. For example: they might have spent so much money on chocolate that they can't pay their bills. They might have consumed so much chocolate that they are morbidly obese (which is defined as 100% overweight). They might be unable to eat other foods because their chocolate intake is making them queasy. They might be isolating from other people and losing relationships in order to sit at home and eat chocolate, and avoiding events at which chocolate is not served. Instead of eating chocolate, chocolate would be devouring them.

Addiction is cunning, baffling, and powerful. Without help, it is too much for the addict to overcome. As pastors and spiritual care counselors, we can detect the beginnings of addictions in ourselves, notice when the addictions of others are just blossoming, and point them in the direction of recovery, a twelve-step program, and a higher power that most of us call God. We cannot cure anyone's addiction, nor can any human being. What we can do is recognize it, and know how to reliably find help. That help will come from this God-given program of recovery. In A.A.'s "Big Book" they write:

> Our description of the alcoholic, the chapter to the agnostic, and our personal adventures before and after make clear three pertinent ideas:
> 1) That they were alcoholic and could not manage our own lives.
> 2) That probably no human power could have relieved our alcoholism.
> 3) That God could and would if he were sought.

Addiction is a medical and spiritual problem that needs a medical and spiritual solution. Effective treatment of addiction includes these elements: 1) The safe detoxification of the addict, 2) Education about the disease, 3) Practice in doing the first five steps of A.A., with the guidance of a counselor, chaplain, and other professionals, 4) Planning for ongoing recovery needs, 5) Successful participation in the spiritual program of Alcoholic Anonymous or a similar twelve-step group, such as Narcotics Anonymous or Gamblers Anonymous. It is reasonable for pastors and spiritual care providers to notice that addiction is developing, to refer for assessment, and to support people in their journey of treatment and recovery. Good treatment programs include all five elements.

The majority of people in recovery are recovering with Alcoholics Anonymous or Narcotics Anonymous alone. If addicts can get well with a twelve-step program, then that is the best plan. If they are attending meetings, but unable to maintain stable abstinence, then an outpatient program is in order. If they are attending outpatient, but are unable to get very many clean and sober days in a row, then inpatient treatment is indicated. If they relapse promptly after inpatient, then a halfway house or extended care are in order. Treatment providers like Hazelden offer services throughout the entire continuum of care to meet a variety of needs.

The Twelve Steps form a plan for spiritual growth and for the successful management of addiction. In step one, addicts admit powerlessness over the addiction, and the unmanageability of life. In step two, addicts find hope by coming to believe that a power greater than themselves could restore them to sanity. In the third step, they may make a decision to embark on a program of recovery, deciding to turn their will and their lives over to the ear of God (as they understand God). Steps four and five involve taking "a searching a fearless moral inventory" and admitting out loud the exact nature of their wrongs. In steps six and seven, addicts become ready and then ask God to remove their defects of character. This creates an openness to spiritual growth. In steps eight and nine, addicts identify the people they have harmed, become willing to make amends, and make the amends unless that would injure someone. This brings restoration and justice back into life. In step ten, addicts continue to take their own inventory, and promptly admit their wrongs. This keeps moral relapse at bay. In the eleventh step, the recovering addicts pray for knowledge of God's will and the power to carry it out. This develops faith and reliance. The spiritual awakening that's mentioned in the twelfth step comes about as a result of working the first eleven, and is secured by passing on a message of hope to others and by practicing these principles in all one's affairs, not just in terms of recovery from addiction.

This twelve-step process is much more than a "just say no" program. It is not about not doing drugs. It is about another way of life, physically clean, mentally alert, emotionally sound, and spiritually alive.

The results of successful participation in a twelve-step program of recovery are so positive that addicts and alcoholics often report being glad to have their addictions, because the addictions have been admission tickets to a new way of life that is more satisfying than if they had never been addicted at all.

REFERENCE

1. Anonymous, *Alcoholics Anonymous* (3rd Edition), A.A. World Services, New York, 1989.

SUGGESTED READING

Anonymous, *It Works, How and Why,* N.A. World Service Office, New York, 1993.

May, G. G., *Addiction and Grace,* Harper, San Francisco, 1988.

Nace, E. P., *The Treatment of Alcoholism,* Brunner-Mazel, New York, 1987.

Nakken, C., *The Addictive Personality,* Hazelden, Center City, 1988.

Thompson, P., *Finding Your Own Spiritual Path,* Hazelden, Center City, 1994.

Vaillant, G., *The Natural History of Alcoholism Revisited,* Harvard, Cambridge, 1995.

CHAPTER 20
The Terminally Ill Pediatric Patient*

Sr. Frances Dominica

As in life, so in death, spirituality cannot be separated off from all that goes to make a person the unique individual God is creating. Body, mind, and spirit are woven together intricately and inextricably. Constantly being made aware of this by the children who have taught me so much and of whom I now write, I would be untrue to them if, in attempting to describe their understanding of death and dying, I focused on anything other than the whole person.

Of all the children who have stayed in Helen House in the fourteen years it has been open, 70 percent have suffered progressive intellectual impairment as a consequence of their illness. The fact that these children are not articulate in no way indicates that their spirit is imperfect. Indeed, again and again we are aware that they exude a spirituality which defies description but affects all those with whom they come in contact.

Statistics indicating longer life expectancy and a significant drop in infant mortality make no difference to the child who knows that he or she is dying or to that child's family—except insofar as they may well feel isolated and lonely because they are different. Their very difference provokes feelings of embarrassment, inadequacy, and fear in others.

We are constantly reminded that, unlike our Victorian forebears, we treat death as a taboo subject. (Unlike our sisters and brothers in developing countries, too, where death is treated as a natural and important part of life and where over 7 million children under the age of

*Reproduced from *The Way Supplement*, Summer 1996, "The Spirituality of Children," by permission of the editors, Heythrop College, Kensington Square, London W8 5HQ.

5 die each year of gastro-enteritis alone.) So adults protect children from the reality of death by not talking with them about it, consciously or subconsciously hoping that their children will not need to worry themselves with it.

But children always have been aware of death as a part of life, if not through close personal encounters with it then through books, stories, nursery rhymes, games, films, and, of course, today through the omnipresent, influential medium of the small screen. Fictional representations of death, fantastic (i.e., based on fantasy) or realistic or—worse—a mixture of the two, may be scary or gory or exciting, but they fall into a different category from the face of death captured by the cameras for a news program or a documentary. Yet both fictional and factual are at one remove, a safe distance from everyday personal experience of life.

A child's initial first-hand encounter with death may well be an insect lying upside down on the window-sill or a mouse the cat brought in. The death of a pet may be a cause of real grief, frequently solved, however, in the child's thinking by the suggestion, often the child's own, of a new kitten, rabbit, goldfish, or other suitable replacement. There is also a certain matter-of-factness about the situation shown by many small children exemplified by a five year old: "Mummy didn't want me to see Sammy (the family gerbil) but I sneaked in and I poked him. His eyes were open but it's all right 'cos he's really dead." Three little girls, four, six, and eight, engaged the services of their clergyman father to conduct a funeral service and burial for their hamster. The four year old was tearful, the eight-year-old suitably solemn, while the six year old busied herself with ensuring that everything was done according to the book. Just as the burial began, the corpse got up and started to walk away. Totally devoid of sentiment, the six year old took command: "Quick, daddy, hit it on the head so it's properly dead and we can finish the funeral."

Anthropologists and psychologists in recent years have studied children's perceptions of death, some of them devoting their entire career to the subject. Twenty-five or thirty years ago the commonly held assumptions were that, by and large, children were not much aware of the reality or the personal risk of death and, if they were, they had a built-in resilience which enabled them to cope at the time and soon forget it. We now realize that this is not true. In recent studies considerable attention has been paid to the age at which children grasp the essential components of the concept of death. It is unlikely, for example, that a two year old will be able to grasp any of the components, but most eight year olds of normal intelligence will have a fully developed idea.

The nine most frequently quoted components are shown in Table 1.

Much of our knowledge on the subject is drawn from Western Judaeo-Christian tradition and so is only partial but it must not be forgotten that a child's cultural and religious background is highly relevant to his or her perception. Children's understanding and perception of death is not influenced only by age; the great influences arise however from actual experience, such as the death of a grandparent or sometimes, tragically, the early death of a parent or brother, sister, or friend. It is often hard for children to articulate their thoughts and feelings about death, not least because adults tend actively or passively to discourage them from doing so. When young children do *speak* of death they will often mirror their parents' views and attempted explanations—"she was very ill and the doctors and nurses couldn't make her better so Jesus took her to heaven to be with him." But the familiar story ending, "and they all lived (died?) happily ever after" implied here is an unhelpful stance for children—as indeed it is for adults—struggling with strong emotions of anger, guilt, confusion, and the out-and-out grief and hell of separation from someone they love and ache for. Besides which, not all children think heaven is a good place to be. Some think it may be boring or even frightening—and the known is preferable to the unknown. Some children do not believe in life after death anyway.

Table 1.		
Component		Average Age Attained (in Years)
Realization	The awareness of death	3
Separation	The location of the dead—where are they?	5
Immobility	The child's notions—are the dead active or inactive?	5
Irrevocability	Permanent and irreversible or temporary and reversible?	6
Causality	What brought about the death? violence, old age, sickness?	6
Dysfunctionality	Ideas of bodily functions other than the senses	6
Universality	The child's ideas of mortality—everybody, nobody, some exceptions?	7
Insensitivity	Does the dead person dream, feel, think, hear?	8
Appearance	Does the dead person look different or the same?	12

Source: [1]

If, in good times, family members communicate openly and honestly with each other, then it is likely that they will do so in difficult times. Unfortunately the converse is true. A death in the family will not suddenly enable private, reticent people to bare their souls to one another, at least not for long. Children may choose not to talk about death—their own or anyone else's. "It helps me to talk about it but I don't see why a child or a person should be forced into having to talk about it, not if they don't want to," commented a ten year old. Sometimes children find it easier to talk to someone they trust outside the immediate family. This may well be one symptom of their strong desire to protect their parents from further pain: "If I talk about it with them they either get cross or cry." In this, as in many ways, we see children reversing roles and assuming parental concerns and responsibilities for their mothers and fathers.

Paul was twelve when he first visited Helen House. He suffered with cystic fibrosis but, his parents told us, he knew little about the disease or the prognosis. On his first two visits to us for respite care his parents chose to stay with him. Then one day he telephoned from home. "Sorry to bother you but I'm bored at home and I'm fed up with my parents. Please can you book me into the Snoopy bedroom next week—and they won't be coming with me." His parents took a good deal of persuading, but he was determined. Having elicited a promise from us that we should not initiate a discussion with Paul about his illness or its outcome, and having reluctantly accepted our proviso that if *he* initiated the discussion we could not break our rule about never deceiving or lying to a child, his parents left him with us. He said good-bye, transparently triumphant, and they had scarcely driven out through our gates before he turned to one of the team and said, "I got cystic fibrosis real bad. I'll probably be dead this time next year. What's it like?" I do not know what answer she gave, but had it been other than brief and to the point he would have been on the other side of the garden kicking a football around or heavily into the Super-Nintendo.

It is never easy knowing how to respond to such questions. We have not ourselves died. We do not know what it is like to die, nor do we have tangible evidence of what life on the other side of death is like. We may have faith to rely on, but we do not have reason; we may have belief, but we do not have experience. It is all right to say, "I do not know" or "we do not understand" when these are the honest answers. We must not say anything we do not believe. Children will accept honesty, however frustrating, but they will not accept perceived pretense, humbug, or deception.

Paul resumed the conversation several times more, at intervals of days or months, when he felt like it. Our role, as we understood it, was to be open and ready to enter into dialogue and to follow his lead.

Paul's parents did not want to believe that he knew he would die in the foreseeable future and even when they did accept the fact, I do not think that either they or Paul talked about it much together. We subsequently learned from the pediatrician looking after him that on one of Paul's hospital admissions a case conference was planned. As the doctor walked past Paul carrying Paul's medical notes and accompanied by other members of the ward team, Paul stopped him. "Are you going to have a meeting about me?" The consultant said they were, but what made him ask? "When no one was looking I made a yellow mark on the cover of my notes so I would know which were mine," came the reply. And then, "Can I come to the meeting?" He did, and this was the start of much more open communication between patient and professionals.

Increasingly, enlightened and sensitive pediatricians involve their child patients in discussion and decision making where this is possible and seems appropriate. It takes courage but is almost always helpful to all concerned. It is a little easier, though still deeply distressing, to discuss the probable death of a child with the parents than it is with the child concerned. Similarly, research has shown that parents more often talk to their well children about the death of their brother or sister than they do to the dying child. It is desperately hard to tell a child that he or she will soon go on to a future which we have not ourselves experienced and cannot accurately describe or measure, and that we cannot go with them, they must go it alone. "I wish all four of us could die at the same time so nobody need be sad," was the comment of an eleven-year-old girl who knew her own death was not far off.

John came to stay with us a number of times in the last eighteen months of his life. Intelligent, ten years old going on sixty, meticulously polite, his emotions tightly controlled, it was difficult to know what went on inside him as he wrestled with an inoperable brain tumor. Then he came on an unaccompanied stay of a week or so and a little boy of four died in Helen House. Suddenly John's anger was unleashed and he railed against the injustice of life and death. "I hate sunshine and green grass and flowers and trees and all the things that remind me of football and my bicycle and the things my brother can do and I can't any more." A few weeks later he wrote:

Dear Mother Frances,
　　　Thank you for your letter, other people's letters are always much more interesting than your own. Nothing interesting happened here—nor ever will. I only have my next visit to you to look forward to in life, and I always think of you all when I'm depressed.

I'm not always sure whose side God is on. I do hope he is on mine. . . .
Sorry it was such a dreary letter.

                                                                    John

In another letter he wrote: "I know God is there but he never seems to be there when you need him. Will he be there if I fall over? or if I fell down stairs?" This from a child who daily experienced problems associated with balance.

Ann Goldman, pediatric oncologist, and Deborah Christie, child psychologist, undertook a study, published in 1993, of thirty-one children between the ages of three years and sixteen years, dying from progressive malignant diseases, to see whether the child's impending death was discussed between the child and the family. Twenty-six of the thirty-one children had been told that their disease had recurred. Twenty-eight of the families had another child over three years old and twenty-one (75%) of these had told the siblings that their brother or sister was going to die. The twenty-two senior staff in the department where the children were treated were unanimous in advocating an open honest approach in talking with children about their own death. In the light of these facts it is perhaps surprising to learn that of the thirty-one children the approach of death was virtually unacknowledged by six families (19%), seven (23%) children were felt to know but chose not to discuss death, in two (6%) families discussion with the child was blocked by the family, nine (29%) died unaware, in seven (23%) families what the children felt was unknown.

The mother of a child who died at the age of seven as a result of neuroblastoma is convinced that he was aware for some time of the probability that he would die, but most of the time he was intent upon a simple examination of the facts of his illness and treatment. His mother overheard a conversation between him and his five-year-old sister when they discussed where they would each like to be buried. Hamish was in no doubt that he would like to be buried in a churchyard not far from home where several relatives were already buried. "Then we would all come out at night and have lovely spooky parties." His mother felt strongly that it was important for him that they should be open with each other about his death and a few days before he died he gave her the opening. "Yes," she said, "you probably will die." He reacted as if she had asked him to go for a very long walk on a stormy day. "I'd really rather not," was all he said.

Twelve percent of the families who have stayed at Helen House since it opened in 1982 have two or more children affected with the same genetic illness. For those who do not suffer progressive intellectual impairment the distress of the longer surviving of the children of each family is unthinkable. Children with life-threatening or life-limiting illness and who are able to observe and to reason are usually very well-informed about the course their illness will take anyway, largely through noticing what happens to other children with the same condition. How much more so if it is your brother or your sister who is at a more advanced stage of the same illness as you!

A very articulate five year old with spinal muscular atrophy lived eleven months after her sister died. She often spoke of Zoë being in heaven and would ask to see photographs of her or to watch a video of them together when they were both bridesmaids shortly before Zoë died—"to remind me what she looks like so I'll recognize her when I get there." In the months before Leanne died she often put on her child's make-up before she went to bed at night—"so I'll look really pretty when I meet Jesus." But mostly she was very busy living and was totally occupied with the present moment. She became critically ill about four months after her sister's death but said clearly that she didn't want to go and find Zoë yet. Through what seemed to be sheer will-power, she survived another seven months.

Leanne clearly knew that she was going to die and said so, but she also had elaborate plans for when she was grown-up. She knew just what kind of man she was going to marry and she planned to have lots of babies. Indeed she practiced being pregnant, persuading her mother to make her a maternity dress and stuffing a cushion up her front!

Holding on to two ideas at once is seen not only in young children. A seventeen-year-old boy in the advanced stages of muscular dystrophy spoke of his approaching death and, almost in the next sentence, of planning to work in computers. "I know I'll be dead before I'm twenty-two . . . but that's all right." "Are you afraid?" After quite a long pause he said, "No, but, you know, I don't really think too much about it, I just get on with living." Told that his cheerful attitude to life had helped another muscular dystrophy sufferer, Peter said that although he knew what might happen to him, "you can decide to be miserable or you can decide to be happy and being miserable only makes things worse and worse."

A nineteen year old, also living with muscular dystrophy, was very anxious, angry, and deeply depressed. He was a man of few words, although he did express some of his feelings through drawing and painting. He was staying in Helen House when another teenager died. With a little encouragement he soon made a card for the other boy's parents and joined them and several members of the team sitting at the round dining room table planning the funeral. He asked to come to the funeral, first buying flowers. He placed these on the coffin and stayed for the funeral service. Afterwards he expressed the wish that his funeral could be "lovely just like that." He said it had taken all his fear away and although he knew it would return he would always be able to think of it and remind himself not to be afraid. For a young man who could fairly be described as taciturn, this openness was remarkable.

A visit to the Ashmolean Museum was the trigger for a nine year old to release some of his feelings about his inevitable death. Fascinated by the Egyptian mummies, their tombs and artifacts, he asked why they put "all those things in their tombs."

"Because they thought they would need them in the next life."

"Why were they wrapped in bandages?"

"Because they wanted to take their bodies with them."

"Yes, I want to take mine."

Fifty-year-old accompanying him: "I'm not sure. As I get older and more worn out I think I'd rather like a new one."

Pause.

"Yes, Maybe I could have one that worked. . . . Anyway I know what heaven is like. It's like a lovely pub. You have a drink and forget all about the things that make you sad. My uncle does anyway."

An eight year old whose twin, Beth, had died had a different concept. "Heaven is different for everyone. Heaven is where there are all your favorite things and favorite people. My heaven will be a huge gymnasium with trampolines and ropes and bars. All my friends will be there and Beth and Jenni."

Just as children who believe in heaven picture it differently, so they have different ways of describing the transition from here to there—and what part of you it is that goes and why you don't come back. Kelly was three when children asked her where Jamie was. "In heaven with Jesus." "And why can't he come back?" "'Cos he likes it there." But Elizabeth, aged five, was angry with God: "You've had our Katie long enough now; we need her back please."

Helping his mother to set a coal fire, a four year old reflected, "He's gone somewhere else like the coal. Just the ashes left behind," and a seven year old mourning the death of his dog said, "He's left his skin behind." But Jane was puzzled when she saw her sister's body. Playing with the doll's house an hour or two later she asked, "But how can she be in heaven with Jesus if she's in that little room?" And later: "I thought when you were dead there was only your head. I thought all your skin peeled off."

Many children who know that they will die soon are wise way beyond their years, with a maturity many of us will never attain. Occasionally we sense that we can only, with Moses, put off our shoes from our feet, for the place on which we are standing is holy ground. This child, wheelchair bound, spirit imprisoned in a diseased and handicapped body, does not wait for heaven but seems to walk and jump and leap with God here and now. Those of us who stumble along beside them can never be the same again. Two such have left an indelible mark on my soul. Jane and Garvan were both ten when I first met them. Jane died when she was thirteen, Garvan when he was twelve.

Jane tried to take her own life when she was ten. The burden of guilt she carried was too heavy. She and her one-year-old sister both had spinal muscular atrophy. Their parents' marriage was breaking and Jane believed the demands her illness made on them were the major cause of the friction.

Jane's relationship with God has to be concealed from her father who became very angry at the mere mention of God or Christianity. Prayers her grandmother sent her had to be hidden. But she was strong in her faith and her praying was part of her living.

> Dear Lord, please look after everyone in the world, especially my friends and family. Most of all look after my sister Laura as she has the same thing as me but worse. She has a tube down her nose to be fed through and she is sucked out often. Please look after her and pray that one day she may be healed of her ulcer. Also Lord, please look after my mum. Please pray that she will win the court case. Pray that she will be able to cope with Laura and I and that she will no longer have migraines. Also Lord please look after me and pray that one day I will be able to walk too. Please look after my dad. Please look after all the handicapped and sick people in the world and pray that they will be able to cope. Please look after everyone. Pray that we all become closer to you and forgive us all for our sins.
>
> Amen.

Her mother did win custody of the children. After Jane's death I found a note in her handwriting on a small scrap of paper:

> Why do I feel like this? We've won the court case. My mum has got custody of my sister and I. Oh why why why! All I have to do now is win my life. And I don't know how.

Yet through all this she busied herself with living, often proving to be an accurate observer of other people's ways of carrying on. "When you're in a wheelchair people either treat you like a baby, or deaf or stupid. I'm not any of those. My body is handicapped but inside I'm just ordinary and I like people to treat me ordinary and do ordinary things with me." With all her adult cares and concerns she loved to play and delighted in being a little girl again.

She openly talked of her illness and death. She was angry with her mother for agreeing to new treatment, still experimental. She refused it for herself and did not approve of Laura having it. "God made me like this for a reason. You shouldn't interfere."

Jane asked to be confirmed in our Anglican chapel so that she could receive holy communion in the Roman Catholic Church when she attended with her grandmother. She made it clear that she wanted to have a headstone after she was dead. Her mother would need somewhere to visit. We went to London on December 20 to see Bonnie Langford in *Peter Pan*. We were caught up in that wonderful make-believe world. Bonnie even gave us gold dust—and some to take home to Laura—so that when the grown-ups were asleep in bed we could learn to fly.

On Christmas Day Jane developed a lethal chest infection. The television played quietly in the corner of her bedroom and we saw Bonnie Langford flying again. Then we saw Jane herself in Helen House, talking with her beloved friend, the Duchess of Kent, with whom she had had countless early morning telephone conversations.

Jane died the following morning. Laura, now four years old, said, "But I wanted to die first," and five days later she died. They lay together in the "little room" at Helen House until their funeral, Jane's arms enfolding her little sister.

Garvan, from a wonderful Christian family where God is talked about as often and as naturally as the rest of us talk about what we have done at work or who is going to win the Cup Final, must speak for himself:

> As I'm sitting here, I'm Garvan, right—but this isn't really me, my body is just a reflection. When I die I will leave my body behind and that reflection will fade. But the real me won't die. My real self will leave my body and will go up to God. At the moment when I die, I believe Jesus will be standing right beside me with his arms outstretched, ready to take me to his father. Imagine the sheer excitement of meeting him for the first time!
>
> I think of God as friend and guardian and the person who loves me. And of course He *is* the Father, He is not just any father. He's the Father of all of us, every one of us, me, you.
>
> Jesus said, "Don't be afraid, I am the light," and He is the Light; He shines, but we can't see it, but in the end we will see it. You see, God has the answers, we have the questions, and only in the end, when we come to the end of our life, He will tell us the answers. He'll have the answers.
>
> Dying isn't really dying. It's just like opening an old door into a new room, coming from an old room into a new room, which is the place where you're going to live; Heaven, where you came from.

Where you came from you have to go back to. That's your real home. I mean, we will all have to go one day, where it will be the happiest life of all. I mean, this earth is very happy but there are riots and things! But when we go into the other life, no sickness, no pain, no tears, just full of happiness and joy. I'm looking forward to that day. Heaven is so beautiful God can't describe it to us. We'll only know what it is like when we get there. I'm glad really that Jesus kept it a secret, because it will give us a surprise, it will give us such a big surprise.

And when I die, I do believe that Christ will look after my family and whatever they need He will provide for them. I shall always look down on them if I go before them. I will be there in the midst of my family. They might not see me, but I'll be there, watching them, looking after them, all the time.

On Easter Day, days before he died, I visited him and his family at home. He was sitting in a large armchair, wrapped up in a duvet, his face radiant and transfixed as he watched Alec McCowan recite St. Mark's Gospel on television. "I always loved the gospels," he said, "but I've never seen anything as wonderful as this!"

I returned four days later. He was very sick and death did not seem far off. "Do I have to die now?" he asked. Foolishly I reminded him of all that he so genuinely and fervently believed. "Yes," he said, "but I love my family and my home and life so much, I don't want to go yet." The next days were not easy. The transfusions he had referred to as his "life-line" were no longer possible. He refused the medication prescribed to ease his physical distress in the belief that it would hasten the end. To the last he was concerned about everyone else's well-being. "Are *you* all right, Frances?"

Garvan never lost consciousness. His struggle at the end and his agony of parting in no way denied his faith, indeed it made it the more real, for in the torment of a death not so unlike his Lord's he was united with the One who had been his friend and his example in life, the One whom he so loved.

REFERENCE

1. B. Kane, Children's Concepts of Death, *Journal of Genetic Psychology, 134,* pp. 141-153, 1979.

CHAPTER 21
The Terminally Ill Adult Patient

Reverend Jon Nyberg

"Everyone wants to go to heaven, but nobody wants to go today," might be thought of as humorous, but it is true of many people in our culture, and it gives a good indication of our human condition. North American culture has traditionally avoided the reality of death because of its emphasis on youth, beauty, fitness, and success. In former generations, and in numerous other cultures, death was and is looked upon as a normal part of living, as the conclusion of a life lived. Life began at home, and life ended at home, attended to by family members in a loving atmosphere.

Somewhere in the past our culture formed the idea that death is an obscenity. Numerous euphemisms have been developed allowing people to avoid using the words "death" and "dying," especially in the health care setting. For many years people have not died in hospitals, they have *expired.* In some hospitals, it is not unusual to refer to death as "R.H.C.," meaning "respirations have ceased," to avoid using the word "death." In hospice, the term "R.H.C." means "routine health care," and this has caused problems for persons who transfer out of hospital employment into hospice!

Avoidance of the word "death" gives a false sense of control. If one doesn't have to say it, one can feel that death is far away, and it doesn't have to be considered. Yet the Psalmist's words, "The days of our life are seventy years, or perhaps eighty, if we are strong" [1], are still fairly accurate, longevity wise. No matter how hard we try to live longer, the average age of dying persons is still within the seventy to eighty year range. In the past few years, the discussion and acceptance of death have slowly become more common in our culture, but the reality that we are all terminal does not make us comfortable. Cultural denial of death is still with us.

In my years as a hospital and hospice chaplain, I spent untold hours with persons who were dying, and with family members who were in anticipatory grief. I have seen deaths occur which have truly been blessed events. I have also witnessed deaths which have been so painful and seemingly unfair that I still feel pangs of anger and frustration as I recall them. Yet, I have a great deal of time with families in bereavement who, having experienced the death of someone close to them, have made great progress in moving toward reclaiming their shattered lives.

There is no set of rules to follow in how to die. Popular culture in the past quarter century has given some credence to "stages" of dying, made popular in the books of Elisabeth Kübler-Ross [2]. She maintained in her writings that patients went through stages of denial, anger, bargaining, grieving, and acceptance from the time they received their terminal diagnosis until death occurred. While many persons do exhibit these feelings, they do not do so in any structured order of occurrence. Indeed, on any given day the dying patient may jump from denial to acceptance and back again, or may find themselves feeling any of the other emotions listed as "stages."

Patients don't, in other words, die "by the numbers." Rather, the experience of dying is as unique to the individual as is personality, history, emotional makeup, and spirituality. How they react to being in a terminal condition is consistent with the way they have lived their life. Persons who have been quiet and withdrawn all their lives often are quiet and withdrawn in relating to their dying. Some may state "This is my fate," "It is God's will," or "It is my time to go," and retreat from life, waiting to die. Others, who perhaps have been outgoing and gregarious in life, may fight to the last breath. They may even wish to spend their last days informing others about what they are experiencing. Whether the person withdraws quietly until death occurs, puts up a vigorous and energetic fight until the end, or acts somewhere in between, it is important for caregivers to allow that person to die in the way they have chosen to do so. This allows the dying person to retain some control in the midst of a situation in which they seem to have lost much control already.

SPIRITUALITY

Spirituality is as varied in definition and scope as is the person. Spirituality is *not necessarily* the same as religious faith. One definition we might consider is that spirituality is the means by which we live and make sense out of life. It is the way we find coherence and meaning as we move through our lives individually and corporately. In defining one's existence, the statements "I am a child of God" or "I am a child of the universe" are equally valid. Both definitions depend on where the patient is grounded, and are meaningful for that person. Spirituality is developed internally, although external experiences can shape and help determine the type and level of spirituality a person possesses. To put it another way, spirituality is *the substance of who someone is*. A spirituality which is positive and maturing can be the basis for an affirming journey toward the end of this life.

When a person receives a terminal diagnosis, it forces them to come to grips with their own mortality in a real way, not as an exercise of the mind in a philosophical way (although some persons deny their diagnosis or prognosis by intellectualizing).

The reality is that death *will* occur, and it will occur "*for me.*" This hits hard, and it is hard to accept, because preconceived cultural notions or fantasies that death is far away (or that "the other guy" always dies), are no longer a source of comfort. It is devastating to give up the notion that there will always be a tomorrow. Facing up to one's own mortality often is a spiritual crisis.

As my own spirituality is grounded in the Christian faith, and is located within the Reformed Tradition of the Presbyterian Church, the Bible has many clues for me as to how Spirituality affects the dying patient. The passage which reads, "So we don't lose heart. Even though our outer nature is wasting away, our inner nature is being renewed every day" [3, p. 16], was often illustrated working with my hospice patients. This was particularly true with one patient and family with whom I had become quite close.

This patient had been doing relatively well for some time after entering the hospice program. She was not able to get out of the house very much, which was a bother to her as she had been an active, "outdoors" type most of her life. Some days she did not feel well enough to get out of her pajamas and robe, but she still was a gracious host, offering coffee to me on my visits. Her faith was strong, although she had not participated in church for some time. We became close friends, and I always looked forward to my visits. Her physical condition began to deteriorate more rapidly over time, and eventually she slipped into a coma. The family called me one morning and asked me to stop by for prayer. When I arrived, they told me that she had not been responsive to any of the family members for the past twelve or so hours. I went into the small room where they had placed her bed, and sat down in a chair next to her. I said, "It's me, the chaplain. Do you want a prayer?" Her eyes opened and she looked directly at me. She was unable to speak, but her smile told me she was saying, "Yes." She closed her eyes, and I said a prayer with her and with her family. Within the span of a day, she died.

Even though her "outer nature" had wasted away to almost nothing, her "inner nature," her spirituality, was still active. Although her power of verbal response had been taken from her, she spoke volumes to me with her smile. She left this world with her inner nature in tact.

SEARCHING FOR MEANING

When the spiritual crisis of a terminal diagnosis happens, the dying patient might look around and ask, "What has my life meant?" "How will I be remembered?" or even, "Will I be remembered?" Does the fact that the dying person has walked this earth, has perhaps married and raised a family, spent years in the working world make a difference? Of course. But faced with a short time to live, these questions are asked as the meaning of one's life is sought in earnest. Perhaps it is because a person's time frame has become shorter, or perhaps it is because the dying person feels that he or she will be cheated out of a longer life that they ask these questions. Anger can also be expressed as questions are asked, "Why was *I* picked to get sick? Because my life has had less value?" "Am I being struck down because I am not valued by God as much as the next person?"

The quest for meaning is real, and it is a *deeply personal* quest. I remember talking to a young man who was an AIDS patient who was questioning the meaning of his life. He related to me that he could find very little importance or meaning to his existence. He discounted his career, minimized his life history, and with his disease he could not look forward to much of a future. I asked him to do some further life review, to give me the essentials of his autobiography. He told me about his early life, his family, his education, and his career. He had been a teacher. His story concluded with his account of first having been diagnosed with HIV, living with the constant threat of full blown AIDS, then having that threat realized. He was feeling spiritually discounted as well, for he had long since severed any religious connections. His experience in the religious world had brought him ridicule, condemnation, and banishment, which he did not wish to discuss. He no longer was able to feel any comfort in a belief in God. He was searching for some meaning to his life, something to help him feel valued. The fact that such an illness would claim him while he was still young had broken his spirit. He was further devastated by the fact that the church had not honored his life as having any value, nor had it remained a place for him to find care and solace. All the institutions and structures around which most people might find meaning to their lives had been denied him, and he felt that the totality of his life had been a terrific waste of time.

He talked about his career as a teacher. He described the many young lives which he had touched, year after year, day after day in the classroom. He recalled the many hours he had devoted in preparing lesson plans, all the time he took in teaching what his pupils needed to know, and the time he spent with them. Each school year built upon the previous one, and the end of each year meant that another group of children was better prepared to face adulthood. Each student had been enriched and encouraged by what he had taught them. By doing this life review, he began to see that he had, indeed, made some important differences in many young lives.

Just as his family had influenced who he was, his influence on the many lives he taught was a positive force. Lives and careers were shaped and built on the foundation he had helped lay for class after class of students. As he talked, I believe that he began to understand how valued a person he was, and that his life *did* have meaning.

The point of most of the funerals I have either conducted or attended in my life has been that each human life has a great deal of meaning to the lives with whom it comes in contact. In spite of what we know about the dead person's life, some details are not discovered until after the death. Often, bereaved families want to hear details about their loved one's experiences that they did not have the privilege to share, like a college roommate telling stories about the deceased, or a coworker talking about the experiences they shared at work. The natural (cultural) tendency is to keep quiet so as not to "upset" the family, but this can be far from what the family wishes. After the dying person is gone, families want to learn *more* about their loved one, to keep memories fresh and alive within their hearts.

At the time of a person's death, especially if it is unexpected or sudden, questions of the meaning of the person's life might be formed in the minds of the person's loved ones. These questions may never be answered at all, but some are realized many years after. Flashes of meaning often occur in a survivor's mind during significant times, i.e., a wedding, the birth of a child, or the death of another loved one. Times of introspection also trigger mental exercises examining the meaning of a dead person's life.

It is beneficial, if time permits, for individual family members to sit down with the dying person and tell that person just what he or she has meant to them. In this way, the meaning of the dying person's life can be shared while the person is still alive, when the whole family can celebrate their relationship with one another.

In the funerals at which I officiate, I attempt to help those attending to feel blessed as they leave the service, by having them recall one good memory of the deceased. To carry that memory with them is important, for it does, in a way, keep the deceased person alive in the hearts of the bereaved. This can help maintain a spirit of celebration of the person's life, and perhaps soften somewhat the hard, empty feelings.

UNFINISHED BUSINESS

With the onset of a terminal illness, there is often a sense of urgency in the dying patient to complete unfinished business. Some unfinished business is financial, some is spiritual. Some people have lists of things that "just have to be done" before death occurs.

One of the most helpful and sometimes quite difficult things for the dying person to do is to make final funeral arrangements. By doing this in advance, the family is not burdened at the time of death by decisions which have to be made in haste. Writing one's own obituary can actually be an enjoyable experience, especially for those who like to talk about themselves! It is an excellent way to get facts and information right the first time, and it prevents the last minute rushing around to obtain information.

Another piece of unfinished business is the distribution of possessions to the survivors before death occurs. This can prevent ugly incidents from occurring after death. One of my seminary professors once told a story about being called to a home when a parishioner died. As he drove up on the driveway, the dead man's sons were having a fist fight on the front lawn. Both wanted their dead father's lawn mower, and with no will or pre-death determination of what items were to be given to whom, this was how the sons attempted to solve their problem.

Unfinished business can sometimes mean doing the hard work in reconciliation of estranged relationships. Some reconciliation is not possible, but if it *can* be done, it helps the dying patient and the family. I recall a patient who, along with the rest of her family, had been estranged from a sister. As the patient lived out her last days, she herself made the attempt to contact this estranged sister, and was successful. The sister not only responded, but also was willing to visit the patient in her home. Other family members also gathered at the bedside, and they were all able to reconcile. The patient died with the knowledge that the family was united, at least for a while. Unfortunately, not too long after the sister was buried, an argument ensued, which brought back all the hard feelings, and the family split up again, but for the patient, seeing her family reunited during her lifetime was important and rewarding.

Unfinished spiritual business can cause a great deal of anguish in the heart of the dying patient. Some hold onto memories of incidents when a spiritual institution might have done them wrong, resulting in their leaving the membership of a particular congregation or denomination. It might have been a small issue to begin with, which might have been reconciled early on, but through the passage of years the attempt to be reconciled became less and less important. Now, with death approaching, the patient might be convinced that there is no chance of reconciliation, and may feel both helpless or hopeless. They may feel that God abandoned them a long time ago, and they no longer have a chance to reconnect with God.

Several years ago, I supervised a Roman Catholic sister who had been assigned to work our inpatient unit. There had been a patient there who could be described as a "lapsed Catholic." I had visited with the patient a couple of times, and had politely indicated after my second visit that she really was not interested in spiritual matters. I accepted her wishes, and did not visit her again. One afternoon the Sister came into my office and inquired if it would be all right for her to visit this patient. I told her that the patient had indicated that she did not wish any more chaplain visits, but I saw no harm in the Sister visiting just as a friendly visitor, not as a student chaplain. I did tell the Sister that she needed to identify herself as she entered as a Sister, but to make sure that the patient understood that the visit was not an official Chaplain visit. The Sister visited often, usually twice a week for several weeks. As time progressed, the chart notes indicated that the Sister's visits were getting longer and more theological in content. In a supervisory meeting with the Sister, we discussed what was going on. She told me that the patient had become very open about her estranged relationship with the Roman Catholic Church, and she was actively seeking reconciliation. Nearer the time of the patient's death, the Sister arranged for a priest to come to the unit. The patient made her confession and received the sacrament of the Sick. A few days later the patient died peacefully, and was buried from a local parish.

Thus, her unfinished business was resolved. Even though my pastoral care focus as a hospice chaplain was ecumenical, this patient was not comfortable in relating to me, a Protestant, as she could to a fellow Catholic. My own experience would have been second-hand, at best.

The fact that the Sister was there to give pastoral care made it much easier for the patient. The Sister's kind way of dealing with the "lapsedness" of the patient's faith history made it easier for the patient to mention the things which were troubling her. There was no condemnation, but rather a great deal of grace in the listening and understanding which was present with the Sister. I was very grateful that she spent quality time and expended some good energy, for it brought about reconciliation with God and her church. It also gave the patient a chance to clear her mind and soul, to relax, and ultimately to let go from this life into the arms of God.

CHANGE OF OUTLOOK

In spite of the fact that the so-called "control" that one would like to have over his or her life is an illusion, there can be a great opportunity for the dying patient to look ahead to what is left in life as a liberating experience. When a person knows that their time on earth is limited, some fascinating things happen. Their outlook changes. What *was* important might seem less so, and those things formerly overlooked as less important become very much an integral part of life's existence. I like to think of this in terms of a camera lens. In photography, the shorter length of the lens, the wider the scene of the photograph is obtained. A wide angle lens is much shorter than a regular or a telephoto lens. The wide angle lens gives a much wider field of vision. So it is, I believe, with a terminal prognosis. The shorter the time frame a patient has, the more the patient will take in, will delight in, and will discover. Day to day enjoyment becomes a much more important part of life when that life is known to be limited. While the thought of a limited life span might bring terror to the hearts of those not dying, for those who know they are dying it can be a time of expectation and enjoyment, living day to day.

Old ambitions that one might have, plans to become richer, to gain more formal education, to "become a success," are dashed by terminal diagnosis. Often, and unfairly, plans for retirement such as fishing, golf, a cabin somewhere, or travel are lost when disease comes calling on a family. As unfair and often tragic as this is, it changes the way people look at the day to day activities of life. *This* day, *this* experience, *this* family time become very important. Once again, things that appeared to be very important just a few weeks or even days ago, are no longer that important. The *Here* and *Now* become important. What we can take in with our shorter lens is precious and rewarding.

Family history or tragic circumstances within that history can generate feelings of urgency to be finished with this life. Sometimes families who have had a history of losing a child or children live with a spirit of thanksgiving that those lost children are now safe, and are not having to grow up in our present culture with all its dangers. One patient who had lost three young children in a fire years before looked at me and stated that she could not wait to rejoin them. She had never really gotten through her grief over their loss, and her terminal illness, she felt, was a gift, so that she would not have to wait so long to be reunited with them. This was in spite of the fact that death would take her from her surviving children. The urgency to have this life end, to join in death those who have gone before, can be much more important than wishing to remain here with loved ones who are living.

DREAMS AND VISIONS

Several terminal patients with whom I have worked told me of dreams and visions which they had experienced. Most of these took place several days to several weeks before they died. For some it was traumatic, for others, a comfort.

One woman told me that she had dreamed that the angels had come for her, but she told them that she was not ready to go. As she spoke these words in the dream, she awakened upright in bed. She called for her family to be with her at her bedside, and she wept for quite some time. When she related this dream to me, I asked her how she felt about it. She told me she had been scared by it all. She said, "I guess I thought I was going to live forever. Now I know I won't." This dream broke through her denial. She had talked to me about being terminal before, and we had discussed her religious faith, with its promise of heaven and eternal reward. She had indicated that she was comfortable with looking toward heaven, but after this dream occurred, she discovered painfully that heaven was closer than she had wanted it to be. With this dream her denial system had been shattered. We talked about what this meant, and I helped her reframe the dream into something less traumatic and more positive.

As hard as it is to deal with the reality of terminal disease, there is some freedom in thinking about it. I spent some time with this patient talking about the new-found freedom she could have in living each day that was left for her to the fullest. This now meant that she could smell the flowers as the old Sixties cliché told us to do. But she could start to enjoy the world around her through a new lens.

A hospice patient I worked with for some time had gone through what is popularly known today as an "Out of Body Experience" while in North Africa in World War II. This man had come down with a meningitis, which had already claimed two others in the field hospital ward where he lay. He was basically unconscious, yet he remembered someone standing at his bedside, saying, "That one's dead over there, and this one's dead, too." At that time, the patient told me that he experienced being in a dark tunnel, traveling upward toward a bright light. He did not reach the light, but, rather, found himself being pulled back. Because of this experience, years later, when he was a hospice patient, he told me that he did not have any fear of dying, because he had felt so peaceful in that tunnel. He was ready *at any time* to enter it again.

Several weeks before she died, my mother reported to me that she had "seen the Pearly Gates," in a dream. She was confined to a hospital bed in an extended care facility, and was steadily declining physically. This vision occurred at a time when she began a more rapid course of decline. Since the dream had occurred several days before I had the chance to speak to her about it, she could not go into great detail about what she had seen. She was convinced, however that she had seen a glimpse of heaven. This was a comfort to her, and she never doubted that she was terminally ill at that time. A little over a month later she died peacefully in her sleep. From our last long conversation, there were no fears, or doubts, for her that when her life ended, she would be free of her arthritic body, free of pain, free to move her left side again.

Visions, then, for terminal people, can bring out feelings of confidence, splinter the structures of denial that might have been built over time, or they can underscore feelings of faith and comfort.

HOLY GROUND

Students of Anton Boisen, the founder of Clinical Pastoral Education, or CPE, will remember Boisen's characterizing of patients as "Living Human Documents." This is certainly true in ministry to the dying patient. Dying patients are no less "Living Human Documents" because they are dying. They are living until the last breath, the split second when their earthly existence ends. Because each hour they remain on this earth is a precious time for them, and it is also a precious time for those who minister to them.

Unfortunately, it is not unusual for people in ministry to feel uneasy about visiting dying people for the first time. Once again, our culture, in its quest for youth, health, fitness, and longevity, plays a role in our uneasiness. We are not a culture that is comfortable in dealing with dying people. People frequently ask hospice workers, "How can you do the work you do?" or "How can you visit dying people all day—doesn't that get to you?" Or the comment is made, "I really have trouble visiting people who are dying. I just don't know what to say."

In the story of Jesus' Transfiguration, Matthew records that when Jesus' face "shone like the sun, and his clothes became dazzling white," and Moses and Elijah appeared and talked to Jesus, Peter's response was to suggest building three shelters or booths, one for each of them [4, pp. 1-9]. Peter was so surprised and scared by it all that he had to try to do something. Yet, the voice that resounded from the heavens said, "This is my Son, the Beloved; with him I am well pleased; listen to him!" [4].

Those who do not know what to say during a visit with a dying patient are missing the point of the visit altogether. *One doesn't have to say anything.* The fewer words spoken by the visitor, the better. Let the patient control the visit. The voice from heaven silenced Peter with the words, "listen to him!" *Listen to the patient.* What is heard from the patient is more than just special. When one is in the presence of a dying patient, one walks on *Holy Ground*. What the patient shares with the visitor is no less sacred than the prayers of the faithful on any given Sunday morning.

During my CPE residency, one of our group was a young nun who was dealing with her diagnosis of leukemia. I remember one group session when she talked about the difficult time she was having in dealing with death in other patients, because she was dying herself. She struggled through the quarter, and finally decided that it would be better to save her strength physically and emotionally by not continuing with CPE. We kept in touch with her throughout the rest of the year. We learned that she spent her final year doing new and creative things, including ceramics. She used this newly found skill to fashion the chalice that would be used in her funeral mass.

LEGACY

The dying patient is ultimately a teacher. It is a privilege to share in the last period of a person's life, for the reasons I've stated above. To share the final chapter of life is indeed Holy Ground, and it is also a wonderful place of learning. The dying teach us to cry and to laugh, they instruct us in the art of not taking anything too seriously, especially ourselves; and they allow us to share, in the most intimate way, what living and dying mean to them. Perhaps the best legacy we can receive from dying patients is the legacy of how we, who remain here just a bit longer, can learn to live.

REFERENCES

1. Psalm 90, 10, *The New Oxford Annotated Bible,* Oxford University Press, Oxford, 1994.
2. E. Kübler-Ross, *On Death and Dying,* Macmillan, New York, 1969.

3. II Corinthians 4, *The New Oxford Annotated Bible,* Oxford University Press, Oxford, 1994.
4. Matthew 17, *The New Oxford Annotated Bible,* Oxford University Press, Oxford, 1994.

CHAPTER 22

The Victim of Domestic Violence and Sexual Assault

Sharon Gilbert and
Reverend Dr. Richard B. Gilbert

TWO COVENANTS BROKEN

The domestic violence shelter where I offer occasional supportive care and counseling sent me a referral the other day. They usually give the briefest of information, as I prefer that they simply give general concerns or parameters so that I can walk into the conversation uncluttered by any preconditioned expectations or agendas.

The referral was accompanied by these words. "Jane (the name is fictional) has been talking a lot about God. Sometimes she sings hymns; then she leaps over into a rage as she lashes out at God and her minister. She practically shoves us aside when we try to help her address these concerns. It is as if she doesn't trust us (at least around these issues)." They told her that I am a chaplain and counselor, and what they describe as "a safe friend for our clients and families." While I was not startled by the client's comments (I hear them quite often), I couldn't help but feel the intensity in the voice of the client advocate, her dismay and her curiosity, as well as something in her reporting that suggests to me that something from her story was triggered in this exchange. I made a note to follow up with the client advocate.

At the appointed time I was ushered into a quiet room for conversation. While I sensed that the eyes of the woman in the living room were following me (it is a safety issue for the clients, so the stare was understood and appropriate), something told me that this person was checking me out with a very specific agenda in mind. She was my client.

Jane was dressed well, giving the appearance of a professional woman ready to go to work. It was a noticeable contrast from some of the other clients who were watching me. While watching me carefully she also seemed to be contently reading a magazine.

I invited her to select a place to sit down that was comfortable for her as I introduced myself. Before I could even sit down the calm composure became the eye of a hurricane. She had gone on the offensive. Standing, waving her fist at me, a face red from the intensity yet with tears streaming down her face. She shouted,

> Don't you dare tell me that God loves me. I won't have it . . . Do you hear me? God let his son get beat up and now he let me get beat up, over and over again. My husband, some pillar of the church!, he sat in the front pew every Sunday. Everyone loves him. He greets everyone, sings the hymns louder than everyone, stays after to listen to everyone's stories . . . then comes home and beats me up. I sang a hymn wrong. I didn't quite get the gist of the sermon. I don't look holy enough when I pray. God let his son get beat up and he did nothing to keep me safe . . . even when I prayed. Some shepherd he is.

She paused for a moment, as if to catch her breath. She looked for the tissues to wipe her eye and her nose. I am glad she was willing to pause. It gave me the time to try to regroup. If I had any plan of action, even as non-directive as I try to be, it went out the window. I didn't need to worry. There was no chance for me to respond. She took a deep breath, started to stand up, waving her arms, and the shouting (her litany) continued . . .

> I don't know why I would expect you to be any different. All ministers are alike, aren't they?! How could I tell our pastor that his little pet, the layman he trusted and counted on, was an abuser? How could I tell him about the swings that follow a sermon about love? The yelling when things don't go right at work? The threats when the kids aren't as he wants them to be? My pastor wouldn't believe it. I tried to tell him. I tried to tell him that things weren't right, that I was scared, that some nights I just wanted to run away. He could only say something stupid, like, "Well, there are times when we all want to run away." He couldn't hear a thing that I had to say. He just promised "to pray for me."
>
> Pray? Ha! That's a laugh. A lot of good that does. I pray for peace, and get conflict. I pray for safety and I am afraid to close my eyes and sleep. I asked God to show me what *I* was doing wrong and the only message I got was from my husband, telling me that everything is *my* fault.
>
> Either I am the worst of sinners, the lousiest of Christians, or "The Lord is my Shepherd" means absolutely nothing to me or to anyone. God just doesn't care, or seems to play favorites. Maybe if I

served on more church committees, sang the hymns better, saved more from my "food allotment" to make the offering bigger, my husband would respect me more.

She then slumped down, fidgeted, and started to get up and move toward the door. Many times victims slump down in terror, not only because of the "man" (or anyone) present who has seen the risk taking and shared in the vulnerability, as if the dialog, the honest outpouring, was pounding the nails deeper into her scars, the nails that radiate the pain. . . . "You are a bad person" and "It's all my fault."

Jane seemed different. It wasn't that I was alarmed, and I certainly wasn't dismayed by what she said. I was puzzled, consumed with sadness and, quite honestly, wondering if I could move to the door faster than she seemed to be wanting to do. It wasn't that I was upset with what she said about God. I can't count the times I have felt the same disappointment and emptiness. I was upset ABOUT the minister (not necessarily FOR the minister), because the covenant of community was not a point of connection for her, which is what ministry is to be about. I just was so overwhelmed by her sincerity, the intensity, the very real pain, and what was, for me, a truly remarkable statement of faith. More about that later.

The exchange reminded me of the power of words, silences, rituals, sacraments (as sign and presence), of authority (perceived or rejected, about God and about clergy), and the very real struggle of determining how to respond, how to offer a different model (at least of one minister who was willing to listen nonjudgmentally), and how, over a period of time, to be willing to walk with her as she finds new sanctuary (safety), redefines God (or beliefs for her), and is willing to trust, at least a little bit, so we can begin the hard work that burdens all victims who, after much labor, choose to become survivors. It was the cry in the wilderness, "out of the depths" (Psalm 130), the soaring sourness of two covenants broken. The covenant of husband and wife, the "death" of so many things, buried in the casket of domestic violence. No flowers. No cards. No sympathy. Only pain, threats, control, and abuse. The covenant of a person's spirit, a covenant of trust, safety, hope, and connection. Two covenants broken.

A NEW JOURNEY BEGUN

"Please don't leave. I would like very much to talk more with you."

That was the only thing I could think to say. "Please." A nonthreatening (or the best that I could do) invitation for two wounded "souls" to share, struggle, and move on to something that might be peace, or least relatively peaceful.

Spirituality is always a journey, a wandering here and there, usually forward, but always with twists and turns, with hopes and defeats, with smooth rides and bumpy roads, much like any relationship. Her journey seemed dashed against the rocks, a God who was indifferent or couldn't help her, a collection of rituals and symbols that seemed a pathway to destruction (as used by her husband), a community of believers that would not understand the stories about the man they idolized, so unknowingly fed into her shame and forced her to perpetuate the secrets. A minister who may have been helpful if given the chance, but perhaps didn't get the message because Jane couldn't tell him. Maybe more to the point, a minister who Jane *perceived* would not understand, would not believe her, was not available, and probably would want only to believe her husband. She felt he would coerce her into working even harder to save the marriage (which many ministers feel "obligated" to do), so he symbolically sent the message that there was no way out for her, in the control of her husband, in the eyes if God, and in the opinion of the minister.

A new journey is beginning. This journey probably began, though it may not have felt recognizable, at least from the spiritual perspective, when she courageously took the first step toward healing and freedom by coming into the shelter. The bulldozer of abuse that previously would have knocked her over and paved her under was now clearing a new path and reframing who she is and what she wants life to be. The pathway received new definition as she courageously shouted out and wept through the tough words of hurt, despair, and grief. It was this journey that was beginning and, whether she believed (or trusted) me or not, she did not have to walk this journey alone.

FEAR, NOT DOUBT, IS THE DESTROYER

Some people insist, almost with a tone of judgment, that doubt is bad, a sin, the antithesis of faith. This line of thought suggests to me more control, more lack of respect for what healthy spirituality is intended to be, and religious abuse. If spirituality is a journey then there must be room for meandering, detours, rest stops, repairs, and refueling. There is, in a sense, no "right way" to be living, spiritually. There are healthier choices to follow, but spiritually speaking, faith is always about choices, and that we can choose.

The down or destructive side of faith is fear. Fear that we are unworthy. Fear that we are not forgiven. Fear that we are bad. Fear that we are not loved, or not lovable. Or, in the deepest valley, afraid of God. Fear is seldom developed or determined from within. We learn to be cautious, developing skills about safety and well-being. Trust emerges as relationships are built. Fear does not come naturally, it is learned or acquired, sometimes imposed on us, and it usually comes to us as a result of the actions (or lack of actions) of others. Fear comes through threats, through faulty definitions (spirituality, religion), through harmful actions and, most of all, from words . . . you are a "wretched sinner," you are unworthy of God's love, it is "your fault," you are a bad person. It is disguised in the words of sermons, in some religious literature, quite often in the attitudes, words, and actions of other people, and sometimes we believe it is the result of something God has done or failed to do.

Fear leaves us battered and bruised, stooped over with shame, infertile in imagination, withdrawn from our circle of friends or our spiritual network, diminished in social skills, unsafe and unable to believe. Its oppressive weight can not only leave us feeling that God and love (or whatever the basics of our belief system may be) are withheld from us (and someone or Someone has the right to do this, and should, because I am a bad person), but we may never be "eligible" for it again.

Doubts we can deal with. They are the opposite side of the coin of faith, so intimately a part of faith. It is the right and the need to ask questions, to search, to examine, to redefine . . . to grow. Fear will last a lifetime; it is what being a victim feels like, until we choose to be a survivor.

THE NEED FOR HEALTHY MODELS

Feelings of abandonment and loneliness are very real and they can choke off the last breaths of our integrity, sense of self-worth, and desire to live purposefully. Those feelings are exaggerated beyond recognition when life threats, and the resulting fear and sense of danger, weigh down those oppressive feelings already pulling a person down.

While it does not serve to say one feeling is worse than another, it is fair to say that the burden is magnified to the hot zone of danger and despair, two opposites dragged together by a person's life story, when the victim feels let down the very people who are supposed to be and facilitate the antithesis in feelings. Obviously, for Jane, there is the abusive husband. A survey of her life story would probably indicate a pattern of victimization that started before this relationship. That dimension of the story is right there for us to see. What about law enforcement officers that victimize further, some even arresting both parties in a domestic squabble, or dismiss cries for help (especially true when stalking) as the foolishness of an hysterical woman? Lawyers who do not listen. Physicians who miss or ignore the signs. Family members who feed into the denial. It is all there. How do we respond when the further victimization, perceived or real, but always experienced as real and true, comes from the minister or other religious leaders, people who are to BE sanctuary to his or her people? What role model is there for that victim? Or possibly the ultimate abuse, beyond religious leaders, other parishioners, organized religion . . . "God let me down."

As professionals we must continue to track what messages, intended and unintended, we are sending out to victims. We must slow down the pace, be an agent for stability and peace, but also deliberately, word by word, gesture by gesture, to be a different word. We must talk carefully, in whispers, to people so wounded that the sound system is turned up to full blast. We must anticipate the risks to the client, yes the risks from our presence. It is our responsibility to track and evaluate, in consultation with the client. They have little strength left even to talk; they have nothing left when it comes to defending themselves against us.

When the damaged role model is how we have seen or experienced God, that is a significant loss, a destruction that may rip through our hearts and lives like the most violent of tornadoes, and leave us spit out on another shore with nothing that is familiar, discernible, or safe.

"God is love" and "Jesus loves you" are phrases that may be at the center of the Christian tradition and, in some ways, with different packaging, the other religions of the world. What does it say to Jane who sees no validity in the concept? She sees only that she prayed and God didn't listen, she sought the help of her minister and he/she did not reply, the adoration of her husband by the congregation that shut her out, and somehow this sheep is without a shepherd. More than that, she is without a metaphor. The sheep, in a trusting relationship, that special bond that is known only between the shepherd and the sheep, is gone. It doesn't work any more. It isn't about shepherd and sheep, but sheep, the helpless animals left defenseless by the mighty God to suffer at the hands of the wolves that abuse.

REDEFINING GOD/RENEGOTIATING COVENANT

The spiritual dimensions of loss are real. For "normal" bereavement, the spiritual dimension is a slippery slope often backed away from by religious leaders and caring believers because we feel helpless, without words, and often failing to grasp what is really involved in the conversation.

Loss that results from violence (and the list of experiences lost may, for a time, feel endless), begins as complications, the disabling journey that feeds into distractions, detours, and dead ends when safe passage is so desperately needed. The loss of God is like no other loss. Who do you tell? God? Yes! But probably not now, at least for the victim. Why use limited energy to talk to someone who isn't listening? Victimization has such a cloak of shame that we dare not tell our ministers. Who else can we risk exposure with? It is appropriate, we believe, in life's polite circles, to condemn oneself to a life of misery by condemning the God who let us down.

Before we can speak of and to the victim, it is imperative that we talk with ourselves. Many of us, even the most skilled practitioners and most loyal friends, are not comfortable (and frequently unskilled) in staying with people in their religious struggles. It is just too easy to quote scripture, offer pious promises (that are heard as more empty promises), suggest that the victim has it all wrong when it comes to God, or offer to repair her (or his) theological frame of reference. The victim is broken, but is also deeply wounded. When sanctuary has been ripped from you, it is the work of both caregiver and victim to recreate (or start anew) with sanctuary. We must first touch our own spirituality, how we are feeling about the accusations of the victim, and to hear the voice within us that may also be asking what happened to the shepherd (Shepherd) for this person. It also may touch the raw nerve within us that still is asking about the times we felt unsafe, attacked, or otherwise let down by the God (or spirituality) we had come to know, love, and trust. Unless we are tracking this we will become conflictual with the client (and with ourselves) and may well heighten the level of abuse they have experienced.

Sanctuary. Safety. It may be expressed through ritual or symbols, by claiming designated places and spaces, and through and because of the special people who bear and are safety for us. It may be surrounding the victim, but the victim can't always see it. Sanctuary is presumed as an expression of faith, even a dimmed faith, and faith is rooted in trust. How do we expect victims to trust when they did once, and were let down by a perpetrator, the system, the religious community, and the God they had known and trusted?

Once safety is established (safety from the perpetrator), we must walk (crawl) cautiously, at the pace determined by the victim, being an expression of safety and trust that, when our acceptance is earned, can be let into the heart and "soul" of the victim by his or her own choosing. Before you blow the heresy horn, let me put it bluntly. It is also a theological truth (that I know God can handle). The first time "in," God is accepted at face value. Now God, or at least the religious community, must earn a place in the life of the victim. No longer can we offer pious answers, rituals, and teachings. We are speaking the wrong language, we are pushing instead of listening, confronting instead of guiding. I cannot give answers for God; I can't give any answers. I can speak only of the pain I have felt when the wrong people, the ones I trusted (including God), let me down. I can begin to understand the grief, hurt, and doubt that were choking me with a force as real as that of the perpetrator. I still can't determine what all of this means to the victim. Maybe, just maybe, in the silence of the moment (silence is also a way to communicate important things), there may be a glimpse of something in our presence that hints of trust or that we might be worth the risk on the part of the victim.

Inviting people back to temple or church, telling them that you will pray for them, offering them the sacraments, may help for some, but for others it may just not be where the victim is at that moment. They may be so victimized that they will just say "yes" to what YOU think is best (and give a false reading that we are "getting somewhere" with them), because they are too tired to say no, their co-dependent style pushes to link to us because they believe they must or because victims have no awareness of their right to say no.

FINAL THOUGHTS

Domestic violence is very real, and so are the numbers. Alarming and appalling numbers. It is in every congregation (despite the denial by people who should know better), and denying it will not drive it away. It will drive away the people who need us so much.

If you read this chapter as a person in authority or leadership, as a provider or professional presence, you are in a position to make a difference. Wishing or praying away domestic violence isn't going to work. We must become proactive. Check your building. Are there signs posted throughout (including the lavatories), that give information for victims, including phone numbers for safety? Make sure some of the material relates to children. Talk about it in your preaching and teaching (for ministers), and as you listen to stories and assess them. Offer special education programs (start with the staff, first). Make yourself available to those providing care for the victims. Does your institution walk the walk of liberation or seem more comfortable in the world of victimization? Rethink how you do counseling. Clergy must place safety first, bringing the perpetrator to a measure of responsibility for his or her actions, and then, a long "then" from the time of intervention, *possibly* consider saving the marriage. Don't counsel the victim and the perpetrator together. You may be heightening the danger for the victim.

This may not sit comfortably with your beliefs, practices, biases, or the expectations of those in your workplace. When we duck the tough questions and walk from the places where we are most needed, then we are the new abuser and we become a new name on the list of perpetrators. Get additional training. Also look at your own personal relationships and spiritual journey.

Jane has taken some important steps. The first one was to choose to live safely. The second one was to get to a safe place. The rest will fall out as she is able to shed it and share it, including the need to explore God (and beliefs) and religious practices again, possibly in an all new way. Some have been sustained by their beliefs. However, many have experienced further destruction and loss.

There is a voice crying in the wilderness, the wilderness of violence, threat, stalking, control, fear, and weapons. Will we listen? Will we respond in helpful ways? Will we become the desperately needed sanctuary and spiritual connection?

SUGGESTED READING

Adams, C. and M. Fortune, *Violence Against Women and Children: A Christian Theological Sourcebook,* Continuum, New York, 1995.

Bean, C., *Women Murdered by the Men They Loved,* Haworth, Binghamton, 1992.

Benvenga, N., *Healing the Wounds of Emotional Abuse: The Journey Worth the Risk,* Resurrection, Mineola, 1997.

Briles, J., *Briles Report on Women in Health Care: Changing Conflict to Collaboration in a Toxic Workplace,* Jossey-Bass, San Francisco, 1994.

Clark, R.-L., *Pastoral Care of Battered Women,* The Westminster Press, Philadelphia, 1986.

Falls, K., S. Howard, and J. Ford, *Alternatives to Domestic Violence: A Homework Manual for Battering Intervention Groups,* Accelerated Development, Bristol, Pennsylvania, 1999.

Gaddis, P., *Battered But Not Broken: Help for Abused Wives and Their Church Families,* Judson Press, Valley Force, 1996.

Greider, K., *Reckoning with Aggression: Theology, Violence and Vitality,* Westminster John Knox Press, Louisville, 1997.

Nason-Clark, N., *The Battered Wife: How Christians Confront Family Violence,* Westminster John Knox Press, Louisville, 1994.

Vanderhear, G., *Beyond Violence: In the Spirit of the Non-Violent Christ,* Twenty-Third Publications, Mystic, Connecticut, 1998.

Zimmerman, M. W., *Take and Make Holy: Honoring the Sacred in the Healing Journey of Abuse Survivors,* Liturgical Training, Chicago, 1995.

Symphony

Reverend Denise A. Ryder

It was a symphony
very few have the privilege of experiencing.

The lead percussionists
were the anesthesiologist and the perfusionist.
They entered
and began to tune their instruments,
Making sure all things were in the finest order
for this work of art.

Nurses finished their set-up of sterile wares,
adroitly placed for expert use
at the appointed time.

Soon the patient entered.
Not too nervous,
more expectant of the mystical magic
to be felt in the hands of the virtuosos.
Nervousness left him as he looked
and talked and realized
that he was the object of reverent focus that morning.

Medicines began to work and slowly,
deep sleep came.

The orchestra continued.
As master violinists, the surgeons prepared
and made their entrance right on cue.
Washed and draped, fine tools in finger's reach,
The tempo increases—
and the observer is enchanted by
the concerto playing before her.

In the background, the percussionists
continue with a driving beat.
Few words pass.
Everyone knows their part.
No instructions are needed.

The bypass is complete.

The tempo changes,
the room becomes light—airy.
To the observer's eyes it seems that everyone relaxes,
but it is only an appearance.
The music goes on
incisions are closed.

Rallentando

The patient is going to recovery.

The observer closes her eyes for a moment and prays.
May the Unseen Conductor
direct this orchestra
so miraculously again.

Contributors

Editor

The Reverend Richard B. Gilbert, D.Min., BCC, is the Executive Director of The World Pastoral Care Center; Director of Chaplaincy Services, Sherman Hospital, Elgin, Illinois; and founding director, Connections—Spiritual Links. A Board Certified Chaplain and a member of both The Association of Professional Chaplains and The National Association of Catholic Chaplains, Gilbert brings extensive experience as a parish pastor, health care chaplain, chaplaincy consultant, and bereavement specialist to his work as a speaker, consultant, resource specialist, and author. Extensively published (articles, reviews, and books), Gilbert serves on several national boards and is in the Ph.D. program (pastoral psychology) of The Graduate Theological Foundation. The degree Doctor of Ministry was conferred on him in the field of pastoral psychology. He is an ordained Anglican priest.

The Poet

The Reverend Denise Ryder, D.Min. BCC, is a Board Certified Chaplain and a staff chaplain at St. Joseph's Medical Center, South Bend, Indiana. A leader in The Association of Professional Chaplains, Chaplain Ryder has done statewide work as a trainer and facilitator with critical incident stress debriefing. She is a Southern Baptist minister.

Contributing Authors

David Adams, M.S.W., C.S.W., is a professor, The Department of Psychiatry, Faculty of Health Sciences, McMaster University (Canada) and Executive Director, The Greater Hamilton Employee Assistance Consortium. He is a certified grief therapist and death educator and has concentrated much of his clinical practice and teaching on the impact of life-threatening illness, death, dying, and bereavement on children, adolescents, and their families. He has written extensively and is co-editor of the three volume series *Beyond the Innocence of Childhood* and co-author of *Coping with Childhood Cancer: Where Do We Go from Here?* He is a past chair of the International Work Group on Death, Dying, and Bereavement.

The Reverend Paul Bierlein, M.Div., B.C.C., is Director of Pastoral Care at St. Luke's Hospital, Maumee, Ohio, and coordinator of The Ethical Consultation Team. A Lutheran pastor who has been active in the support of clergy throughout his church, and also as past state leader in the chaplaincy group for Ohio, he has extensive institutional and parish based experience. He has been active in presenting seminars on stress management, preventive self-care, and spiritual wellness, as well as promoting congregational health ministries. He continues to serve in various state and denominational leadership roles for pastoral care, and is active in medical ethics. He is a member of the Society for Bioethics Consultation and the Bioethics Network of Ohio.

The Reverend Laurel A. Burton, Th.D., B.C.C. is Academic Dean and Professor of Pastoral Studies at Methodist Theological School in Ohio, and the first president of The Association of Professional Chaplains. Long respected as an authority on institutionally based pastoral care, health care, and ethics, he is extensively published and frequently sought after as a speaker and a consultant. He is an ordained United Methodist minister.

Inge B. Corless, Ph.D., is Associate Professor and Director of the HIV/AIDS Specialization at the MGH Institute of Health Professions in Boston, Massachusetts, and former program director at St. Peter's Hospice, Albany, New York. She is the editor of *Dying, Death and Bereavement, a Theoretical Perspective and Other Ways of Knowing* and *A Challenge for Living-Dying, Death and Bereavement*, along with numerous articles.

Gerry Cox, Ph.D., is a member of the Sociology faculty of The University of Wisconsin-La Crosse. Extensively published in issues related to Native American traditions and spirituality as well as bereavement issues, he serves on several national organizations and is extensively published. He lives in Lacrosse, Wisconsin.

Rick Csiernik, Ph.D., C.S.W. is an Assistant Professor, School of Social Work, King's College, University of Western Ontario, London, Ontario. A member of the Ontario College of Certified Social Workers, Rick is the past-president of The Canadian Employee Assistance Program Association and serves on the editorial board of *The Social Worker*.

Sr. Frances Dominica, ASSP, is the director of Helen House, a hospice for children and adolescents in Oxford, England. Long an active participant in the International Work Group on Death, Dying, and Bereavement, she is well known for her advocacy and gentle presence in caring for dying children and adolescents and the support of their parents and caregivers.

The Reverend Joseph J. Driscoll is executive director, The National Association of Catholic Chaplains. He is nationally recognized as a speaker, author, and spokesperson for chaplaincy and pastoral care. He has served as a C.P.E. supervisor. He has worked diligently to enhance the role of the chaplain in his own faith tradition and also has been a leader in ecumenical cooperation and support. He is from Milwaukee.

The Reverend Thomas A. Droege, M.A., Ph.D. is a Lutheran pastor and educator whose area of expertise is health and spirituality, with a particular focus on the implementation of health ministries in congregational settings. After a career of teaching and research in practical theology at Valparaiso University, Dr. Droege joined the Interfaith Health Program as Associate Director in 1992. He has served as the principal administrator of the Atlanta Interfaith Health Program, which is forming coalitions of congregations to meet the health needs of disadvantaged populations. Dr. Droege has authored numerous books and articles in the areas of faith development studies, understanding death and dying, and health and spirituality. His most recent publications are *The Faith Factor in Healing* (Trinity Press International, 1991) and *The Healing Presence* (Harper/Collins, 1992). He is from Atlanta.

Sharon Gilbert, B.S. in Elem. Ed. served as the Executive Director of The Caring Place, a non-profit agency that has served Northwest Indiana for twenty years. In addition to providing a shelter for victims and their children, they provide education, advocacy, intervention, and professional development. Their programs include domestic violence, sexual assault, and date rape. They developed "Mayors Commissions" as a respected model for several communities, bringing together government, law enforcement, education, advocacy, the judicial system, and treatment providers. In connection with Valparaiso University they have developed dramas used in schools to raise issues around date rape and sexual assault.

Rabbi Earl Grollman, D.D. has long been admired and respected as a pioneer in the field of bereavement studies and care. With over twenty books published, he has presented internationally on bereavement and also pastoral care. He is a regular keynote speaker and contributes to several publications. He resides in the Boston area.

The Reverend Sue Jelinek, M.Div., B.C.C. is an ordained minister with The United Church of Christ and, until recently, Director of Pastoral Care, The LaPorte Community Hospital, LaPorte, Indiana. A leader in her denomination, she is now a staff chaplain (specializing in oncology) at Children's Hospital, Cincinnati and an active pastoral presence for and to the Gay-Lesbian-Bisexual-Transgendered communities.

Cathi Lammert, R.N., is Executive Director, SHARE-Pregnancy & Infant Loss Support, Inc., with national headquarters in St. Charles, Missouri. As a bereaved parent, Cathi combines her personal experience with her education and professional experience as a nurse. She is responsible for the beginnings of SHARE in the St. Louis area. She has conducted numerous perinatal loss workshops for professionals, clergy, and the bereaved and their families. She also writes for various publications including the National SHARE newsletter. She is the editor of *Caring Notes*, a newsletter for caregivers who assist parents with perinatal bereavement, and recently co-edited the book, *Angelic Presence . . . Stories of Hope and Solace After the Loss of a Baby*. She is responsible for guiding and supporting over 120 SHARE groups throughout the United States.

The Reverend John A. Mac Dougall, D.Min., is a United Methodist minister and the Supervisor of Spiritual Care at Hazelden Recovery Services in Center City, Minnesota. Long respected as a caregiver with the addicted and a trainer of those who provide care for the addicted, he welcomes inquiries about treatment and support through the Hazelden system at 800.257.7800.

The Reverend Robert Miller, M.Div., is an active leader in The Roman Catholic Archdiocese of Chicago and a priest at Holy Angels Church, Chicago. A thriving inner city parish with the largest all-Black parish school in the country, Miller is the author of *Grief Quest*, concerned with male patterns of grieving. He is working on a book of meditations and spiritual reflections.

John Morgan, Ph.D. is professor emeritus at King's College, London, Ontario, where he has had a distinguished career as a pioneer in the field of death education. He founded the King's College Bereavement Conference, still an annual event, has been the author of several books, and is the editor of a lengthy and noteworthy list of textbooks in the various Baywood series. He has distinguished himself as an international educator and mentor, as noted by his presence in The International Work Group on Death, Dying, and Bereavement and in ADEC (Association of Death Education and Counseling).

The Reverend Jon Nyberg, M.Div., B.C.C. has extensive experience as a parish based minister, and, most recently, with the St. Vincent's Hospice of Indianapolis. A state leader for The Association of Professional Chaplains, Rev. Nyberg, a Presbyterian minister, was recently appointed Minister of Pastoral Care at the First Presbyterian Church of Valparaiso, Indiana.

The Reverend Karrie Oertli, M.Div., B.C.C., is an ordained minister affiliated with The Southern Baptist Convention, a Board Certified Chaplain, and recently certified as a Supervisor with The Association of Clinical Pastoral Education. She is on staff at Integris Baptist Medical Center, Oklahoma City.

Cynthia A. Russell, D.N.Sc., R.N., is an associate professor at Valparaiso University College of Nursing. Dr. Russell received her doctoral degree from Rush University College of Nursing in 1991 with a concentration in psychiatric nursing. She also teaches a course on death and dying. She lives in Valparaiso, Indiana.

Edgar P. Senne, M.Div., M.Ed., M.A. (History of Religion), is Professor Emeritus, The Department of Theology, Valparaiso University, where he still does some teaching. He has developed a significant presence both in the study of world religions and in the increase in dialog among these religious groups. After his retirement he became the first director of Hilltop House, bringing quality health care and social support to those who otherwise could not afford it.

Chaplain Jeffrey Silberman, D.Min., B.C.C., is Director, Pastoral Care and Education, Beth Israel Medical Center, New York City. He is a C.P.E. supervisor and an active presence in The Association of Professional Chaplains. He was the founding president of The National Association of Jewish Chaplains.

The Reverend Richard Stewart, M.Div., B.C.C. has just completed his term of service as President, The Association of Professional Chaplains. He was instrumental in guiding the process that brought together the College of Chaplains and The Association of Mental Health Clergy into the Association of Professional Chaplains. He has been a leader in building bridges with the various judicatory leaders and recently retired as director, Section of Chaplains and Related Ministries, The United Methodist Church. He is from Nashville, Tennessee.

The Reverend John Vander Zee, D.Min., B.C.C., is Director of Pastoral Care at the Bloomington Hospital, Bloomington, Indiana, and a leader in The Association of Professional Chaplains. A past president of The Indiana Health Care Chaplains Association, he has served as a pioneer in drawing attention to the needs of the chronically ill. He is an ordained Presbyterian (USA) minister.

Index

Books of Interest in the
Death, Value and Meaning Series
Series Editor: John D. Morgan

All Kinds of Love: Experiencing Hospice
By Carolyn Jaffe and Carol H. Ehrlich

Readings in Thanatology
Editor: John D. Morgan

Mending the Torn Fabric:
For Those Who Grieve and Those Who Want to Help Them
By Sarah Brabant

Widower: When Men Are Left Alone
By Scott Campbell and Phyllis R. Silverman

Awareness of Mortality
Editor: Jeffrey Kauffman

Ethical Issues in the Care of the Dying and Bereaved Aged
Editor: John D. Morgan

Fading Away: The Experience of Transition
in Families with Terminal Illness
*Editors: Betty Davies, Joanne Chekryn Reimer,
Pamela Brown and Nola Martens*

Last Rites: The Work of the Modern Funeral Director
By: Glennys Howarth

Perspectives on College Student Suicide
By Ralph L.V. Rickgarn

What Will We Do?
Preparing a School Community to Cope with Crises
Editor: Robert G. Stevenson

Personal Care in an Impersonal World: A Multidimensional Look at Bereavement
Editor: John D. Morgan

Death and Spirituality
Editor: Kenneth J. Doka with John D. Morgan

Spiritual, Ethical and Pastoral Aspects of Death and Bereavement
Editors: Gerry R. Cox and Ronald J. Fundis

Greeting the Angels: An Imaginal View of the Mourning Process
By Greg Mogenson

Beyond the Innocence of Childhood – 3 Volume Set
Editors: David W. Adams and Eleanor J. Deveau
Volume 1
Factors Influencing Children and Adolescents'
Perceptions and Attitudes Toward Death
Volume 2
Helping Children and Adolescents
Cope with Life-Threatening Illness and Dying
Volume 3
Helping Children and Adolescents Cope with Death and Bereavement